Crisis, Resilience and Survival

Crisis, Resilience and Survival charts the evolution of the global automotive industry, revealing the pressures and challenges facing firms in this huge but turbulent realm of business. Long-term over-capacity and swings of the economic cycle mean that many car companies are in financially perilous positions. Yet failures of auto companies are rare, and many have bounced back from the brink. Using the concept of the 'survival envelope', Holweg and Oliver argue that the ability to design, develop, manufacture and distribute vehicles competitively is not the only factor in ensuring success. Using detailed analyses of two failures (Rover and Saab) and two near-misses (Chrysler and Nissan) they explore how scale, market reach and supportive stakeholder relations can make the difference between success and failure in this global industry. This book will appeal to anyone working in or studying the auto industry, as well as those interested in corporate success and failure.

MATTHIAS HOLWEG is Professor of Operations Management at the Saïd Business School, University of Oxford. He is interested in how process improvement methodologies, such as lean thinking, have evolved and been adapted over time, and what impact they have on the competitiveness of the firm. He is co-author of *The Second Century* and *The Lean Toolbox*.

NICK OLIVER is Professor of Management at the University of Edinburgh Business School, where he served as Dean from 2007 to 2012. His particular specialities are lean methods and organizational resilience. He is co-author of *The Japanization of British Industry*.

Crisis, Resilience and Survival

Lessons from the Global Auto Industry

MATTHIAS HOLWEG
University of Oxford

NICK OLIVER
University of Edinburgh

CAMBRIDGE
UNIVERSITY PRESS

University Printing House, Cambridge CB2 8BS, United Kingdom

Cambridge University Press is part of the University of Cambridge.

It furthers the University's mission by disseminating knowledge in the pursuit of education, learning and research at the highest international levels of excellence.

www.cambridge.org
Information on this title: www.cambridge.org/9781107076013

First published 2016

Printed in the United Kingdom by Clays, St Ives plc

A catalogue record for this publication is available from the British Library

ISBN 978-1-107-07601-3 Hardback

To Sue and Rebecca

Contents

Figures

Tables

Acknowledgements

The production of this book has spanned a long period. It initially started as an analysis of the collapse of the UK's MG Rover in 2005, but grew to encompass the collapse of Saab in 2011 and from there to a more general treatment of crisis, resilience and survival in the global auto industry. Producing this book was only possible because of the help and support of many people, whose contributions came in many different forms.

A special thanks is due to Mike Carver who was central to collecting the data on Rover, setting up interviews, participating in these, and developing the rather complex Rover story. In this part of the project we talked to many of the key people involved with the company in its various guises between 1968 and 2005. These include most of the chief executives during that period; several Board directors and senior managers; representatives from trades unions, and from the British government, including senior figures of Rover's one-time partners Honda and owners BMW; and representatives of companies that were once part of the Rover family but were sold off at various points in its history, including Unipart, Jaguar and Land Rover. Thanks to Rachel Simpson who worked hard to turn a voluminous set of observations about Rover into a preliminary and coherent story.

Many people gave up a great deal of time to help us while we were researching the collapse of Rover, and we are grateful to them for sharing their views and their experiences with us. In particular, we would like to thank: David Andrews, John Bacchus, Peter Bailey, Tony Benn, Tetsuo Chino, Sir Graham Day, Sir Michael Edwardes, Sir John Egan, Dr Walter Hasselkus, Shoku Hayashi, Ray Horrocks, Osamu Iida, Kiyoshi Ikemi, Lord Jenkin, Nobuhiko Kawamoto, Noriyuke Koide, Michael Marshall, Sir John Mayhew-Sanders, Shojiro

Miyake, Jon Moulton, Harold Musgrove, John Neill, Sir Geoffrey Owen, Geoffrey Robinson MP, Mamoru Sakata, Nick Seale, Lord Simpson, Lord Stokes, Trevor Taylor, Peter Thompson, Yozo Usuki, Geoff Williams, Tony Woodley, Joe Yoshinari. We also are grateful to Roland Clement, Ding Dong, Bao Youxian and Ji Guorong for sharing their views on aspects of Rover's recent history in China.

Our work on the collapse of Rover led us to much bigger questions on what drives success and failure in the global motor industry. The prolonged struggle and ultimate failure of Saab in 2011 soon provided us with another case study of an auto company's crisis and collapse. We are very grateful to David Herman, Rolf Sandberg and Jan-Åke Jonsson for speaking to us about their involvement with Saab over the years.

Many of the ideas that we developed when studying Rover and Saab had a strong bearing on events, crises and mergers at other car firms. In this regard we would like to thank Dr Ralf Speth, Carl-Peter Foster, Dr Jürgen Hedrich and Glenn Mercer for allowing us to share and explore our ideas with them.

Furthermore, we are also grateful to Glenn Mercer, Professor Andy Graves, Professor Susan Helper, Professor Richard Lamming, Professor John Paul MacDuffie, Mike Kitson, Dr Steve New, Professor Bill Nuttall, Dr George Olcott, Professor Alan Pilkington, Professor Garel Rhys, Professor Mari Sako, Dr Janet Smart, Professor David Upton, Professor Giuseppe Volpato, Max Warburton, Professor Francesco Zirpoli, and our colleagues at the MIT International Motor Vehicle Program for helpful discussions and comments on various ideas and issues covered in this book. We also would like to thank the Automotive Team at the Department for Business, Innovation and Skills (BIS) for their assistance, including Phil Davies, Ian Broadhurst, Dr Rupert Lewis, Ashley Roberts, Stephen Bates, Dr Alan Begg, Simon Carter, Francis Evans, Ian Major and Ben Rimmington. Furthermore, our research assistants deserve our thanks, in particular Dr Andreas Reichhart, Dr Stephan Schramm, Dr Merieke Stevens, Dhyan

Somanna, Yuepeng Yan, Kristoph Ullrich and Misha Leybovich for their help with the background research.

Lyn Benson worked tirelessly to transcribe the many hours of interview recordings that we accumulated in the course of the research on Rover. We thank the Cambridge-MIT Institute and the MIT International Motor Vehicle Program for the financial support that made the earlier parts of this work possible.

Last but not least, we owe great thanks to Paula Parish at Cambridge University Press. Paula kept pushing us to extend our horizons, and it is due to her that the book has the global reach and perspective that it now has. Paula showed amazing amounts of patience with us as the deadline to complete the book extended beyond any expectation that she, or we, could ever have imagined. Thank you, Paula, for staying with us.

All errors that remain are of course solely ours.

I Why a book on corporate resilience?

Corporate failure is an increasingly prevalent occurrence. Interest in resilience – the avoidance of failure and the recovery from it – is therefore unsurprisingly on the rise: The average lifespan of a company listed in the S&P 500 index has decreased by more than 50 years in the last century, to a mere 15 years by 2010.[1] Company life expectancies are reducing, and so are CEO tenures. Many reasons for this trend have been put forward: technological innovation, low-cost competition, overcapacity, and an increasing focus on short-term financial returns in many business environments. From a free market perspective, occasional failure is not a bad thing, a sign of creative destruction. Firms that are unable to generate sufficient returns should go out of business, or be taken over by stronger, more efficient firms. Yet in cyclical, mature industries this short-termism may deprive companies of the opportunity to develop long-lasting capabilities that generate wealth in the long term.

The 'industry of industries', as Peter Drucker once called the automotive industry, is a perfect setting to explore these challenges.[2] Yet many other sectors, such as aerospace, electronics and industrial equipment, face the same problem: firms are battered by cyclical markets that see demand drop drastically in a downturn, while they struggle to reduce the large structural cost embedded in their business. Recurring crises become the norm. Emerging markets have been both a bane and a boon in this respect – often providing the greatest opportunity for growth and a major threat due to new entrants at the same time. How can firms develop resilience to perennial problems such as global overcapacity and low-cost competition, to withstand the pressures that they face during a downswing in the business cycle?

In short, what does it take to survive in a mature global industry? This is the question we seek to answer in this book.

MANAGEMENT OR CONTEXT?

Our analysis combines the perspectives of two, usually opposing, schools of thought on corporate success and failure. Within writings on general management (by which we broadly mean strategy, organizational behaviour and operations management) there are ample examples of 'best-practice' literature. This literature typically identifies the practices found in relatively successful companies and describes these, often in a highly stylized form, in a manner suitable for consumption and transfer to other environments. Examples of the 'success manuals' of this genre include Peters and Waterman's *In Search of Excellence* (1982)[3], *The Machine that Changed the World* by Womack, Jones and Roos (1990)[4] and Collins and Porras' *Built to Last* (1994)[5] and Collins' *From Good to Great* (2001)[6]. Targeted at practitioners, these books aim for near-universal appeal and applicability which, critics say, can lead them to ignore, or play down, some of the more complex factors that are of crucial importance to the very success they are purporting to explain.

At the other extreme are those, often writing from a political-economy perspective, who argue that corporate success and survival is largely about history and context, with management choice and practice playing a much more limited role.[7] Such commentators are scathing about corporate success manuals and stress the importance of corporate history and context to performance. Viewed from this perspective, many struggling organizations are more or less doomed to fail because of a web of environmental constraints within which they find themselves enmeshed (such as agreements with organized labour, market conditions, national culture and institutions etc.). The success or failure of large firms is more to do with being in the right (or wrong) place at the right (or wrong) time than with how they are managed.

In this book we seek to combine both these perspectives. Whilst we share the view that many of the success manuals are naïve, simplistic and skate conveniently over issues of context, research demonstrates that the application of practices, such as lean principles, is often associated with high levels of quality and productivity and that, other things being equal, this augments competitiveness. The critical political-economy perspective downplays the significance of good management and the choices that managers actually have – although exercising these choices may mean overcoming formidable obstacles which many executives lack the political or other resources to do.

Where we concur with those who stress context is in our use in this book of Freeman's (1984) stakeholder theory[8] to consider how the 'settlements' between auto companies and their various constituencies (suppliers, labour, owners, capital markets, the state and customers) enable and constrain corporate behaviour. We argue that supportive stakeholder relations can be an important mechanism to prevent the failure of an auto company – as a necessary but not sufficient condition for long-term survival, above and beyond good practice in management. We argue that what constitutes 'success' depends on the perspective of the particular stakeholder: for investors it may be predictable and profitable return on their investment, for labour it is a safe and well-paid employment, for government it is employment and a national capability in one of the world's largest industrial sectors. The challenge for auto industry executives is to navigate through this complex landscape of stakeholders, trying, as far as possible, to achieve a balanced, sustainable set of settlements.

An implication of the stakeholder perspective is that major strategic change in large, established organizations such as auto companies, essential at times of crisis, typically requires not only changes to operations and organization, but also sometimes radical adjustment to the settlements between auto companies and their stakeholder groups. Like the 'Swiss cheese' model of failure,[9] which views disasters as a consequence of an unlikely alignment of circumstances, resilience and recovery from crisis requires an unusual – but not unattainable – alignment of enabling conditions. The absence of this alignment can explain long-term trajectories of decline as companies become progressively more and more 'boxed in' by multiple constraints, so that fixing one problem often just creates others elsewhere.

CRISES IN THE AUTO INDUSTRY

The aim of this book is to explore crisis, resilience and survival in the world's automotive industry. We focus on the automotive sector, specifically the 40 or so companies in the world that design, build and sell cars in significant numbers. The auto industry is a mature industry, featuring stable technology (with a dominant design that has been established more than a century ago); high barriers to entry and, as we shall argue, to exit as well; a global footprint; and a strong public profile. The activities of auto firms are heavily embedded in the economies in which they operate and their products are heavily embedded in the lives of those who use them.

The automotive industry has had a huge influence on thinking about management and organization. Not only is it a major employer in many countries, but the ways in which it has organized complex operations such as product development, manufacturing and supply chains have become management principles in their own right, with the approaches used by companies from Ford to Toyota influencing management theory and practice in many other sectors.

The auto industry is also an industry under stress. Two major car companies, Rover and Saab, have failed since 2005, and in 2009 GM, for decades the largest car company in the world, had to be bailed out by the US Government, along with Chrysler. There might have been even more auto company bankruptcies had it not been for support on the part of many governments, even ones ideologically opposed to intervention. Toyota, the star of the industry for more than two decades, faced its first ever loss in 60 years and suffered a bruising public relations disaster involving large-scale product recalls in 2010.

We first embarked on the research on which this book is based in April 2005, triggered by the collapse of MG Rover, the last

UK-owned volume car maker. In the immediate aftermath of the collapse the British media carried stories essentially blaming the collapse on the actions of the consortium of executives, known as the 'Phoenix Four', who had owned the company since 2000. Whilst there were certainly questions over some aspects of the conduct of the Four, it seemed to us that the seeds for Rover's collapse had been sown many years before. Our investigation of the Rover collapse, which is written up in Chapter 5, led us to interview many people who had been involved with the company in one capacity or another over the 40 years leading up to its demise. This was a fascinating process, and one from which we drew a number of conclusions.

First, many of the reasons for Rover's failure had a very, very long history, some of them pre-dating the formation of the company as a conglomerate through the merger of previously independent companies in 1968. Secondly, it was clear that most of the actors involved, even taking into account the benefits of hindsight, were very aware of the issues and problems that the company was facing at the time. Yet it was also clear that this awareness of the issues and problems was not, in most cases, accompanied by possession of the levers to pull in order to rectify them.

Our first impression was that the formation of the conglomerate had, more or less overnight, created an organization so complex that it had overwhelmed the capacity of its management apparatus to coordinate and control it. We published this idea in a paper in 2008[10] but remained unconvinced that the only explanation of Rover's failure was that the management apparatus was overwhelmed by the complexity that it faced. As we describe in Chapter 5, Rover faced a multitude of issues, and many of our interviewees conveyed a sense of being 'hemmed in' by forces and constraints they could not overcome. Although overload was clearly part of the picture, it did not explain everything.

A further source of unease as we delved into the Rover story was that few of the prescriptions found in the management literature seemed to really address a lot of the issues that Rover faced.

Particularly limited in this regard were many of the 'best practice' case studies, which claim to show the 'secret sauce' of corporate success. For the last 20–30 years, in the case of the auto industry, the 'sauce' often equates to an exhortation to 'design and build better cars'. We are not suggesting for a moment that designing and delivering bad products and services is a recipe for success in any industry, but in Rover's case simply fixing its products – which with Honda's help, it largely did during the 1980s – still left many other troublesome issues.

One of the reasons for this lies in the nature and dynamics of the auto industry itself. Many analyses of car companies have typically focused on the efficiency and effectiveness with which car makers design, build and distribute their products. These capabilities are of course important – but since the early 1990s we have seen a convergence in performance on these measures as car companies have learned lean methods from Toyota and other exemplars. However, we argue that success and survival cannot be understood in these terms alone, but require the orchestration of several conditions simultaneously: coverage of multiple vehicle segments; economies of scale through common components and platforms; and a strong position in markets that are growing and developing. Plus, crucially, the ability to reach appropriate settlements with external stakeholders such as the capital markets, owners, the state and organized labour. The recent global financial crisis has graphically highlighted that adjustments to such settlements can make the difference between corporate life or death.

Achieving all of this is a hard act to pull off. As the cases of Rover and Saab show, not all auto companies will make it. With a persistent 30 per cent production overcapacity worldwide[11] and as we write in 2015 continuing austerity in Europe, the industry faces yet more pain in the future. This book maps out how the auto industry has arrived at its current position, who is at risk in the coming years, and what lessons our analysis holds for other companies and sectors.

The book draws on material from a variety of sources. We have conducted detailed case studies of the collapse of Saab and Rover.

These form the basis of two chapters of the book which explore the dynamics of failure in depth. These two case studies are set in context by material on the evolution of the shape, size and competitive dynamics of the global auto industry which is presented in Chapter 2. In Chapter 3 we discuss different models of competitiveness that have been prevalent at different times in the industry, with reference to Ford, GM, Toyota and VW. Chapter 4 introduces our framework for thinking about issues of resilience and survival under four main headings – management and operations, stakeholder support, scale and market reach. Chapters 5 and 6 contain our case studies of Rover and Saab. In Chapter 7 we look at some of the 'near-misses' – auto firms that have experienced crises but survived. In Chapter 8 we look to the future and discuss the implications of our findings for the future of the industry.

Our aim is to take the discussion of failure, resilience and survival in the auto industry beyond consideration of the narrow and well-covered factors of competitiveness based on capabilities in product development, manufacturing and supply chain management and to show that, important as these capabilities are, they are not of themselves sufficient to understand why some companies survive and others do not. To do this, we argue, also requires consideration of the 'settlements' auto companies achieve with their stakeholders relative to those of their global competitors – stakeholders such as labour, suppliers, the capital markets and local and national governments, as well as of course their customers.

2 The evolution of a global industry

Few inventions have shaped our lives as much as the automobile. It not only allows us to freely move around in our personal lives, it also underpins and enables much of our economic activity by being able to efficiently move goods. As we write this book, the global automotive industry has produced a combined 3 billion vehicles[1] since 1900. The annual growth rate of industry output since 1945 has been 6.3 per cent, and this growth – despite distinct troughs during economic crises – has accelerated in the most recent decade.

In 2013 a total of 87,354,003 vehicles were produced globally, of which 65,462,496 were passenger cars. These added to the 1.1 billion vehicles presently in operation on the planet (see Figures 2.1 and 2.2).

The global auto industry comprises around 40 companies (or groups of companies) who in 2014 each manufactured 100,000 cars a year or more. Most of these also produce light commercial vehicles and about half have divisions that produce heavy commercial vehicles. The largest of these are truly colossal – companies such as Toyota, GM and Volkswagen produce around 10 million vehicles a year, employ hundreds of thousands of people in 100s of assembly plants and other facilities around the world. Yet, despite this scale, giant car companies are not immune from failure, as the bankruptcies of both GM and Chrysler in 2009 show.

In this chapter we will describe the evolution of the auto industry, as well as the operation of car companies within it and look at their strategy and operations. Car companies represent an extreme in terms of scale and complexity, but we will argue that many of the processes at work in the auto industry are common to many other organizations – they are simply played out on a much greater scale.

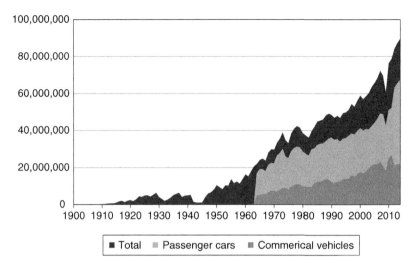

FIGURE 2.1 Global annual vehicle production since 1900
Source: World Motor Vehicle Data, various years

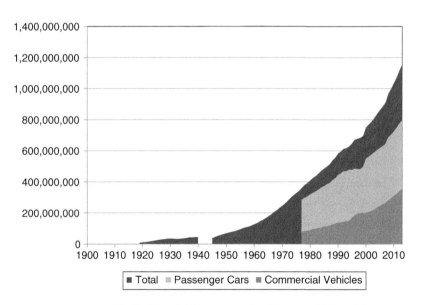

FIGURE 2.2 Worldwide vehicles in operation (data pre-1919 and for
1940–1944 not available)
Source: World Motor Vehicle Data, various years

The auto industry also has six key idiosyncrasies that are key to understanding both the dynamics of the industry and the success and failure of particular auto firms. These are:

1. **Persistent global production overcapacity** – in aggregate, automakers around the world have the capacity to produce far more vehicles than there is demand for. This is not a transient problem – overcapacity has existed for many years.

2. Auto firms have **national and corporate symbolic value** – for developing economies, possession of a car industry symbolizes economic development and progress. For mature economies, the decline of auto-making symbolizes industrial decline and creates political difficulties, especially in communities dependent on the auto industry for employment. Hence there are strong economic and non-economic incentives to enter car-making and equally strong barriers to exit.

3. Car sales are heavily affected by the **economic cycle**. Cars are expensive consumer items with a relatively long service life. Replacement or acquisition of vehicles can usually be deferred if money is tight, so the peaks and troughs of the economic cycle are amplified in the rise and fall in demand for cars.[2]

4. Cars are **complex products**. They contain a multitude of technologies that must be sourced and integrated into complete vehicles, which are then produced to exacting quality standards, within demanding cost constraints, in very high volumes. This demands a formidable capability to coordinate and control, not just within the auto-assembly companies, but across large and complex networks of supply, distribution and sales and support, often located on multiple continents.

5. Cars operate in varied and **demanding environments** – from desert to arctic conditions. The expectation is that they should function reliably for many years with minimal maintenance, in the hands of drivers who have little or no mechanical knowledge. Much modelling, testing and proving is needed before products are released

to the market, and high levels of support are required (e.g. parts supply and servicing) once vehicles are in the hands of customers.

6. For many people, cars are important **'identity' items** – the car that one drives can be an expression of one's self. For many car owners the look, feel and reputation and brand of their car count for a great deal, even more so than price, reliability or other 'rational' criteria.

As we shall describe, these and other features of the auto industry add up to an industry that is high profile, global and ferociously competitive. It is also, we shall argue, an industry in which being operationally capable is no longer a sufficient condition for survival.

EARLY HISTORY AND EVOLUTION

The automotive industry has its origins in both Europe and the USA, where inventors began to work on self-propelled road vehicles towards the end of the nineteenth century. These included Carl Benz, whose 'Patent-Motorwagen' of 1886 is widely considered to have set the blueprint for what became the modern automobile. Key figures in the nascent European auto industry were Nicolaus Otto, who worked with Gottlieb Daimler on the four-stroke internal combustion engine, Rudolf Diesel who proposed a self-igniting engine design, and of course many vehicle designers whose names we still recognise today: Armand Peugeot started production of his first self-propelled vehicle in 1889, Fiat was founded in 1899 by nine partners, including Giovanni Agnelli, and André Citroën started producing vehicles in 1919. At the birth of the automotive industry craft producers such as Panhard et Lavassor, Duesenberg, and Hispano Suiza, employed skilled workforces to hand-craft single vehicles customized to the preferences of the few customers who could afford them.

In the USA, Henry Ford founded the Ford Motor Company in 1903, and started producing his famous Model T in 1908. Many auto brands that rose to prominence were also founded in the early days of the twentieth century: For example, in 1903 David Buick founded his company, which was taken over by William Durant in 1904, who went on to found the General Motors Corporation in 1908. Louis

Chevrolet started producing his model *Classic Six* in 1912 to compete against Ford's Model T. His company was bought out by Durant in 1918, to become part of the growing General Motors Corporation. The Chrysler Motor Corporation was founded in 1925 by Walter Chrysler (who previously had worked for GM). Chrysler grew to become the third of the 'Big Three' US auto producers when it purchased Dodge Brothers and became home to the Chrysler, Dodge, Imperial, DeSoto and Plymouth brands. Many comprehensive historical accounts of the early years of the motor industry have been written,[3] and we refer readers who are interested in detailed historical accounts to these works.

Several important features of today's motor industry stem from this early period. First, the dominant design of the automobile as we know it was established at this time. These included an internal combustion engine burning petrol or diesel fuel; the vehicles rode on four wheels with rubber tyres; they had predominantly steel bodies; and made use of an on-board DC electrical system to power various systems and items of electrical equipment. In the very early days of the industry electric cars were strong contenders for the dominant design, but then, as now, faced challenges with range and performance due to problems of energy storage and the limitations of battery technology.

A further important influence on the industry was in how cars were produced and this was initially driven by Henry Ford, who aimed to relentlessly cut the cost of his vehicles to make them affordable to a mass market, and his counterpart Alfred Sloan at General Motors, who – unable to compete with Ford on cost – devised the notion of building 'a car for every purse and purpose'. The competitive dynamics between these two strategies drove the development of mass, yet differentiated, markets for automobiles and laid the foundation for vehicle 'brand' as a key differentiator between products.

A combination of global expansion and consolidation of the industry via mergers and acquisitions led to the formation of powerful auto corporations who would rule the world for decades to come. Ford began establishing its own overseas operations in 1917, subsequently opening a series of factories in the UK, Germany, Argentina, South Africa and Australia. GM opted more for acquisition. In 1925, GM bought Vauxhall in the UK, in 1929 Adam Opel AG in Germany, and in 1931 it acquired Holden in Australia.

Although car production took place in a number of countries around the world before the Second World War (Nissan produced its first car in 1914, for example) this was generally very low volume and the lion's share of car production took place in Europe and the USA. In 1935, the USA produced 3.25 million passenger cars and 694,690 commercial vehicles which amounted at the time to 77 per cent of total global vehicle production.

1950S–1960S

The post-war period was a period of growth in the auto industry, and for countries such as Japan and Germany, a period of reconstruction. At the beginning of the 1950s, the US was producing around 4 million vehicles a year and the figure grew to average between 5–6 million vehicles per year throughout the decade.

In Europe, the four major car producing countries – the UK, Italy, France and West Germany – all increased output significantly during the 1950s. By 1960 West Germany was producing close on two million units per year, and the other three were each producing 500,000–1 million units per year. In the post-war period, Japan's car industry, which had been nascent prior to the war, began to develop, from almost nothing, to just over 200,000 units per year by 1960.

Initially, the Japanese growth was driven by domestic demand as the country went through 'motorization' – the term for the period when ownership of motor vehicles increases drastically, something which nations experience once economic development passes a certain point. Protected from their much stronger foreign competitors by import tariffs, Japanese car makers initially made cars for the Japanese domestic market. However, as the Japanese car makers learned and developed, so the productivity and quality of Japanese cars began to rise, growing close to world standards; Japan started exporting to the United States and Europe, initially at modest levels. Toyota first started selling cars in the US in 1957, when they sold just 403 units. However, the 1960s saw the rapid rise of Japan as a vehicle-producer:

car output soared nearly 17 fold, from around 200,000 units per year at the start of the 1960s to nearly 3.5 million by 1970.

The 1950s were boom years for the US automobile producers. In 1950, 81 per cent of all passenger cars produced globally were made in the USA, and the USA accounted for 76 per cent of the world's passenger car pool. The 1960s continued to be a boom time for most automakers, albeit with increasing labour unrest as the decade wore on. Early in the 1960s, car production in the USA reached what turned out to be a long-term average of around eight million units per year, excluding light trucks (pick-ups) and commercial vehicles.

Sales were also going well for the major car producers in Europe in the 1960s: most increased their output by about 50 per cent over the decade, although labour unrest became prevalent. Germany and France were the clear leaders in car production, producing approximately 3.5 and 2.5 million units per year respectively, while Italy and the UK both produced around 1.5 million units per year.

During the 1960s, car ownership continued to rise sharply in most markets – apart from the already mature North American market – and car makers grew in size accordingly. In some cases, firms' organic growth was supplemented by mergers and acquisitions in pursuit of size and scale. We will deal in detail with one example, namely the creation and subsequent demise of British Leyland, in Chapter 5.

Meanwhile, import tariffs – which governments had set in place to protect their domestic car industries – began to come down during the 1960s, as pressures for free trade increased. This increased the competition that car manufacturers faced in their domestic markets, as imported vehicles became cheaper to buy. For example, tariffs on vehicles imported to the UK had been as high as 33.3% in 1956. They were reduced to 22% in 1968, and fell yet further in 1972 to 11%. Tariffs on vehicles traded between Britain and the major Western European countries were removed completely in 1977. Free trade, and the resulting levels of imports into many markets, fundamentally changed the nature of the global motor industry.

THE 1970S–1980S: OIL SHOCKS AND IMPORTS FROM JAPAN

At the beginning of the 1970s, European and US producers still dominated the global auto industry. True, the output of Japanese producers had been growing exponentially, but up until that point, this had primarily focused on the Japanese domestic market. Japan's initial experiments with exporting cars, particularly to the United States during the late 1950s and 1960s, had met with mixed success. However, this changed with the oil shocks of 1973 and 1979 which benefited Japan's automakers considerably.

Although the risk of oil crises had existed for some time,[4] US car producers had largely ignored the warning signs and continued to produce large gas-guzzling vehicles. But then in 1973, in protest at American and Western support for Israel, a number of Arab oil producers began to boycott the supply of oil to the West – principally to the USA. Within just two months the price of crude oil quadrupled, and in the USA gasoline jumped from 36 cents per gallon to 60 cents per gallon. Queues developed at gas stations; there were fights as drivers jockeyed for position in the lines and even reports of murders. The American auto industry had been caught by surprise and in Western Europe, new car registrations fell by 25 per cent.

In the USA, the oil crisis came as a boon to Japanese car makers whose much smaller vehicles were very fuel efficient. While the US industry struggled to modify its cars to cope with effects of the shock, Japanese imports poured into America, to the dismay and anger of the indigenous producers. Henry Ford II trenchantly described the arrival of Japanese cars in large numbers as 'an economic Pearl Harbor'[5] and as the decade wore on, friction mounted. Nightly news programmes on US TV showed pictures of unemployed car and steel workers attacking Japanese cars with sledgehammers in protest at the loss of their jobs. By the mid 1970s, the Japanese share of the US market had risen to 9.5 per cent or around 800,000 units (*Automotive News* 2000). In Europe the Japanese took around 10 per cent of the UK market, and 5 per cent of the Western European market as a whole.

Around the world, auto production dipped in response to the oil shock. Though output recovered fairly quickly, the oil crisis was significant because it provided a jolt that disrupted established patterns of car buying around the world – and when the crisis was over, the old pattern did not return. In the USA, this meant that Japanese automakers made significant, enduring inroads into the US car market. Reflecting on this some years later Hal Sperlich, of Ford, observed: 'Suddenly, what they [the Japanese] had was hot and what Detroit had, was not.'[6]

The influx of Japanese cars into Europe at this time was less marked, but the oil crisis dealt a disproportionate blow to weaker players, such as British Leyland, the major UK domestic producer, whose story we recount in Chapter 5.

This is a pattern that we shall see repeatedly in our analysis of crisis and resilience in the auto industry. Persistent overcapacity means that most car makers are financially marginal across the business cycle, apart from those (such as, at the time of writing, the German premium brands of BMW, Mercedes and Porsche) who have managed to carve out niche positions that partially shield them from the intense competition that comes when several producers compete head to head in the same segment, eroding margins.[7] We shall see that in the auto industry shocks such as the oil crisis, much like natural shocks such as epidemics or storms in the case of biological organisms or ecosystems, do far more damage to the weak than the strong.

Other significant changes in the auto industry also occurred in the 1970s, one of which was the move towards more integrated global operations, of which the idea of the 'world car' – that is a car based on a common platform and components but sold, with only minor variations, in many markets around the world – was one manifestation. An early example of this was General Motors' 'J platform' which went into production in 1981 and was the basis for models branded, in different markets, as Chevrolets, Pontiacs, Oldsmobiles, Opels and Vauxhalls. Later attempts at the 'world car' were the Fiat Palio and the Ford Focus, but most attempts were either outright failures against their original objectives or regional successes at best. Ford, for example, took a serious beating in the financial press for taking six years and spending an estimated $6 billion developing its world car – the Mondeo/Contour/Mystique. Although defended publicly, Ford senior management privately vowed never to spend as much on a single vehicle again.

Many major auto companies began to look at ways to consolidate their operations at this time. Ford created 'Ford of Europe' as a pan-European organization responsible for the design, production and distribution of all Ford vehicles in Europe. This contrasted with the previous situation, where vehicles had been engineered and produced largely on a country-by-country basis. The creation of Ford of Europe, which involved merging Ford's British and German subsidiaries, recognized a growing need to think of Europe as a single trading block and to allow Ford to enjoy the economies of scale arising from this. Ford was not alone in reconfiguring its operations. GM took similar steps, centralizing its European R&D in Germany and moving increasing amounts of its production to Spain. Other key European industry players, such as Renault and Volkswagen, expanded their product ranges and developed manufacturing facilities in key markets across Europe.

The early 1980s saw pronounced trade friction between Japan and Western economies, particularly the USA, over the increasing share of the US market that Japanese producers were now taking. Detroit was in crisis, and the US auto producers demanded protection from Japanese imports. They got it, in the form of 'voluntary' export restraints (VERs), which limited the numbers of Japanese autos that could be imported into the USA. Although reluctant to accept these, the Japanese did so out of a concern that if they did not, full-scale trade barriers would be erected, which would greatly limit their access to foreign markets.

At the same time there were similar tensions in Europe. The CEO of Peugeot-Citroën, Jacques Calvet, was particularly outspoken in his criticism of Japanese penetration into European markets. Calvet led a campaign to protect the European car market in order, he said, to give the indigenous European producers time to adjust to the competitive threat coming from Japan. Calvet was one of the most ferocious critics of investments into the UK by Nissan, Honda and Toyota during the 1980s and early 1990s and argued that Japanese cars built in the UK should count as 'imports' into Europe – and hence be part of the import quotas. His stance did not prevail, although European import quotas on Japanese vehicles remained in place until as late as 1999.[8]

As a response to these import restraints, the Japanese built plants in the USA and Europe. Honda was the first Japanese auto firm to start production in the USA: its factory in Marysville, Ohio, which opened in 1982, was followed rapidly by Nissan's Smyrna plant in 1983, and Toyota's joint venture with GM in Fremont, California (NUMMI), in 1984.[9] In Europe, Nissan opened a plant in UK, in 1986, soon to be followed by Toyota and Honda, both in 1992. By 2014, Japanese auto firms had no fewer than 12 assembly plants Europe and 21 in North America.

The quotas imposed by the voluntary export restraints applied to the number, rather than value, of imported vehicles so the Japanese response was to go upmarket in search of more value per car. Ironically, this meant that the quotas did not so much reduce the Japanese threat to local car producers, but in fact increased it. Because Japanese producers were restricted in the number of vehicles they could export to the USA, they concentrated on exporting their more profitable variants and introduced premium brands, such as Toyota's Lexus, Nissan's Infinity and Honda's Acura brands. Cheaper, entry-level cars were produced locally. As a result, throughout the 1980s, the Japanese captured increasing market share in the USA, and opened assembly plants in North America as fast as GM, Ford and Chrysler closed them. Figure 2.3 shows how the combined share of the US market of indigenous car makers fell from close to 100% in the 1950s to less than 50% by 2010.

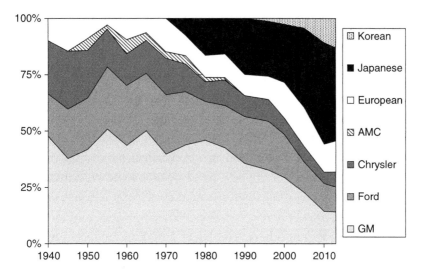

FIGURE 2.3 Market shares in the US passenger car market since 1940
Source: Ward's Yearbooks, various years

By the mid 1980s, in the space of just 25 years, Japanese auto producers had secured approximately a quarter of the global market for passenger cars, from virtually zero in 1960. In 1985, car production in Japan accounted for 23.1% of total global production, of which 57.9% was exported. Over the same period, the US share of global car production more than halved from 52.4% to 25.0%.

Although trade friction had been one consequence of Japan's advance into Western markets, Western auto companies also began to look with increasing admiration at how Japanese companies were managed. Theories as to what made Japanese car makers so successful abounded. Was it the much greater commitment of Japanese workers to their companies? Was it consensual decision-making? Was it bottom-up improvement activities such as quality circles, and the famous just-in-time system pioneered originally by Toyota, but adopted to varying degrees by all the other Japanese auto-producers? More and more Western industrialists made visits to Japan to learn about the success of Japan's major manufacturers, and the auto industry was centre-stage. Publications about Japanese management, and particularly Japanese manufacturing methods, ballooned.[10]

Prior to this time, most post-war overseas investment in the auto industry had come from firms from the developed world investing in plants in the developing world – either to cut labour costs, circumvent import duties or to access new markets. But what happened in the 1980s, led primarily by the Japanese, was the reverse: a wave of investment into developed countries which already had their own strong, indigenous producers. Competitiveness in the car industry came to be seen in part as a test of industrial prowess between nations and regions.

One side effect of the new trend was for some Western producers to tackle their falling domestic market share by seeking out new, developing markets themselves. The 1980s saw oversees investments by Renault, VW and others. The larger European producers realized that it was necessary to build presence in developing, as well as in established, markets and so began to set up production facilities overseas, in much the same way as the USA had done during the 1920s. Volkswagen, which had already established overseas facilities in Brazil (1953), Mexico (1964) and the USA (1976), started looking to markets such as China, and entered into an agreement with the Chinese government to start car production in Shanghai in 1984. Trade liberalization and opening of China to foreign investment under Deng Xiaoping set in train a motion that two decades later would see China rise to become the largest single market for passenger cars. The impact of this strategy on VW's sales and production volumes is shown in Figure 2.4. Auto companies that for one reason or another did not pursue these new opportunities, perhaps because they were relatively small and lacked the resources to do so, risked finding themselves far behind the early movers once these markets developed.

But developing countries did not just want to be a home for the factories of foreign-owned car makers. Many also wanted to develop their own automotive industries. In practice, this entailed attracting foreign inward investment, as well as entering into technology tie-ups and other relationships.

South Korea is a case in point. With strong support from government, Hyundai Motor was established in 1967 and quickly

FIGURE 2.4 Volkswagen: production volumes and net income, 1970–2004
Source: VW annual reports, various years

developed and was producing 4 million cars annually by 1990. Korea's Daewoo had been producing cars in various guises since 1937, while Samsung Motors was founded as late as 1994. Samsung actually began selling cars in 1998, just as the effects of the 1997 East Asia financial crisis began to bite. Samsung sold a 70 per cent stake in Samsung Motors to Renault in 2000, who renamed the company Renault-Samsung Motors and later increased its stake to 80 per cent.

Overall, car production in South Korea rose from 106 units in 1965, to 18,498 in 1975, to 264,458 units in 1985, and surpassed 1 million units for the first time in 1991. This growth has continued and in 2015 South Korea is the fourth largest car producer in the world.

THE 1990S: LEAN PRODUCTION, MERGERS AND ACQUISITIONS

'Lean production'

The advance of the Japanese car industry during the 1970s and 1980s was impossible to miss, and many in the industry were well aware of the competitive threat posed by the Japanese – although the precise nature and basis of the apparent Japanese advantage was still debated. The year 1990 saw the publication of *The Machine that Changed the World*,[11] a book which rapidly became a bestseller. The book was based on a five-year research programme (the International Motor Vehicle Programme or IMVP) focusing on competitiveness in the world's auto-industry. The researchers set out to measure, as systematically and objectively as possible, the size of the competitive gap that many believed existed between the Japanese auto producers and those in the rest of the world.

Up until then, there had been various theories about the success of Japan's auto firms on the part of non-Japanese observers, including favourable exchange rates, higher automation, smaller, simpler products and labour culture (which advocates viewed as a consequence of greater worker commitment and critics saw as greater intensification and exploitation of labour). *The Machine that Changed the World* challenged many of these interpretations in that it appeared to demonstrate far greater superiority on the part of the Japanese producers, in both productivity and quality and placed the credit for this on the way that Japanese auto producers organized the processes by which cars were designed and produced. But if the IMVP findings were deeply worrying for Western auto manufacturers, there was also a message of hope. The performance levels of the Japanese transplant factories in North America, a number of which had been set up in the 1980s in response to trade friction, were actually quite close to those of the plants of their parents in Japan. American workers, on American soil, but under Japanese management could apparently produce cars at similar levels of efficiency and accuracy as the parent plants in Japan. This, according to Womack, Jones and Roos, proved that Japanese 'lean production' principles were in fact transferable across national boundaries, and were not culturally specific to Japan.

The IMVP research focused on assembly plant performance – the final assembly of the complete vehicles – but the IMVP also addressed supplier relationships and new vehicle development,[12] which (as we shall discuss in Chapter 4) showed that Japanese superiority was not limited to vehicle assembly, but extended to their ability to design and engineer new vehicles as well. Japanese producers were also able to produce a greater variety of models, with about half the engineering hours and much shorter development lead times, than their Western counterparts.[13] This allowed Japanese firms to operate shorter model replacement cycles and to proliferate models and segments, something which piled even more pressure onto struggling Western auto firms.

The productivity differences highlighted in IMVP's first round of benchmarks were startling (see Figure 2.5), so much so that when they were first published some of the European producers questioned their validity. Others, like Carl Hahn at Volkswagen, saw their potential and used them to develop and drive internal efficiency improvement projects. VW's 'KVP', short for continuous improvement process in German, was a direct translation of Toyota's kaizen methodology. Over time, as Western manufacturers adopted lean

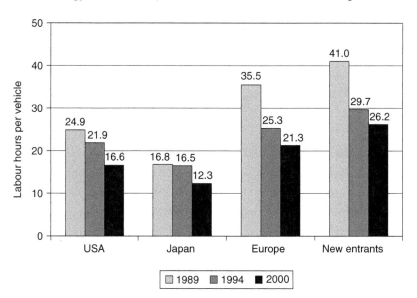

FIGURE 2.5 Productivity differences by country: 1989, 1994 and 2000
Source: Holweg and Pil (2004)

production practices, the productivity differentials narrowed as lean practices diffused through the industry and manufacturing practices converged across firms and regions.

The decade of mergers

Just as *The Machine that Changed the World* was published and global admiration for Japanese automakers was peaking, Japan's economic bubble burst and Japan entered a prolonged period of recession followed by stagnation – dubbed the two 'lost decades'. Prolonged recession in their domestic market caused a number of the Japanese car makers – whose ability to develop and manufacture cars efficiently was so celebrated – to run into financial difficulties. At the same time the US economy entered a period of sustained growth, leading to the recovery of the US producers, and to some extent a restoration of their confidence. Within a few short years the tables appeared to be turned. Although on measures of operational performance Japanese automakers were still ahead of their Western counterparts,[14] the stagnation of Japan's economy on which many Japanese car makers were quite dependent for a significant proportion of their sales pulled down their financial performance, partly because of a reluctance on the part of Japanese auto companies to cut capacity (and jobs) and cancel contracts with suppliers. Thus, despite their operational prowess, a number of Japanese automakers became takeover targets for their now financially stronger Western counterparts.

In 1999 GM bought a 20 per cent stake in Fuji Heavy Industries (Subaru). In 1996 Ford increased its small shareholding in Mazda, which it had held since 1979, to 33.3 per cent and practically took over the running of Mazda. These stakes proved to be short-lived – GM disposed of its interest in Fuji in 2005–6, just six years after acquiring it and Ford sold off most of its holdings in Mazda in 2008–10.

Chrysler, too, flirted with ownership of a Japanese automaker. Chrysler had taken a 15 per cent interest in Mitsubishi Motors in 1971 and had a 50:50 joint venture with Mitsubishi in the US in the late 1980s in the form of Diamond-Star Motors. Chrysler had sold off its holding in Mitsubishi in 1992–3. As part of a global expansion strategy, Daimler took over Chrysler in 1998, and in 2000, the merged Daimler-Chrysler took a controlling 34 per cent stake in Mitsubishi Motors. However, a scandal due to a recalls cover-up, the stagnant Japanese economy, and a big loss in the USA all dragged Mitsubishi Motors down and by 2005 it was back in the hands of the Mitsubishi Group.

Perhaps most dramatically of all, Nissan, Japan's second largest car maker, entered into a strategic alliance with French automaker Renault in 1999. Louis Schweitzer, CEO of Renault at the time, saw Renault as being 'too small, too isolated, too French', and was looking for a partner. He had proposed a merger with Volvo in 1997, which was blocked by Swedish unions. Then, when the negotiations between Nissan and the newly formed DaimlerChrysler failed to conclude in 1998, he moved quickly and four weeks later the contract between Renault and Nissan was signed.

So here was an interesting paradox. Many of the Japanese car companies who at the start of the 1990s had been operationally strong (with efficient production and high product quality) were now financially weak, and vulnerable to acquisition by their Western competitors whose operational performance was poorer. The exceptions were Toyota and Honda, both of whom continued to perform well and who remained independent.

In Europe, mergers and acquisitions swept up most of the smaller independent specialist producers from the late 1980s onwards. Ford bought Jaguar in 1989; BMW acquired the Rover Group, including Land Rover, in 1994, only to break it up again in 2000. BMW retained the new Mini and the plant in which to build it and sold Land Rover to Ford. As we shall see in Chapter 5, Rover's fading volume cars business was sold to a British consortium for just £10 in 2000. GM acquired 50 per cent of Saab in 1989 and assumed full ownership in 2000. Ford added Volvo to its growing family of premium European brands in 1999, and also picked up Land Rover a year later, following the break-up of the Rover Group by BMW. Ford formed its 'Premier Automotive Group' (PAG) from these acquisitions, a group that comprised the Lincoln, Mercury, Aston Martin, Jaguar, Land Rover and Volvo brands. While estimates are hard to confirm, sources claim that Ford invested US$17 billion in its PAG,[15] only to dismantle it again after Alan Mulally became CEO in 2006 when Ford needed cash to get through the 2007–8 financial crisis. Ford sold Jaguar Land Rover to Tata in 2008 for US$2.3 billion, and Volvo to China's Geely Group in 2010 for US$1.8 billion.

Volkswagen too had been on the acquisition trail, acquiring Seat in 1986, Skoda in 1991, and Bentley in 1998. VW was outmanoeuvred by BMW, who retained the naming rights to 'Rolls Royce', so a gentlemen's agreement saw VW retain the original Rolls Royce and Bentley factory in Crewe and the Bentley brand, while BMW established a new factory for its Rolls Royce brand in Goodwood, UK.

The prevalent belief in the auto industry during this period was that small car companies could not survive alone. Hence there was a scramble to seek protection under the wing of a larger player, or to merge with a player of a similar size (Renault-Nissan, Daimler-Chrysler, Rover and BMW). The conventional wisdom in the 1990s was that no car manufacturer producing fewer than 1 million units per year would be able to sustain its operations independently, and that eventually the industry would consolidate into six major manufacturers (or groups).

The consequence of this was an industry structure that included many cross-ownership ties, some large groups, and some smaller, independent manufacturers. While the mergers and acquisitions of the 1990s created some nominally very large firms, realizing actual operational benefits was more elusive. In extreme cases, as in the Daimler-Chrysler merger, personal and corporate vanity seemed to overrule the potential complementarities to be gained from joining forces. Jürgen Schrempp, then CEO of Daimler-Benz, in an allusion to the old British Empire, stated that he wanted to create a global company 'where the sun never sets', and acquired stakes in Chrysler,

Hyundai and Mitsubishi. But amidst subsequent corporate scandals at Mitsubishi, and continued losses at Chrysler, it soon transpired that there was actually little operational synergy to be gained. Differences in product architecture, market segments, regional coverage, and not least, organizational culture proved to be too great.[16] Daimler sold Chrysler to Cerberus Investments in 2007, after Chrysler posted losses of US$1.5 billion in 2006. Schrempp, who resigned in 2005, has since entered German corporate history as the CEO who presided over the greatest destruction of market valuation of any German company since 1945, an estimated €40bn.

In fact most of the big auto mergers that took place in the 1990s unravelled sooner or later, as the difficulties of integrating different corporate cultures and dispersed development activities became apparent, and it became clear that aggregate production volumes alone were insufficient to create viable car companies. One notable exception to this is Renault-Nissan, which on most measures has been a success, confounding the sceptics. The two firms have complementary strengths – Renault in design and marketing, Nissan in manufacturing and engineering – and complementary global presence: Renault in Europe and Latin America, Nissan in Asia and North America. In addition both firms had compatible product architectures and operate in the volume segments, so that they have been able to share platforms, components, production facilities and purchasing to a degree that Daimler and Chrysler were never able to.

The 1990s thus represented a period of turbulence and change for the auto industry. The decade began with the Japanese automakers as an apparently unassailable force. US and European producers were in a humiliating position – re-learning skills in how to manage and organize new product development and manufacturing from their Japanese rivals. Analyses of the auto industry focused largely on the USA, Europe and Japan – in *The Machine that Changed the World*, only about 10 per cent of the assembly plants studied lay outside these three regions, and non-US, European and Japanese plants from everywhere else in the world were lumped together under the category 'NICs' – newly industrializing countries – and were limited to Mexico, Brazil, Taiwan and Korea.

As the Japanese economy stagnated following the burst of the bubble in 1990, the spotlight soon moved away from the Japanese automakers. Some argued that the Japanese advantage had been overstated all along and that the success of the Japanese automakers in the 1970s and 1980s had been due to the confluence of a particular set of social, economic and market conditions rather than to distinct and replicable management practices.[17] But in the course of the 1990s many Japanese auto companies were forced to accept cash injections from the foreign automakers, graphically demonstrating that operational excellence of itself does not deliver sustained success. It was not that the Japanese ability to make cars diminished – indeed, throughout this period, Japanese cars continued to top the league tables on measures of quality and customer satisfaction. Table 2.1 shows ratings of 36 car brands for breakdowns and faults, drawn from the UK's Consumer Association publication *Which?* for 1995 to 2009. Of the top 10 brands, 9 are Japanese.

Faced with a prolonged downturn in their domestic market and a reluctance to downsize (partly out of a sense of obligation to their employees and suppliers) many Japanese auto firms simply ran out of cash or suffered such depreciation in share price that they became attractive takeover targets. This occurred at the same time as a flurry of mergers, acquisitions and alliances as companies struggled to achieve the economics of scale believed, at the time, to be necessary to survive in the auto industry. Other East Asian producers also expanded massively, particularly the South Koreans with Hyundai for example expanding its output from 676,000 to 2.4 million vehicles per year between 1990 and 2000. This massive expansion of capacity laid the foundations for trouble and this broke in 1997, when the East Asian financial crisis led to the near bankruptcy of most of the South Korean producers. Hyundai and Kia engaged in a defensive merger and Daewoo was acquired by GM and became one of GM's global low-cost

Table 2.1 *Average ratings for faults, problems and breakdowns 1995–2009*

Rank	Brand	Average rating*
1 =	Honda	5.0
1 =	Lexus	5.0
1 =	Mazda	5.0
1 =	Toyota	5.0
5	Subaru	4.4
6	Daihatsu	4.3
7 =	Suzuki	4.2
7 =	Hyundai	4.2
9	Nissan	4.0
10	Mitsubishi	3.8
11 =	Proton	3.7
11 =	Mercedes	3.7
13 =	BMW	3.3
13 =	Isuzu	3.3
15 =	Kia	3.1
15 =	Daewoo	3.1
15 =	Audi	3.1
18	Skoda	3.0
19	Volkswagen	2.9
20	Jaguar	2.8
21 =	Seat	2.7
21 =	Porsche	2.7
23	Volvo	2.5
24 =	Chrysler	2.4
24 =	Ford	2.4
26 =	Jeep	2.3
26 =	Peugeot	2.3
26 =	Saab	2.3
29	Vauxhall (GM)	2.2
30	Citroën	2.1
31 =	Alfa Romeo	2.0
31 =	Smart	2.0
33	Fiat	1.9
34 =	MG Rover	1.8
34 =	Land Rover	1.8
36	Renault	1.8

*Ratings are calculated from the UK's *Which?* consumer magazine, in which brands are scored on a scale of 1–5 according to (a) breakdowns (excluding accidents, punctures, flat batteries); (b) problems – annoyances and inconveniences (e.g. squeaks, rattles) (c) parts that have required replacement or repair (excl. routine replacements, accidents and misuse). The data cover every year from 1995 to 2009 inclusive, apart from 2004–5 and 2005–6 when data were reported in a different format. 1=worst, 5=best.

brands. GM subsequently re-branded Daewoo vehicles as 'Chevrolets' across several regions of the world.

2000–2010: PLATFORMS AND THE RISE OF EMERGING MARKETS

In the 1980s and early 1990s much attention focused on manufacturing reform. By the mid 1990s product development and engineering management were receiving far more attention than had previously been the case. Car makers around the world strove to drive down product development lead times and to take time and cost out of the product development process. More responsibility was put on to first-tier suppliers, who underwent considerable consolidation, fostering the development of global first-tier 'full service' suppliers. In the latter part of the 1990s we began to see the emergence of 'mega-suppliers', global giants capable of supporting multiple automakers around the globe, and by 2012 the largest of these such as Bosch, Denso and Continental had sales to rival some of the smaller automakers.[18]

Related to the growth of mega-suppliers, during this period there was speculation that cars would become much more 'modular', in the way that personal computers are, largely comprising standard components and subsystems, produced by mega-suppliers with the role of car makers reduced to a few activities such as integration and marketing. In practice, modularity made limited advances as it limited the ability of car makers to finesse the complete vehicle in pursuit of a particular look and feel. As the Product Development Director of a European premium producer commented to us, when describing how his company had investigated buying 'corner' (wheel and suspension) modules: 'You get plenty of it, but it's not always quite what you want'. It was also becoming apparent that the Japanese system of product development reported in *The Machine that Changed the World* – revolving as it did around relatively autonomous development teams under strong project managers – had drawbacks as well as advantages. The strong, autonomous product development teams that were so effective at coordinating the efforts of engineering and other specialists in order to develop individual new models quickly and effectively had a side effect – they encouraged a proliferation of models and variants that shared relatively few components. This in turn pushed up costs.

Vehicle platforms

As a response, car makers increasingly turned to the 'product platform' concept.[19] The key idea behind a *product platform* is that one common base supports many different variants. In the auto industry, the term 'platform' is typically used to describe the basic underbody of the vehicle – floorpan, engine compartment, suspension and running gear, etc. The main benefits of sharing a 'platform' between several models is the ability to standardize production equipment, save time in product development by re-using parts and components, and of course, economies of scale in purchasing of components. In short, platforms allow manufacturers to provide *external* variety (in terms of different models and bodystyles), while keeping *internal* variety to a minimum. On the downside, a criticism of platforms is that vehicles on a shared platform can become too similar to provide a meaningful differentiation. The main issue in using platforms successfully is to standardize aspects of the product the customer does not care about, or does not even see, while making sure that the salient aspects of the vehicle are distinct. As Bob Lutz[20] argues: 'You could make the argument that [platforms] detract somewhat from peak engineering excellence. But my retort to that is, So what? If the design is good and the brand is good, that doesn't matter...'

The platform accounts for a significant share of development costs of the new vehicle (which on average, overall, amount from $1bn for a new model that shares existing parts, to $6bn for a new model on a new platform).[21] However, the same platform can support several variants, which may be tuned to look and feel quite different to the end-user. Body shape, engines, suspension, steering settings, trim and so on can all be altered to create apparently different cars, all based on the same platform. The platform concept

Table 2.2 *Platforms, models and production volumes in Europe, 1990–2000. Source: Pil and Holweg (2004)*

	1990	1995	1996	1997	1998	1999	2000
Number of platforms in use (all Europe)	60	60	57	56	53	51	45
Number of bodytypes offered (all Europe)	88	137	139	148	157	162	170
Average number of bodytypes per platform	1.5	2.3	2.4	2.6	3.0	3.2	3.8
Average production volume by platform (in '000s)	190	171	185	194	199	215	249
Average production volume by bodytype (in '000s)	129	75	76	73	67	68	66

thus offers car makers scope to address many different market niches, whilst economizing on underlying engineering and development costs. An ability to share platforms enables manufacturers to increase their product range and reach in a fragmenting market, while still benefiting from economies of scale. However, as we shall see in the case of Saab in Chapter 6, platform-sharing must be executed with some care, particularly for premium products, if it is not to undermine brand value.

The mid 1990s saw a drastic reduction in the number of platforms in use in the industry and an increased number of variants per platform. As Table 2.2 shows, the number of platforms in use in Europe fell from 60 on 1990 to 48 in 2002, but at the same time the number of body types offered more than doubled. One car maker who took this concept further than anyone else was Volkswagen, whose platforms are shared across its Volkswagen, Audi, Seat and Skoda brands. Its A4/PQ34 platform formed the basis of no fewer than seven vehicles that were in production simultaneously – the VW Golf Mk. IV/Bora and New Beetle; the Audi A3 Mk.I and TT Mk.I; the Skoda Octavia Mk.I; the Seat Leon Mk.I and the Toledo Mk.II.

We argue later that this ability to simultaneously reach more market segments, across more territories, whilst enjoying economies of scale below the surface and without compromising brand identity is a critical success factor for the volume car makers – but an act that not all can pull off successfully.

If a key challenge for the volume producers was to squeeze maximum market reach from the minimum variety of underlying fundamentals, the smaller, more specialist producers faced a different challenge. Driven by the high costs of new model development, smaller auto producers began to find it more and more difficult to fund their new model programmes, and consequently were not able to replace their models so frequently (or to extend their model ranges to increase their market reach). As segments proliferated, and the sales to be had from any one segment diminished, the specialist producers came under more and more pressure. As we shall see in the chapter on Saab, this manifested itself as a restricted set of models (and hence limited coverage of a limited number of market segments in an increasingly fragmented market place) and long model lives in an industry where product life cycles were becoming shorter. With more models but shorter model life cycles, vehicle makers had smaller production volumes and less time over which to recover the fixed costs of new product development. Low-cost manufacturers at the bottom end of the market could remain competitive through low production costs per unit for less technologically sophisticated products. Low-volume specialist manufacturers like Porsche and Ferrari could happily survive on their large margins. However, the companies serving the upper to middle segment of the market suffered. Companies such as Volvo, Jaguar and Saab were squeezed between the high development costs necessary to remain competitive at the upper end of the market, whilst being unable to expand their volumes due to limited demand because of their specialist brand images. This made the specialists receptive to the advances of the volume makers who were seeking to acquire premium brands.

Table 2.3 shows the average usage of platforms by vehicle manufacturer in 2013. As can be seen, by now the platform concept has been widely adopted across all main car makers. The three largest individual platforms are the Toyota's 'MC-M' (2,787,808 units across 29 models), VW's PQ35 (2,699,722 units across 22 models) and Hyundai's 'HD' (2,618,011 units across 22 models).

Emergence of new markets

Another significant development for the auto industry that began in the 1990s and developed significantly in the 2000–2010 period concerned the rise of emerging markets, the most significant of which, so far, has been China. China largely pursued a policy of economic isolation from the establishment of the People's Republic in 1949 until shortly after the death of Mao in 1976. During this period the emphasis was on trucks – car production was very limited at only a few thousand cars a year for use by high-ranking officials. In the 1980s, a few foreign car makers began to make investments in China which, at the insistence of the Chinese government, took the form of joint ventures with indigenous Chinese firms. Examples included Volkswagen, Jeep (Chrysler), Peugeot-Citroën and Suzuki.

In 1994 the Chinese government published its seven-year 'Automotive Industry Policy', the aim of which was to build up the auto industry in China as a 'pillar' industry. The policy had a number of aims, including the encouragement of car ownership, the establishment of a number of large-scale car-producers (in place of the 120 or so producers of trucks and cars that existed at the time), to improve the components industry and the creation of an indigenous automotive product development capability. To be allowed to operate in China, foreign auto firms had to establish joint ventures with Chinese car makers. China essentially made technology transfer to local firms a condition of access to its potentially huge market.

Table 2.3 *Platform volumes and number of models by car firm. 2013 data. Source: IHS Global Insight.*

Group	Production volume	No. of models	Volume per model	No. of platforms	Volume per platform	Models per platform
Toyota	9,487,653	114	83,225	30	316,255	3.8
Volkswagen	9,357,741	88	106,338	27	346,583	3.3
GM	8,153,540	102	79,937	22	370,616	4.6
Hyundai	7,652,056	72	106,279	12	637,671	6.0
Renault-Nissan	7,153,885	151	47,377	25	286,155	6.0
Renault	*2,563,909*	*52*	*49,306*	*10*	*256,391*	*5.2*
Nissan	*4,589,976*	*99*	*46,363*	*22*	*208,635*	*4.5*
Ford	5,754,897	45	127,887	24	191,830	1.9
Fiat-Chrysler	4,258,533	70	60,836	24	177,439	2.9
Chrysler	*2,302,314*	*22*	*104,651*	*9*	*255,813*	*2.4*
Fiat	*1,956,219*	*48*	*40,755*	*18*	*108,679*	*2.7*
Honda	4,024,789	39	103,200	10	402,479	3.9
PSA	3,040,698	48	63,348	12	253,392	4.0
Suzuki	2,669,898	44	60,680	9	296,655	4.9
BMW	1,907,149	24	79,465	8	238,394	3.0
Daimler	1,792,893	26	68,957	21	85,376	1.2
Mazda	1,292,430	23	56,193	14	92,316	1.6

Table 2.3 (*cont.*)

Group	Production volume	No. of models	Volume per model	No. of platforms	Volume per platform	Models per platform
Mitsubishi	1,133,439	31	36,563	16	70,840	1.9
Tata Automotive	869,812	28	31,065	15	57,987	1.9
Jaguar Land Rover	*376,357*	*12*	*31,363*	*7*	*53,765*	*1.7*
Land Rover	*301,493*	*7*	*43,070*	*4*	*75,373*	*1.8*
Jaguar	*74,864*	*5*	*14,973*	*3*	*24,955*	*1.7*
Subaru	767,658	15	51,177	7	109,665	2.1
Brilliance	524,152	20	26,208	2	262,076	10.0
Isuzu	398,523	11	36,229	5	79,705	2.2
Proton	166,577	8	20,822	6	27,763	1.3
Geely Group (incl. Volvo)	950,957	36	26,415	8	118,870	4.5
Volvo only	*357,092*	*12*	*29,758*	*4*	*89,273*	*3.0*
Tesla	3,368	1	3,368	1	3,368	1.0

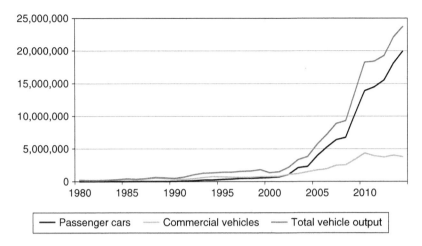

FIGURE 2.6 Growth in vehicle production in China since 1980
Source: World Motor Vehicle Data, various years

Foreign automotive firms flooded into China during the latter part of the 1980s and into the 1990s: Peugeot-Citroën (PSA) teamed up with the Dongfeng Motor Corporation (now the second biggest auto-maker in China); GM did the same with the Shanghai Automotive Industry and First Automobile Works (both companies now among the top five Chinese car makers); and Honda also tied up with the Dongfeng Motor Corporation.[22] This soon led to a massive increase in production capacity, and by 2005, the Chinese domestic market had grown to become the second largest vehicle market in the world after the USA, with 5.8m vehicles sold and by 2009 was the largest car market in the world, with sales of 13.5 million units (helped by the financial crash, which dragged sales in the USA down to around 10 million units). In 2014 approximately 23 million vehicles of all types were sold in China, the vast majority of which were also produced there, as Figure 2.6 shows.

The 2001–2010 period was characterized by a near-religious belief in the auto industry that the future of the industry, and manu-facturing in general, was determined by the development of auto sales in the so-called BRIC (later BRICS) countries, denoting Brazil, Russia, India and China, with South Africa added later.

The Chinese market in particular was a major driver of global growth in the industry, and for many vehicle manufacturers the revenues earned in China were crucial to their financial health. The auto companies with the largest sales in China tended to be those that had been early movers – Shanghai-Volkswagen, FAW-Volkswagen, Shanghai-GM, Shanghai-GM-Wuling (SGMW), followed by Beijing-Hyundai and Dongfeng-Nissan. By brand, VW was market leader in 2013 with 15.1% of the market, followed by GM with 14.5%, and Hyundai with 7.6%. Not all ventures were successful. For example, in 1997 Peugeot withdrew from their Guangzhou joint venture after 12 years in which only 100,000 cars were produced. Honda moved in following Peugeot's exit. Peugeot was later to re-enter the Chinese market with a different local partner.

Brazil, Russia and India each also developed into important auto markets, but individually each was very much smaller than China. Car production in Brazil, for example, grew from 1.4 million in 2000, to 2.8 million in 2010. However, production was largely of small vehicles for the local market in Brazil, and for export to neighbouring countries in Latin America.

Russian car production only grew marginally from 969,000 to 1.2 million during the period 2000–2010, but generally comprised larger vehicles, and the Russian market also showed strong demand for imported luxury vehicles. Lada is market leader in Russia with 17 per cent of the market, followed by Renault, Kia, Hyundai, Chevrolet, Volkswagen, Toyota and Nissan that each hold market shares of 5–8 per cent.

India had similar auto production levels to China in 2000, but has grown more slowly than China, reaching a production level of 2.3 million cars by 2010. Although a large market overall, 49 per cent of sales in India are accounted for by Maruti, which produces low-cost Suzuki-designed vehicles for the entry-level market. The best-selling Maruti 800 (produced from 1983 to 2014) was based on a 1979 Suzuki design with an 800cc engine, and sold for an equivalent of US$3,500 (depending on specification). Hyundai has been the second-best selling brand in India, with 21 per cent of the market, followed by Tata Motors and Honda with about 6 per cent each.

Although the growth of these markets is commonly cited as evidence of the globalization of the auto industry, this is actually something of a misnomer. The process is better described as a 'regionalization', during which auto companies adjusted their manufacturing footprints in order to follow rising demand in emerging markets. However, some activities, such as R&D, remained relatively concentrated so production in the developing regions was generally of adaptions of the models that had been designed and developed elsewhere.

Table 2.4 illustrates this changing manufacturing footprint by taking snapshots of vehicle production and numbers of assembly plants in a cross section of countries and regions every 10 years from 1970 to 2010.

The auto industry underwent a dramatic shift in manufacturing footprint from 2000 onwards, with its centre of gravity moving away from developed markets, into emerging markets. In 1970, we estimate that the USA, Western Europe and Japan were home to around 60% of the world's car assembly plants and 90% of global production of autos. By 2010 these figures had halved, to around 37% and 47% respectively as Figures 2.7(a) and 2.7(b) show. Capacity, measured by numbers of assembly plants, had increased at about 25% for each 10-year period since 1970, and at an even higher rate during the period 1990–2000 (although actual production lagged the establishment of capacity). The table vividly illustrates the role BRIC countries have in driving the dynamics of the industry, accounting for virtually the entire growth since 2000.

The decade of 2000–2010 ended in a global recession due to sub-prime mortgage lending in the USA that triggered a banking crisis and led to the collapse of a number of financial institutions in 2008. The recession depressed vehicle sales in many markets, particularly in Western Europe and the USA. In 2009 global car sales dropped by

Table 2.4 *Passenger car production by region (number of vehicle assembly plants in brackets). Source:* Wards World Motor Vehicle Data, Motor Vehicle Facts and Figures, *various years. Production data exclude light trucks and commercial vehicles, and thus underestimate production levels for the USA and Canada. Assembly plants produce both passenger cars and commercial vehicles.*

	1970	1980	1990	2000	2010
North America	7,473,565	7,307,566	6,965,884	6,391,349	3,338,182
(USA and Canada)	(48)	(54)	(76)	(87)	(61)
Latin America	645,119	1,490,756	1,423,321	2,730,915	4,730,305
(Argentina,	(22)	(26)	(37)	(65)	(47)
Mexico and Brazil)					
Western Europe	10,773,062	11,080,224	14,981,950	15,945,373	12,219,306
(Germany, France,	(70)	(83)	(95)	(122)	(89)
Italy, Spain, UK,					
Benelux,					
Scandinavia,					
Austria, Portugal)					
Eastern Europe	510,976	1,259,406	886,538	1,022,323	2,359,496
(Czech Republic,	(10)	(10)	(10)	(23)	(28)
Hungary,					
Romania,					
Slovakia,					
Slovenia, Poland)					
Japan	3,178,708	7,038,108	9,947,972	8,359,434	8,307,382
	(27)	(32)	(36)	(42)	(30)
South Korea	14,487	57,225	986,751	2,602,008	2,792,210
	(4)	(6)	(9)	(14)	(13)
India	37,440	30,538	176,821	604,970	2,316,931
	(9)	(11)	(16)	(26)	(38)
China	196	5,418	42,409	604,677	9,494,018
	(9)	(10)	(15)	(30)	(39)
World	23,698,919	30,183,777	38,110,006	41,625,644	51,040,227
	(251)	(310)	(393)	(553)	(673)

15 per cent compared to 2007. Vehicle manufacturers around the globe faced cash flow crises as sales fell from the peak. In the USA, sales in 2009 dropped to 64 per cent of pre-crisis levels, and both General Motors and Chrysler were forced to enter Chapter 11

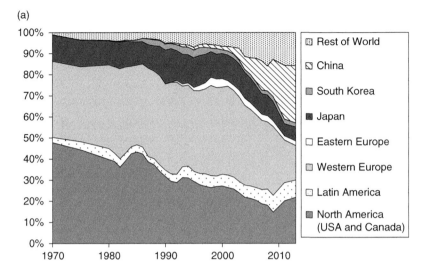

FIGURE 2.7(a) Global car sales by region since 1970

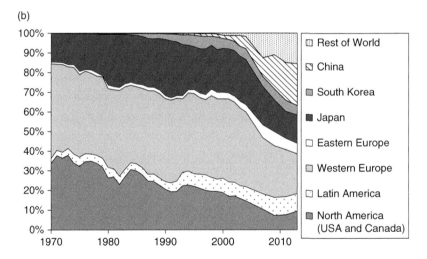

FIGURE 2.7(b) Global car production by region since 1970
Source: various

bankruptcy proceedings and required $17.4bn from the US Government's TARP (Troubled Asset Relief) Program. We shall return to this in Chapter 7 where we discuss the case of Chrysler and the significance of stakeholder support to troubled auto firms in more depth.

2010 ONWARDS: GLOBAL SALES PATTERNS AND NEW TECHNOLOGY

Since 2010 many of the issues that have dominated the auto industry since the turn of the millennium continue to be salient. By 2010 the industry (in global aggregate) had recovered to pre-crisis production levels, although some individual markets, such as Europe, have still not fully recovered as we write this in 2015. Passenger car production in the UK, for example, dropped to below 1 million units in 2009, and only returned to pre-crisis levels of 1.6 million by 2014. The car market in the USA also recovered to pre-crisis levels by 2014, but remained almost 1 million units below its peak volume of 2000. All three key 'developed' markets remain below their peak sales levels experienced around the turn of the twentieth century.

BRIC countries and global growth

Most growth, in both sales and production, is occurring outside the developed regions. Accounting for 37 per cent of global vehicle sales, BRIC countries have become the most strategically important region for vehicle manufacturers. China alone currently accounts for 26 per cent of global sales. Continued strong demand in China often masks underlying concerns such as the sustainability of current sales levels in the face of slowing GDP growth, growing pollution and congestion levels, and rising household debt. The other BRIC nations have shown far slower growth, and tend to have issues of their own, of which the 2014–15 geopolitical situation with respect to Russia and the Ukraine is simply the latest example.

Table 2.5 shows global vehicle registrations for all types of vehicle from 2005 to 2013, broken down by various regions and countries. We present this to show the latest global sales footprint of the industry. A number of points emerge from this. First, the domination of Asia and its neighbours is very clear, with around 50 per cent of global registrations of vehicles of all types. The USA and Europe are now each only responsible for 15–20 per cent of global sales. The

Table 2.5 *Vehicle registrations by regions and top 10 countries (comprising passenger cars and commercial vehicles), 2005–2013.* Source: OICA.

Regions/ countries	2005	2006	2007	2008	2009	2010	2011	2012	2013	% global share 2013
Asia, Oceania and Middle East	20,437,962	21,851,980	23,620,567	24,252,051	28,255,489	35,128,757	35,337,911	38,228,305	40,454,477	47%
BRIC	10,719,913	13,139,442	16,146,009	17,406,269	20,649,760	26,724,527	28,327,716	29,845,565	31,943,162	37%
EU 15 + EFTA	16,942,079	17,161,729	17,297,311	15,813,252	15,228,050	14,696,720	14,683,816	13,420,004	13,181,878	15%
NAFTA	20,242,979	19,899,024	19,301,479	16,240,451	12,859,351	14,203,961	15,597,614	17,526,688	18,764,371	22%
Central + Latin America	3,069,988	3,432,895	4,295,855	4,655,363	4,654,465	5,479,164	5,942,931	6,146,341	6,239,432	7%
China	5,758,189	7,215,972	8,791,528	9,380,502	13,644,794	18,061,936	18,505,114	19,306,435	21,984,100	26%
USA	17,444,329	17,048,981	16,460,315	13,493,165	10,601,368	11,772,219	13,040,613	14,785,936	15,883,969	19%
Japan	5,852,034	5,739,520	5,309,200	5,082,233	4,609,333	4,956,148	4,210,224	5,369,721	5,375,513	6%
Brazil	1,714,644	1,927,738	2,462,728	2,820,350	3,141,240	3,515,066	3,633,253	3,802,071	3,767,370	4%
Germany	3,614,886	3,772,394	3,482,279	3,425,039	4,049,353	3,198,416	3,508,454	3,394,002	3,257,718	4%
India	1,440,455	1,750,892	1,993,721	1,983,071	2,266,269	3,040,390	3,287,737	3,595,508	3,241,209	4%
Russia	1,806,625	2,244,840	2,898,032	3,222,346	1,597,457	2,107,135	2,901,612	3,141,551	2,950,483	3%
UK	2,828,127	2,734,360	2,799,619	2,485,258	2,222,542	2,293,576	2,249,483	2,333,763	2,595,713	3%
France	2,598,183	2,544,165	2,629,186	2,614,829	2,718,599	2,708,884	2,687,052	2,331,731	2,201,068	3%
Canada	1,630,142	1,666,008	1,690,345	1,673,522	1,482,232	1,583,388	1,620,221	1,716,178	1,779,860	2%
World	65,957,595	68,374,448	71,563,264	68,297,366	65,594,533	74,894,082	78,090,955	82,166,701	85,393,803	100%

significance of sales in the BRIC countries, dominated of course by China's huge market, also stands out, with close on 40 per cent of global registrations in 2013. Third, after China and the USA are taken out of the equation, individual countries, even those with large economies, generally have small shares of the global pie – in the region of 2–6 per cent. This sets the scene for a key point that we shall pick up in Chapter 4 – that auto companies face a very broad and varied set of markets and having the 'reach' to address these – whilst retaining underlying economies of scale – is a key ingredient of resilience for an auto firm.

Going forward, many predict for car demand in BRIC countries to rise further. Some signs seem to point in this direction, however, this largely rests on developments in China. Car demand in China is slowing, and regulatory changes could change the picture rapidly here. As we write this book, the other BRIC countries, Brazil, Russia and India, are all showing signs of stagnation, and even declines in demand (caused, in Russia's case, by geo-political factors surrounding the situation in the Ukraine). It is clear that emerging markets may present strong growth potential, but they are also inherently volatile. As Martin Winterkorn, CEO of VW put it in 2014: 'Of the BRIC countries, only China is left standing.'[23]

Alternative powertrains

In the opening pages of this chapter, we observed that the dominant design of the contemporary automobile was established in the early 1900s and has not changed fundamentally since then, notwithstanding swathes of incremental innovations which over time have hugely improved the efficiency, performance and functionality of cars.

We close this chapter with some observations about the implications of technological change for resilience, specifically the status and likely significance of alternative powertrains (propulsion methods) for the industry. Partly driven by soaring oil prices in 2008, and partly by tighter emission standards arising from concerns over climate

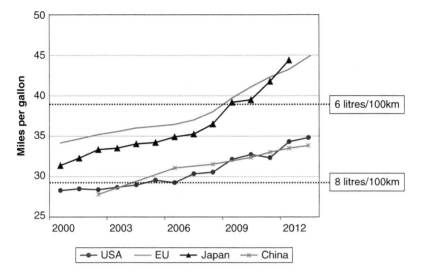

FIGURE 2.8 Average passenger car fleet fuel economy (CAFE) by country. Data based on standard testing cycles.
Source: ICCT

change, the auto industry has been giving the most serious attention to alternative powertrains that we have seen in decades. Although greenhouse gases are produced by almost all industries, especially power generation, the transportation sector attracts particular attention. Transportation produces roughly 30 per cent of global CO_2 emissions, and 75 per cent of these stem from road transport. It is unsurprising, then, that car makers have been under pressure to improve fuel efficiency in the quest for lower emissions. Figure 2.8 shows the average fleet fuel economies by country (noting that these data are based on standard testing cycles, while actual average consumption tends to be up to 30 per cent higher).[24]

Although car makers' advertising routinely proclaims levels of fuel efficiency that would have been unthinkable a few years ago, in some markets, such as the USA, average fuel consumption has not decreased significantly over time. This may seem odd since engine technology and downsizing have indeed led to more efficiency, however, the increase in vehicle equipment and size has meant that a high proportion of these improvements are offset by increases in weight and power consumption.

The quest for greater fuel efficiency and emissions reductions has led to exploration of alternatives to the internal combustion engine. The main contenders for new powertrain and fuel combinations so far have been all-electric vehicles with batteries as the power source (BEVs), hydrogen fuel-cell vehicles (FCVs), and hybrid vehicles that combine propulsion by a traditional internal combustion engine with that by electric motors powered by batteries ('hybrid' electric vehicles or HEVs). For some of these hybrids batteries are charged primarily by the internal combustion engine, usually with some regenerative braking; others also have the option of plugging in to mains electricity ('plug-in' hybrids or PHEVs). Figure 2.9 maps the various energy sources, fuel and powertrain combinations currently in use, or under active investigation.

From the perspective of resilience, these developments are interesting, because they raise the prospect of a disruption to the established order in the auto industry that will challenge the incumbents in various ways, creating advantage for some and disadvantage for others, and opening up the field to new competitors, such as the Californian producer of luxury electric vehicles, Tesla. In an industry whose products carry considerable symbolic value, driving a particular car can be a potent way to signal one's green credentials, as certain Californian politicians have been quick to spot. So far, Toyota has been one of the most successful manufacturers in the hybrid space with its Prius hybrid vehicles (launched in 1997), while several other manufacturers offer mass-produced electric vehicles. Examples are the GM Volt (launched in 2010, and sold as the Ampera in Europe); the Nissan Leaf (2010); and the Renault Fluence ZE (2011).

As of 2015, sales of all-electric vehicles have been very limited, accounting for less than 1 per cent of sales across all established car markets, (with the exception of markets with strong state subsidies such as Norway, for example), although sales of hybrid vehicles are more significant, and growing. In Japan, an astonishing 30 per cent of

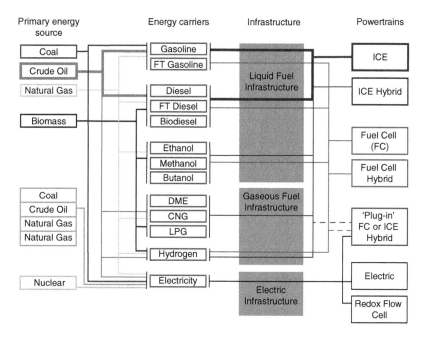

FIGURE 2.9 Energy source, carrier, infrastructure and powertrain pathways

passenger cars are already hybrid vehicles, compared with an estimated 3 per cent in the USA.

Predictions of growth of sales for either electric, hydrogen or hybrid vehicles are hard to make as sales depend significantly on national regulation and taxation schemes, and some car makers, for example Nissan, have already been caught out by making wildly optimistic estimates. Economically, electric vehicles are considerably more expensive to buy than traditionally powered vehicles, and there are justifiable concerns over life cycle, range and recharging times all of which make electric vehicles less attractive to many buyers. Electric vehicles are best suited for regular and city duty cycles. Furthermore, while EVs may be zero emission during use, their environmental benefit diminishes when the CO_2 emissions inherent in producing grid electricity are taken into account and when emissions associated with their production and disposal are factored in.

If we compare four electric and hybrid 2012 models in the compact segment on the basis of their CO_2 emissions per kilometre driven, some of the challenges of electric vehicles from an emissions perspective become clear. The hybrid (HEV) Toyota Prius achieves 107 g/km, the electric vehicle (EV) Nissan Leaf 111 g/km, and the standard ICE Golf Bluemotion third with 121 g/km, while GM's Vauxhall Ampera electric vehicle had the highest emissions (petrol mode: 131 g/km; UK electric mode 126 g/km). This short comparison highlights a fundamental problem with electric vehicles: their well-to-wheel emissions (considering the CO_2 emissions of the fuel production, as well as vehicle usage) are highly dependent on the carbon intensity of the electricity that is used to charge their batteries. On the current UK energy mix, there is virtually no reduction in greenhouse gas emissions. In France, where electricity is largely generated from nuclear power plants, emissions are a quarter of the levels in the UK. In China, where much of the electricity is generated from lignite, emissions are more than *double* for electric cars, at an estimated 278 g/km.[25]

A number of the new entrants, Fisker, BetterPlace, Coda and Th!nk have gone out of business. Only Tesla has managed to establish itself as a new player in the luxury car market. Many established auto firms have successfully adopted hybrid and electric powertrain technologies and have added them to their portfolios. Commercial success is less clear.

The question of what powertrain will become the dominant design to replace the internal combustion engine (ICE) is not yet resolved. Electric cars and fuel cell vehicles seem likely contenders, yet new battery technologies, such as metal–air electrochemical cells or redox flow batteries, or a breakthrough in solid hydrogen storage, could all significantly change the economic viability of alternative powertrain technologies. For the medium term, the electrification of the existing ICE powertrain is the most likely interim solution. It offers lower emissions in urban settings through start–stop technologies and kinetic recovery systems, while at the same its large-capacity electrical infrastructure also feeds the many electric and electronic systems on board. The electric motor offers much greater energy efficiency (90 per cent versus 26 per cent for the internal combustion engine, which produces much wasted heat). Electric motors offer zero emissions in use, and EVs can use the existing grid infrastructure to recharge battery packs.

As things stand, it seems most likely that hybrid vehicles will function as an interim stage from the ICE to the next powertrain design, and that those makers most exposed to regimes that support and encourage low-emission vehicles may enjoy the advantage of extensive, local, test-and-development environments. In Japan, tax breaks exist for fuel efficient vehicles. By 2013 the hybrid market share accounted for more than 30% of the 2.9 million standard passenger vehicles sold, and about 20% of the 4.5 million passenger vehicles sold each year (including the kei cars of up to 600cc displacement). This has had a measurable effect on fleet fuel economy, which has improved by more than 70% since 1995, and has averaged 6% annually over the past five years. In Western Europe, hybrids represented just a 1.4% market share of new car sales in the region. Hybrids accounted for about 3% of the US light vehicle market in 2014, nearly half of which were Toyota Prius models. The EV market in comparison remains very small – in the USA it is 0.3%, and in Europe ranges from 0.8% in France to 0.1% in Italy. EV sales in Japan were 0.9% of the market in 2014. The exceptions are Norway and the Netherlands, both of which have very favourable tax regimes and where EVs account for 6.1% and 5.6% of the market, respectively.

SUMMARY

In this chapter we have presented a brief review of the history of the auto industry to set the scene of our exploration of crisis, resilience and survival. We have been selective in what we have covered because our purpose has been purely to provide some context in terms of how the industry has evolved, and of the landscape through which car companies have to navigate. At different periods in the industry's history, different models of organization and management have been prominent. In the next chapter, we review four of these, each represented by a different company, which in its own way has served as a model that others in the industry have followed.

3 Competing in a global industry

In the previous chapter we reviewed the evolution of the auto industry and noted how key innovations in approaches to management and organization have seen the industry grow from a craft operation – making single cars for wealthy customers – to the mass production of a wide variety of cars, affordable to an increasingly large proportion of the global population. Each of these innovations, or *paradigms*, has been the subject of intense analyses elsewhere and we will not reproduce these in detail. We point more specialist readers to some of the classic studies in the area.[1]

Our aim in this chapter is to provide an overview of four broad approaches to management and organization in the auto industry, each represented by a particular car company which represents the pinnacle of what was possible in the auto industry at a particular point in time, within a set of parameters bounded by standards of cost, quality, product variety and so forth. The four companies are Ford, General Motors, Toyota and Volkswagen.

FORD: THE BIRTH OF MASS PRODUCTION

'Any colour you like so long as it's black'

The first major innovation in management and organization in the auto industry was Henry Ford's mass production approach, which represented a step change in production efficiency. By reducing the cost of producing motor vehicles, Ford created an entire new market of car buyers. In his autobiography, Ford wrote:

> I will build a car for the great multitude. It will be large enough for the family, but small enough for the individual to run and care for. It will be constructed of the best materials, by the best men to be

hired, after the simplest designs that modern engineering can devise. But it will be so low in price that no man making a good salary will be unable to own one – and enjoy with his family the blessing of hours of pleasure in God's great open spaces.[2]

Over time, Ford made many improvements to his production processes, which allowed him to reduce the price further over time. Ford's famous Model T originally cost $850 in 1908, but by 1920 the cost of a T had fallen to just $260. Falling prices meant a growing market and Ford produced over 15 million Model Ts between 1908 and 1927.

The heart of mass production, which turned the economics of the motor industry upside down from 1908 onwards, was not the moving assembly line, as many believe, but standardization and interchangeability of parts. The economics of mass production were very different from those of craft production, where the cost per car of building one vehicle differed little from the cost per car when 1,000 identical ones were made. Since parts were hand-made and subsequently adjusted by 'fitters' in order to fit together under craft production, the amount of labour required per vehicle stayed largely constant, irrespective of the number of units produced. Furthermore, most vehicles at the time were customized to individual requirements, so standardizing parts was not a priority.

The notion of standardization and interchangeability of parts was a critical enabler of Ford's mass production system, although the concept originally stemmed from the arms-making sector.[3] Initially proposed by Eli Whitney and later implemented by Samuel Colt, the ability to standardize parts meant that assembly operations could be streamlined, making the role of the 'skilled fitter' (and therefore the fitters) largely redundant. The moving assembly line which was implemented by Ford in his Highland Park factory in 1913 for the first time was a logical evolution of the concepts of continuous flow production and of standardization of parts and jobs. As Robert Hall argues, 'there is strong historical evidence that any time humans have engaged in any type of mass production, concepts to improve the flow and improve the process occur naturally'.[4]

Ford's vision was to produce the maximum number of vehicles at the lowest possible cost that became the hallmark of mass production, and the cornerstone of motor industry economics of the twentieth century.[5] As Peter Drucker put it: 'The essence of the mass production process is the reversal of conditions from which the theory of monopoly was deduced. The new assumptions constitute a veritable economic revolution.'[6]

Henry Ford's approach literally changed the world – by producing large volumes of cars he reduced the cost per unit, and hence made cars affordable for the general population. His new 'mass production' approach, a term first used in an article in the 1925 edition of the *Encyclopaedia Britannica*, worked well for almost two decades. Ford was able to reduce the labour hours for assembly of the vehicle from 750 hours in 1913 to 93 hours in 1914, and the sales price for a Model T reduced from $1,200 in 1909 to $690 in 1914 (see Figure 3.1). However, the introduction of the moving assembly line also brought

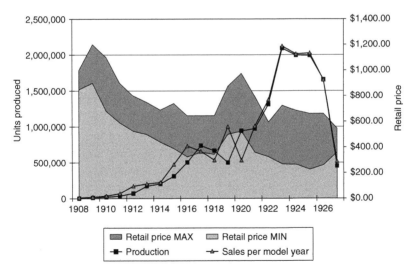

FIGURE 3.1 Model T production, sales and retail price band 1908–1927
Source of data: Ford Benson Research Center

labour challenges. The new type of mass production work was not well received by the work force, and staff turnover soared to unsustainable levels.[7] And although sometimes misinterpreted as a philanthropic move by Henry Ford, his 'five-dollar-day' was primarily geared to making the workplace sufficiently attractive for workers to stay. A secondary effect was that his own workers were soon able to buy the cars that they made, hence stimulating demand even further.

Market constraints

Ford certainly achieved efficiency gains, but at the price of limiting product variety. This worked fine in the largely undifferentiated US market of the early twentieth century, but had significant limitations as the market matured. The limitations of pure mass production emerged quite suddenly, and apparently as something of a surprise to Ford. In the USA in 1927 more car buyers were by that stage no longer buying a car for the first time, but moving on to their replacement car – this was a sure sign that the market was reaching a state of replacement demand in which the dated Model T (which from 1914 to 1926 was indeed only available in one colour, black), however low the price, was no longer attractive to many customers. But if Ford could not offer the levels of specifications and variety expected by the customers, one of its major competitors, General Motors (GM), certainly could. How GM was able to do this is the subject of the next section.

GM: THE MULTI-BRAND ENTERPRISE

'A car for every purse and purpose'

The fundamental weakness of the Ford system, namely its limited ability to offer a variety of different models, was soon exploited by General Motors (GM). GM was founded by William 'Billy' Durant in 1908. Durant had been a leading manufacturer of horse-drawn vehicles in Flint, MI before he entered the nascent automobile industry. At its inception, GM's main operation produced Buicks, but within 10 years GM would acquire more than 20 auto companies including Cadillac, Chevrolet and Oakland (later known as Pontiac), and Oldsmobile, also forming the General Motors Corporation (GMC) Truck Co. Alfred Sloan became GM's CEO in 1923, a position he would hold until 1946, thereafter becoming Chairman, until 1956. Unlike Ford, whose vision had revolved around the creation of a mass market for cars by driving the cost down, Sloan recognized that the US auto market was maturing and sought to offer 'a car for every purse and purpose'. A key element of this strategy was the capability to offer customers a choice of products and brands, suited to their particular circumstances. Sloan envisaged a progression of brands, so car buyers could move up from mass or entry-level brands such as Chevrolet, to prestige brands, such as Cadillac, as their circumstances changed, whilst remaining within the GM brand portfolio. Of course, offering multiple brands from the same organization and operations was a challenge and Sloan, writing about GM's expansion between 1918 and 1920, observed: 'I had been struck with the disparity between substance and form: plenty of substance, and little form. I became convinced that the corporation could not continue to grow and survive unless it was better organized.'[8]

For the first half of the 1920s, Ford's sales led those of GM by a considerable margin, and in 1925 Ford outsold GM by a margin of more than 2:1, as Table 3.1 shows. However, Ford was slow to develop its replacement model for the Model T. By the time the T's replacement, the Model A, was introduced in 1927 the T had been in production for 18 years. In 1926 the tables were turned and GM outsold Ford by nearly 2:1. Ford's share of the US market dwindled from 55 per cent in 1921 to 30 per cent in 1926. Ford briefly pulled ahead of GM in 1929 and 1930, but since then GM's sales have consistently exceeded those of Ford, usually by a very substantial margin (see Table 3.1).

For many commentators the reason for GM's superiority over Ford was that GM was able to marry Ford's mass production model (thereby offering low prices and opening up mass markets) with the ability to offer a wide choice of models to the customer. This was important as auto markets matured and consumers were no longer

Table 3.1 *US sales 1900–1970. Source: Automotive News, The 100-year almanac. 1996.*

	1900	1910	1920	1925	1926	1927	1928	1929	1930	1931	1940	1950	1960	1970
Ford	–	20,255	463,451	1,525,380	1,337,4522	499,335	550,034	1,528,518	1,236,955	656,973	778,169	1,772,797	1,958,197	2,794,065
GM	–	28,519*	379,729	653,747	952,140	1,231,738	1,447,681	1,438,895	1,032,685	931,914	1,788,545	3,288,752	3,171,528	3,920,414
Total car & light truck sales	2,288	177,796	1,612,095	3,423,602	3,587,421	2,928,683	3,479,175	4,339,694	2,988,768	2,187,321	3,926,881	7,199,592	7,209,414	9,850,276

*Note: 1910 sales for GM include 18,932 units by Buick, and 9,587 by Cadillac.

content to receive simply a basic car. Along with the idea of market segmentation, Sloan was mindful that demand could also be actively stimulated and in the 1930s introduced the idea of annual refreshments of models every year (creating the concept of the 'model year' which is still with us today). These refreshments largely involved cosmetic or other minor updates to each vehicle each year, in between the more substantive major replacement cycles, and spawned the notion of built-in obsolescence.

Also supporting GM's growth was the introduction of the General Motors Acceptance Corporation (GMAC) in 1919. Recognizing that demand is profoundly affected by the ability of consumers to buy, GMAC provided car buyers with the funds to finance the purchase of their vehicles. At the time, many retails banks believed that consumer credit was a risky proposition so consequently financing for cars was largely offered by brokers and independent firms, rather than banks. As early as 1913, a $500 car could be driven away with $125 down payment. In 1919, 65 per cent of Fords were bought on credit, although the Ford Motor Company did not itself provide the credit.

The provision of credit represented an opportunity for GM. In 1919, the cheapest car in GM's line-up was the Chevrolet 490 (introduced in 1915 for $490, hence the name). However, by 1919 the 490 actually cost $715. To put this in context, according to US census data, average income in the US that year was $605, which meant that to purchase the car outright was beyond the reach of many. Thus, the market opportunity for GMAC was huge, especially in the light of Ford's reluctance to enter vehicle financing. By 1924, 75 per cent of cars in the USA were bought on credit. Not everyone's credit was good, of course, and GMAC had to write off $2 million in first year, but its 'time payment plan' became a very popular option for car buyers, and fuelled GM's sales. GMAC also set up an insurance business to complement its financing operations. By 1926 it was providing credit to 40 per cent of all GM dealers. Ford responded by setting up the Universal Credit Corporation (UCC) in 1928. However, Ford was forced to sell its shares in UCC in 1932 to finance its manufacturing operations, and it was not until in 1959 that Ford Motor Credit came into existence to provide vehicle financing.

Volume and variety

In analysing the relative success of the GM system relative to the Ford system, it is hard to disentangle the effects of offering multiple brands and models in a maturing market from the provision of finance for the vehicle. However, both illustrate a theme that runs through this book – that success and survival in the auto industry goes beyond simply the ability to design and make good cars.

In combination the measures taken by GM meant that it eclipsed Ford through its ability to reach new and bigger markets, although Ford continued to excel in straight production efficiency. GM's approach has subsequently been termed 'flexible mass production' to capture its combination of high volume production coupled with product variety, although GM's approach was also characterized by considerable *in*flexibility. Increasing numbers of models, variants of models and of course annual refreshments, meant that factories found it difficult to cope with all the variety, especially as production equipment was limited in its flexibility. Changing over equipment from one configuration to another in order to produce a different variant was time consuming and cost valuable production time. Components and vehicles were therefore typically made in large batches in order to achieve the economies of scale so critical to mass production and stored until they were needed, a process characterized as 'batch and queue'. Lead times and inventory levels rose. The system was also prone to quality problems, as high levels of inventory and slow progress of materials through the factory made it difficult to pinpoint problems, thereby impeding their resolution.

Notwithstanding these issues, having gained the position of the world's largest car maker in 1931, GM maintained this position for an astonishing 77 years, indicating that its basic model of management and operations, whatever its flaws, was competitive against other models.

The signs of the first real challenge to GM's model began to emerge in the 1970s, and the challenge this time came not from Ford, but from Japan, specifically from Toyota, in the form of the 'Toyota Production System', a distinct configuration of practices later to be dubbed 'lean production'.

TOYOTA: THE BIRTH OF LEAN PRODUCTION

'Costs do not exist to be calculated. Costs exist to be reduced.'[9]

The foundation of the Toyota Motor Company dates back to 1918, when the entrepreneur Sakichi Toyoda established a spinning and weaving business based on his advanced automatic loom. Toyoda sold patents to the Platts Brothers in 1929, and these funds enabled his son, Kiichiro, to establish an automobile operation in 1933. The romantic version of the story is that Sakichi told his son on his deathbed: 'I served our country with the loom. I want you to serve it with the automobile.'[10]

In the 1930s the Japanese market was dominated by the local subsidiaries of Ford and General Motors which had been established in the 1920s so the establishment of Toyoda's automotive business was therefore fraught with challenges. Nevertheless, Kiichiro prevailed – helped by the newly released Japanese automotive manufacturing law in 1930 – and began designing his first car, the Model AA, making considerable use of Ford and GM components.[11] The company was re-named 'Toyota'. Truck and car production started in 1935 and 1936, respectively, and in 1937 the Toyota Motor Company was formally established. Car production ceased during the Second World War and although Toyota's factories were still intact at the end of the war, they faced all the problems of post-war industrial Japan – a shattered economy, old equipment, very limited resources and few orders. In the whole year of 1950, the entire output of the Japanese auto industry was equivalent to less than three days' of that of the US producers.

Kiichiro's cousin Eiji Toyoda went to the United States in 1950 to study American manufacturing methods. Going abroad to study competitors was not unusual; before the war a Toyota delegation had visited the Focke-Wulff aircraft works in Germany, where they observed the 'Produktionstakt' concept, which later developed into 'takt time' at Toyota – the beat or rhythm that paces production. Eiji Toyoda was determined to implement mass production techniques at Toyota, yet severe capital constraints and low production volumes in the Japanese market could not support either the dedicated machinery or the large batch sizes that were common at Ford and GM. To address the conditions faced by Toyota simple, multipurpose production equipment was needed, capable of producing small runs in one configuration and then able to be quickly switched over to another.

The individual most responsible for developing the Toyota Production System (TPS) so it could produce large variety in small volumes economically was Taiichi Ohno. Ohno had previously worked in Toyota's spinning and weaving business before moving into the auto division. It has been suggested that this experience and his lack of preconceptions about auto manufacturing were instrumental in his development of the just-in-time (JIT) approach. Ohno argued that Western production systems of the sort used by Ford and GM had two flaws. First, he reasoned that the production of components in large batches resulted in large inventories, which consumed costly capital and warehouse space whilst they were waiting to be used. This also slowed down the identification of errors, resulting in the production of even more defects before corrective action was taken. The second flaw was the slowness of the system to accommodate switches in preferences and demand – because a great deal of inventory was 'trapped' in the system, the lags could be considerable. A production system that could produce in small lots and could be quickly reconfigured was inherently more responsive to changing demand from the market.

Ohno gradually extended his concept of small-lot production throughout Toyota from the engine machining shop that he was managing – see Ohno (1988) for a complete timeline.[12] He focused on reducing cost by eliminating waste, a notion that developed out of his experience with automatic looms that detected when a thread broke and stopped themselves automatically, in order not to waste material. Ohno referred to the loom as 'a text book in front of my eyes',[13] and this 'jidoka' or 'autonomous machine' concept became an integral part of the Toyota Production System. Ohno also visited the USA in 1956, and incorporated ideas he picked up during these visits, most notably the 'kanban supermarket' to control material replenishment. Ohno describes the two pillars of TPS as autonomation, based on Sakichi's loom, and JIT, which he claims came from Kiichiro who once stated that 'in a comprehensive industry such as automobile manufacturing, the best way to work would be to have all the parts for assembly at the side of the line just in time for their user'.[14] In order for this system to work, it was necessary to produce and receive components and parts in small lot sizes, something which was uneconomical according to the traditional thinking of production management of the time. Ohno had to modify the machine changeover procedures to produce a growing variety in smaller lot sizes. This was helped by the fact that much of the machinery Kiichiro had bought was simple, general purpose equipment that was easy to modify and adapt. Changeover reduction was further advanced by Shigeo Shingo, who was hired as external consultant in 1955 and developed the SMED (single-minute exchange of dies) system.[15]

Taken together, these individually simple innovations gave Toyota a capability to produce a high variety of cars in comparatively low volumes very cost-effectively and, eventually, at very high levels of quality, thereby challenging the conventional logic of mass production that underpinned the operations of companies such as Ford and GM. Once they coalesced into a coherent pattern, these changes were hailed as revolutionary, a paradigm shift in how products were made, yet they were in fact a sequence of adaptations to the particular circumstances faced by Toyota at a particular period in its history.

The Toyota system evolved over many years and in due course extended into the supply base, assisted by the close, long-term 'keiretsu' relationships between Japanese car makers and their key suppliers. Although many of the concepts had been put into practice by the 1950s the evolution of the TPS was in fact a continuous, iterative learning cycle that spanned decades. This 'dynamic learning capability', which delivers continuous incremental improvement of processes (and products), lies at the heart of the TPS. As Fujimoto concluded in a seminal review of the Toyota Production System:

> Toyota's production organization ... adopted various elements
> of the Ford system selectively, and in unbundled forms, and
> hybridized them with their ingenious system and original ideas.
> It also learnt from experiences with other industries (e.g. textiles).
> It is thus a myth that the Toyota Production System was a pure
> invention of genius Japanese automobile practitioners. However,
> we should not underestimate the entrepreneurial imagination of
> Toyota's production managers (e.g. Kiichiro Toyoda, Taiichi Ohno,
> and Eiji Toyoda), who integrated elements of the Ford system in a
> domestic environment quite different from that of the United
> States. Thus, the Toyota-style system has been neither purely
> original not totally imitative. It is essentially a hybrid.[16]

The TPS was not formally documented for external consumption until 1965 when kanban systems (card-signals that 'pull' products through a production system) were rolled out to Toyota's suppliers; there had simply not been a need to do so whilst practices operated solely within the confines of the Toyota company. As a result, the development of TPS was largely unnoticed – and only started attracting real attention during the first oil crisis in 1973.

As we described in Chapter 2, the oil crisis gave sales of fuel-efficient Japanese cars a huge boost in the USA and Western auto manufacturers started to wake up to the huge strides that the Japanese auto producers had made in terms of the quality and reliability of their vehicles. This was an enormous dent to the pride of Western auto producers, particularly those in the USA, who sought protection behind import quotas. Studies such as *The Machine that Changed the World* provided systematic evidence of the gap between Japan and the rest of the world in terms of both productivity and quality, with Toyota leading the way in Japan. Not only were the Japanese able to produce cars with fewer labour hours and fewer defects than their Western counterparts, but their plants could also handle greater model variety, and their product development teams develop new cars faster and more efficiently than their US and European counterparts (Clark and Fujimoto 1991). GM's 'flexible mass production' model, which had more or less dominated the high volume auto industry for the best part of 50 years, was challenged by Toyota's 'lean production' approach, which rapidly became the model that car makers around the world sought to emulate. Toyota's prowess was also seen in its large share of the Japanese domestic market, at over 40 per cent, and its rapidly growing output, from about 150,000 units per year in 1960, to 1.6 million in 1970, 3.4 million in 1980 and nearly 6 million in 2000. In 2008, Toyota (temporarily) overtook GM as the world's largest car maker, by volume.

Toyota's approach addressed many of the shortcomings of so-called flexible mass production, particularly in areas of quality and cost but also in terms of flexibility, because despite its name 'flexible mass production' was not actually very flexible, other than in comparison to the early version of mass production that it replaced.

The Toyota Production System has many strengths, but Toyota's greatest product successes have typically been in high volume markets. Although quite successful, Toyota's luxury Lexus brand has not (yet) displaced many established producers of premium brands particularly the German companies such as Mercedes, BMW and Audi whose sales have continued to grow faster than those of Lexus, as Figure 3.2 shows.

As we saw in Table 2.1, independent consumer evaluations have rated Toyota vehicles highly for many years and most Toyota models have class-leading reliability, despite improvements by non-Japanese producers over the last two or three decades. Yet,

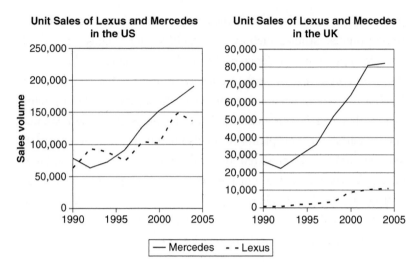

FIGURE 3.2 Unit sales of Lexus and Mercedes in the UK and US markets
Source: Ward's Yearbooks and SMMT

despite their alleged inefficiencies, German producers such as Mercedes have continued to out-sell Lexus, especially in Europe. We speculate that it may be the very absence of 'leanness', manifested by a reluctance to make compromises in design and by a propensity to over-engineer the vehicles, that creates the image and brand value that support brands such as Mercedes in the premium segment of the market.[17] This suggests that the next point of inflexion in the industry will be around a model of organization that combines production efficiency, market variety, high quality and reliability and *brand* appeal. The auto company that currently looks very strong in this respect is VW, and it is to this company that we now turn.

VW: PLATFORMS AND BRANDS

Efficiency through scale and sharing

Volkswagen AG has its origins in Nazi Germany in 1937, set up to build the famous 'Beetle' car for the German population ('KdF-Wagen'). The car, designed by Ferdinand Porsche, entered production in 1936. Post-war, under British occupation, VW restarted production at Volkswagen's Wolfsburg plant. Heavily reliant on the commercial success of the Beetle, VW grew rapidly until the 1970s, when other vehicles began to offer serious competition.

Although the Beetle remained in production in Germany until 1978, the introduction of the Golf Mk I in 1974 was decisive in propelling the company forward. With the success of the Golf, Polo and Passat models, VW continued to grow and under Carl Hahn's decade-long leadership became Europe's largest car producer. In the merger mania of the late 1980s and 1990s VW acquired Seat and Skoda, and made significant investments overseas. These investments later paid off, giving VW strong positions in Southern and Eastern Europe, Latin America and especially China. However, the expansion proved to be ambitious, and overstretched VW's resources, causing a major financial crisis in the early 1990s.

Ferdinand Piëch, grandson of Ferdinand Porsche, took over from Carl Hahn in 1993. In his 21 years at Audi, Piëch had been the architect of turning Audi around from being a sleepy producer of family sedans, into a technology leader providing desirable premium cars that competed with marques such as BMW. Key Audi innovations included the quattro all-wheel-drive system, fully zinc bodies, novel safety features, and 5-cylinder engines. The company was – in Piëch's words – three months away from bankruptcy (see also Figure 2.4 on VW's financial performance during the period of 1970–2004). Piëch had risen through the ranks at Audi to gain overall control of Volkswagen in January 1993, a company he described to *Automotive News* as 'a duck grown too fat to fly'. A cornerstone of VW's turn-around was a radical renegotiation of working hours with the workers' representatives, who are represented on the firm's supervisory board in Germany. In return for agreeing not to cut a projected 30,000 jobs (out of the 108,000 workers in Lower Saxony), Piëch persuaded the unions to agree to a 28.8 hour working week – which remained in place until 2006. Once in charge of VW, Piëch embarked on radical cost cutting, reducing the 127,000-strong workforce in Germany by 10 per cent. He also introduced a new concept, 'platform sharing'.

He claims to have been inspired by BMW, which at the time was sharing the floor pressings for its 5-series and 7-series models. Piëch adopted this idea at VW in 1995, and the first of three stages of VW's 'platform strategy' came to fruition.

Traditionally, each new vehicle had been designed independently. This changed with the Audi A4 platform (also known as PQ34), which also hosted the Golf Mark IV. This platform was subsequently shared with the Audi A3 and TT, the Golf derivatives of the Bora and Jetta, the Shanghai-VW Lavida, the New Beetle, the Seat Leon and Seat Toledo, and the Skoda Octavia.

Leveraging structural engineering across several models, including sharing of engines and transmissions, allowed Ford-style standardization of production equipment and processes *within* a vehicle segment and therefore delivered economies of scale. It also allowed VW to share powertrains (engines and gearboxes) across models much more easily, as this required only standardization of the engine bay and mounting points.

The second stage of VW's strategy was to add a 'module strategy', which not only shared platforms between models, but also core modules of the vehicle. Modules are found in areas such as steering, suspension, braking, fuel system and exhausts, as well as interior parts such as dashboards, HVACs (heating, ventilation and air-conditioning) systems and the like. These core modules can be shared by different vehicles on the same platform, as well as with vehicles of similar size. Such modularization allows VW to share core components across, as well as within vehicle classes, achieving even greater economies of scale.

The third, and most recent stage was agreed in 2007. This involved abandoning bespoke platforms for a certain size of a vehicle, and the adoption of four modular architectures across the entire range. In German these are called 'Baukasten', referring to the ability to mix and match components in the greatest possible way. The main innovation from the PQ platforms was the standardization of the most fundamental part of the platform – the engine bay area to the dashboard. All other areas of the vehicle – forward of the engine, wheelbase, rear of the vehicle and even width of the track – can be scaled according to the vehicle dimensions. This means that the 'platform' no longer is a platform in the traditional sense, but rather an architectural blueprint that can be applied to many vehicles across a number of different segments. This marks a considerable advantage in terms of flexibility over the simple sharing of platforms and components within a particular vehicle segment.

VW's four architectures, presented in 2012 as they entered production, are:

- MQB, the transverse architecture. This hosts the VW Golf, and will host a further 24 vehicles across the Audi, Seat and Skoda brands. All vehicles will share new modular engines (both petrol and diesel) along with all possible alternative powertrains (compressed natural gas (GNG), hybrid and EV);
- MLB, which is the equivalent of MQB, but for in-line engines. This platform is in use for the Audi A4, A5, Q5, A6, A7 and A8. In addition to the difference in engine mounting, MLB vehicles will largely have aluminium bodies;
- MSB, which was initiated in 2011, and will provide a more generic set of core modules for large SUVs and sportscars across the VW, Audi, Porsche and Lamborghini range;
- NSF, which is the current small family car platform used in the VW Up! and its derivatives. It is built around a 1 litre three-cylinder engine, while also capable of supporting EV, CNG and hybrid propulsion technologies.

The main benefit of extending the platform idea to a modular architecture is that all engines are now mounted in the same angle, so transmission and suspension can be standardized as well. With the MQB all engines receive a uniform assembly position, which leads to a considerable reduction of the number of variants and the complexity going down the assembly lines by using a modular assembly strategy. The core vehicle architecture is based around common key components (seat frame, HVAC module, engines/transmission packages, electronic modules, electric architecture) which increases economies of scale and purchasing power. Branding is achieved by a unique upper structure (such as the body), with 'plug and play' inner pressings to allow for body style variations with minimal additional parts.

The main risk of such high levels of commonality is a lack of differentiation between different brands and products within the VW portfolio which could mean that sales between models on the same platform are likely to experience a substitution or cannibalization effect by cheaper brands. Relatedly, there is a risk that different models lose their distinctive nature, reducing their market appeal. As we shall see in Chapter 6, this latter point was a major problem for GM when it used its mid-market platforms in Saab vehicles. However, VW appears to have largely avoided such problems (so far) through the use of bespoke interiors, different haptics, and unique settings for different models' steering, suspensions and powertrains so as to keep both 'look and feel' distinct for each vehicle.

The platform concept is a very significant development in the industry because it promises a route to address some of the fundamental dilemmas and trade-offs in the industry, for example between product variety on one hand and market reach on the other. Importantly, well-executed platforms can also support not just multiple models, but multiple and distinctive *brands*.

Partly on the back of its multi-brand platform strategy, partly because of its aggressive globalization, VW has grown from a predominantly European producer 30 years ago to being one of the top three car producers in the world, where it vies with Toyota and GM for the top spot. In 2014, VW produced 10.1 million vehicles in 100 assembly plants in 27 countries.

Financially, VW is currently strong, but the financials also point to the growing problem of complexity that running multiple brands from limited platforms and common architectures inevitably brings. While the aggregate results may smooth over the details, the profitability of its core VW car operations in Europe is surprisingly low at 2.3% – compared to Toyota's 8.8% or Hyundai's 9.5%[18], as Table 3.2 shows.

Table 3.2 *VW financial results, in €bn. Source: VW Annual Reports.*

	2009	2010	2011	2012	2013	2014
Revenues	105.2	126.9	159.3	192.7	197.0	202.5
Net profits	1.0	6.8	15.4	21.7	9.1	10.8

In 2014, VW's CEO Martin Winterkorn announced an aggressive €5bn cost-cutting plan, partly based on reducing the number of new models. Also in 2014, Michael Macht, the VW board member responsible for production, left the company due to the delays and quality problems associated with the MQB modular production toolkit.

While there is little doubt over VW's strengths, in 2015 there were concerns starting to surface relating to whether the company has become too complex to be managed effectively. Platform and module sharing provides great efficiencies in design and production, and has allowed VW to provide enormous variety across brands, segments and regions. Sharing however also requires considerable coordination effort, and a strong, central mindset to enforce discipline.

EVOLVING PERFORMANCE FRONTIERS,
CONVERGING PRACTICES

In this chapter, we have described four distinct paradigms or company models in the auto industry over the last 100 years. Ford's mass production model increased efficiency and opened the mass market for the automobile, but was limited by the growing sophistication of the market. GM's model exploited the demand for variety through multiple models and brands, as well as vehicle financing, whilst offering, for a number of decades, adequate quality and productivity. GM's approach dominated the mass global market for cars for many years, until Toyota's lean production methods introduced a step change in terms of productivity, quality and vehicle reliability. Toyota has grown rapidly, temporarily knocking GM off the top spot, but there are signs that its lack of distinctiveness in design restricts its appeal in some geographical markets, in particular Europe, and in certain market segments. Volkswagen's approach to platform and component sharing has allowed it to cost-effectively pursue a multi-brand strategy and through Audi, it has enjoyed considerable success in the premium sector. Yet even VW – to date – has not been able to conquer all markets, and has had persistent difficulty in penetrating the US market with the VW brand since the 1970s. Although VW was a strong brand in the US market in the 1960s, its sales declined, partly in the face of Japanese competition. Despite a long-standing history, and even operating an assembly plant in Virginia from 1973 to 1987, today, at 2.5 per cent market share, VW sells fewer cars in the USA than does niche producer Subaru.

For VW, the difficulties of managing the enormous complexity of its operations stemming from a multi-brand, shared-platform model, are beginning to show, leading some observers to believe that there are limits as to how much commonality can be handled by a firm producing in the order of 10+ million vehicles per annum across so many brands.

It is interesting to note that the paradigms we have described oscillate between gains in *efficiency*, and increases in *variety* provided to the market place. This relates to a fundamental tension in automotive manufacturing, the *standardization–customization* trade-off. Firms clearly need to standardize products in order to achieve economies of scale. But as they push for efficiency and volume, they tend to lose out on variety and market segmentation, and vice versa. If they push product variety, they increase market presence but lose scale, and fall behind on costs and margins. The tension between the need to standardize on the one hand, and the need to customize on the other, represents an inherent tension in the automotive industry and many evolving practices can be understood as attempts to square this circle.

When we consider the approaches of dominant auto firms over time, we can see how these approaches shift from variety to efficiency, and back again (see Figure 3.3). With each new paradigm the overall *performance frontier* does move forward, while generally there

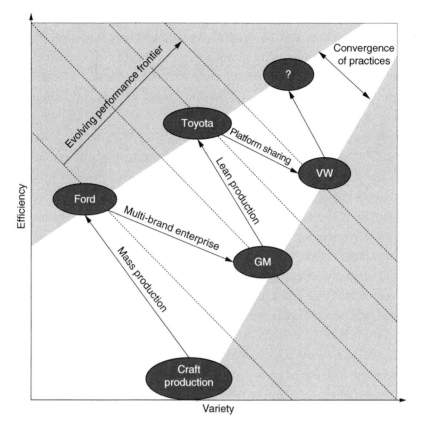

FIGURE 3.3 The evolution of management paradigms over time

is a step backwards in terms of the opposite frontier: so, when Ford introduced mass production, it enjoyed massive gains in efficiency. However, in contrast to craft production, mass production meant a step backwards in variety. Equally, on many measures GM was not as efficient as Ford in production terms, but it was able to offer much greater variety to the market.

The other feature to observe is the *assimilation and convergence of practices*: Ford may have been the first to introduce the moving assembly line, but within a fairly short space of time GM had also installed moving assembly lines in its factories. As the industry has matured, and practices converged, the relative performance advantage each new paradigm provides may have become smaller. This convergence can be seen in the labour productivity of global assembly operations. The performance advantage of the Japanese highlighted in 1990 in *The Machine that Changed the World* had narrowed by the end of the 1990s. Since then, virtually all manufacturers have adopted some version of lean production. Similarly, quality has improved to such a degree that in 1998 JD Powers, who survey vehicle quality, had to change its methodology, as fewer and fewer defects were recorded. In order to be able to continue to discriminate between vehicle manufacturers, it extended the number of items recorded to 233 categories. Lastly, VW may have led in the adoption of platform sharing and proliferation of models and brands, but by 2013 platform-sharing was common across all major car manufacturers. In fact one might argue that the use of platforms has shifted the economies of the entire industry: the proliferation of segments, and cross-over vehicles, has only been possible because of the ability to share much of the vehicle structure with other models.

We have now reviewed the evolution of the industry, and illustrated how four companies – Ford, GM, Toyota and VW – have, in different ways, pushed the 'frontier of performance' in the industry forward. This should be seen in the context of a quest to reconcile the market's need for variety with the need for productive efficiency. In the next chapter we shall build on these ideas and discuss the core capabilities of a successful car company, and look at three additional factors crucial to understanding survival and resilience in the auto industry – stakeholders, market reach and scale.

4   Concepts: Stakeholders, operations and context

Car companies are huge organizations, which design, make, sell and support complex products in high volumes, all over the world. In order to understand survival and failure amongst auto firms we shall focus on three areas: (1) the relationships between auto firms and their *stakeholders* (2) the ability of auto firms to run their *operations* effectively – essentially, designing, making, selling cars to competitive standards – and (3) key features of the *context* in which auto firms operate. Many analyses of competitiveness in the auto industry have tended to concentrate on the second of these, to the neglect of context and stakeholder relations. Our argument is that to understand survival and failure in the auto industry, consideration all three areas – operations, stakeholder relations and context – is necessary.

Manufacturers operating in competitive market conditions need to be capable of conceiving, designing, making, distributing and selling products to competitive standards, at appropriate prices and in economic quantities. They need to do this while maintaining sufficient margins between revenues and costs so that they can make provision for the development and renewal of products and infrastructure. This is a typical 'operations' perspective on success and failure. It is this perspective which dominates much commentary on the auto industry – and, indeed, much of the general strategy and operations management teaching in business schools around the world. From this perspective, efficient companies who make products that are comparable to, or better than those of their competitors in terms of price, quality, style and reliability are successful and grow; those that do not go out of business. To this, one could also add the need for sufficient financial flexibility to ride out perturbations such as economic downturns or other events (e.g. natural disasters, product recalls) to which the auto industry is vulnerable, and which can precipitate crises. The operations perspective represents a powerful, Darwinian logic of survival-of-the-fittest.

This perspective is compelling and persuasive, but it only provides a partial explanation of why some auto companies thrive and survive and others do not. As the woes of some of the Japanese automakers showed in the late 1990s, and the 2008–9 global financial crisis demonstrated more graphically still, auto companies that are capable of designing, making and selling reasonably competitive products, efficiently, can still get into trouble. And the fact that a business runs out of cash – as a number did during the global financial crisis – does not automatically mean that it ceases to exist. Stronger businesses may take over weaker ones and make changes that restore profitability. Failed businesses may receive state aid, or even be taken into state ownership, if the likely consequences of their collapse are sufficiently severe and far-reaching to justify a public rescue. In the auto industry, GM and Chrysler were in this position in 2009, as was Rover (then called British Leyland) in the mid 1970s. The French state injected $1.1 billion into Peugeot-Citroën (PSA) in early 2014, taking a 14 per cent stake in the struggling automaker. Several financial institutions – AIG, Fannie and Freddie Mae in the USA and RBS, Northern Rock and Lloyds TSB in the UK – were all rescued by their respective states in 2008–9 due to a need to prop up the financial system as a whole.

The support that distressed companies receive from parties who have an interest in their success and survival – in other words, their stakeholders – can take many forms. Stakeholder support is particularly significant in times of crisis, but operates, albeit less visibly, in the background for much of the rest of the time. This support may be given for a variety of reasons and can come, in different forms, from a range of stakeholders – customers, suppliers, labour, financiers and so on. The key point is that organizations' relationships with their stakeholders are additional, and sometimes crucial, factors in understanding failure and survival because these relationships can give access to support and resources that are quite independent from the core operations of designing, making and selling products.

STAKEHOLDER RELATIONS

All organizations exist within an environment and growth, development and continued existence depend on their ability to secure resources from the environment in order to sustain themselves.[1] A high proportion of these resources are passed on to other organizations, for example to suppliers and to employees, for materials, services and other forms of support in a form of corporate food-chain. To understand failure and survival of organizations – where 'failure' is typically a consequence of being unable to muster sufficient resources for continued operation – we need to understand the environment within which an organization is embedded and its relationships with the players in that environment who can provide (or withhold) support at times of crisis.

For commercial enterprises operating in a market environment the sources and direction of resource flows are largely taken as read. Under normal commercial conditions, resources flow to firms from customers via sales of products and services. These resources are then distributed to the various groups who participate in the activities of the firm: labour, suppliers of parts, materials and services, equipment suppliers, providers of capital (e.g. banks and investors) and so on. All of these participants have claims on the resource stream – suppliers demand certain prices, labour seeks acceptable levels of wages and salaries, the providers of capital demand interest on their loans or a certain level of return on their equity.

Viewed through this lens, a firm is not just a set of material and information flows, but a node in a network of resource flows. Various groups make claims on these flows and sometimes their claims compete. Funds that are distributed to shareholders as dividends are not then available for investment – and vice versa. Generous wages (very desirable from the perspective of labour) mean higher costs and therefore lower margins (which is bad news for investors) unless prices are raised – which is disadvantageous to customers. Cost reductions sought from suppliers permit lower prices for customers or better profits for the car assemblers.

This conception of a firm as embedded in a network of other organizations[2] on which it depends for various forms of support – anything from cash to legitimacy – underpins what is commonly known as the 'stakeholder' perspective on organizations.[3] Stakeholders, simply defined, are 'groups without whose support the business would cease to be viable'. There are also broader definitions of stakeholders such as 'any group who can affect a business' or any group who can 'be affected by the realization of an organization's purpose'.[4]

Over time, organizations arrive at a collection of 'settlements' with their multiple stakeholders. By settlements we mean social (and in some cases legal) contracts between stakeholders. Embodied in a settlement will be a shared understanding between actors as to what constitutes appropriate behaviour, what each party is expected to contribute to the relationship and what it can expect in return. Like any form of agreement, settlements are subject to negotiation and may be relatively stable, or constantly contested, like an unresolved border dispute between two nations. Settlements can build up over many years and once established may profoundly affect the competitive position of a firm.

The concept of the settlement applies to an organization's relationships with various stakeholder groups, for example labour, suppliers, shareholders and customers. The balance and the nature of settlements may vary considerably across different contexts and often reflect national differences. For example, a 'settlement' between a Japanese auto firm and its core employees in Japan is likely to involve some explicit or implicit commitment to long-term employment security on the part of the company and a preparedness to work flexibly and to offer suggestions for process improvement on the part of the employees. For many years, the settlement between the Big Three US auto firms and their workers, represented by the United

Automobile Workers (UAW), included significant health care benefits and 'jobs banks' for workers who were laid off. For the Big Three, these benefits and health care costs added US$1,600 to the cost of a car, compared to US$200 at Toyota.[5] Yet these benefits were woven into the fabric of the employer/employee settlement and the UAW, unsurprisingly, resisted their removal. It was not until GM and Chrysler entered Chapter 11 in 2009 that this particular settlement was broken, and many of the benefits conceded by labour. This illustrates an important point – that settlements, once established, can be difficult to change and in aggregate can profoundly influence the competitive position of a firm. In effect a firm is held in a 'web' of settlements with its different stakeholders, a web that exerts both supporting and constraining forces.

The nature of these settlements determines the balance of returns between different stakeholder groups as well as the competitiveness and sustainability of the firm. Management teams and boards of directors generally act as arbiters in this balancing process, and through a myriad of choices and negotiations (for example, about wage levels, prices and conditions under which to supply parts, levels of dividends) firms arrive at 'settlements' with their various claimants – labour, suppliers, financiers and so on. Within a sector, there may be coordination between firms on settlements, for example national norms with respect to working hours, pay rates or health care provision.

Of course, executives do not have a blank slate when it comes to settlements with stakeholders, but face constraints on how they can act. One source of constraint is competition in the product market. Competitors, through their prices, quality, service and other attributes, set standards for an industry. A company that violates these standards, by demanding higher prices, or offering inferior quality or delivery, risks losing customers to competitors who offer a better deal. Market discipline means that winners are rewarded with more sales and/or higher prices, which in turn provide more resources for distribution to the various claimants. Losers are punished by reductions in resource through lower sales volumes, or find that their products cannot command such high prices. These processes can set in train virtuous circles of growth and development or vicious cycles of decline.

Market discipline is most visible in product markets and customer buying behaviour. But similar processes are at work with respect to transactions with other stakeholders. If firms offer less favourable settlements to suppliers, workers and shareholders than competitors do they will struggle to attract and retain these key supporters. On the other hand, if a firm is too generous in its settlements, its cost base will be high, meaning there is insufficient resource left over for future investment. If some stakeholders are too obviously privileged at the expense of others, goodwill and cooperation from those who feel disadvantaged will be reduced.

A stakeholder map of a typical auto firm is shown in a simplified and stylized form in Figure 4.1. The diagram shows how auto firms are embedded in an extensive network of stakeholders to whom they are bound via a series of settlements. A key option in times of crisis, we shall argue, is for firms to re-negotiate or break existing

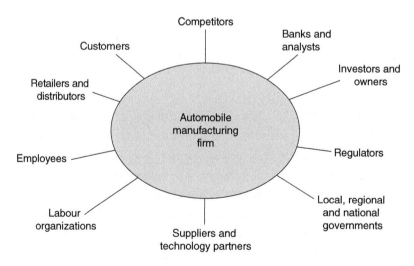

FIGURE 4.1 A stakeholder map of an auto firm

settlements with stakeholders, as they search for the elbow room to allow remedial action. For example, labour might be persuaded (or forced) to accept short-time working, or pay restraint, or new working practices. Suppliers may be asked to offer longer payment periods, or to reduce prices. Financiers may be asked to reschedule loans – and so on.

What is the significance of the stakeholder perspective to an analysis of failure and survival in the auto industry? In our view, the perspective is helpful because it highlights several factors that are often overlooked by analyses of success and failure that focus solely on the prowess of auto firms at designing and building cars. The stakeholder perspective gives a more rounded analysis and explains outcomes that a pure operations perspective cannot – such as why companies that are reasonably competent at making cars cease to exist, and why others that do not have particularly outstanding products soldier on for long periods, despite financial weakness.

Three key points follow from the stakeholder perspective. First, multiple stakeholders mean that firms are located in a web of pressures and constraints. The need to match or beat products offered by competitors spurs the renewal of models and the reduction of costs, because without this most *customers* will eventually go elsewhere. The need to comply with standards with respect to safety or emissions set by *governments* and *regulators* constrains design options. The closure or relocation of factories, which may be desirable in terms of cost, may be shunned due to pressures from *labour unions* or other economic and political lobbyists. For example, in 2012–14 French automakers Renault and PSA both faced acute political pressure to retain employment in France, which influenced key location decisions in favour of retaining French factories. Thus, the practical strategic options available to management teams may in reality be more limited than they might appear, unless existing stakeholder settlements are breached.

Secondly, the stakeholder perspective highlights how firms are *embedded* in their environments. Degrees of embeddedness can vary considerably from firm to firm. Auto firms are typically highly embedded in their environments. An organization such as a pop-up restaurant, there for one night only, is the antithesis of an embedded enterprise. But what does embeddedness mean in practice and why do we characterize auto firms as embedded enterprises?

In part this is to do with the nature of cars themselves which are heavily embedded in the lives of those who own and use them. Notwithstanding the swings of the economic cycle, this embeddedness gives stability of demand for the product over the long term – because people's choices about where to live, where to work and how they spend their leisure time are all influenced by access to vehicles. A decision to stop owning or using a car would have profound consequences and therefore will not be taken lightly. Embeddedness is manifested in other ways too. Extensive infrastructures (roads, fuel stations, service stations, parking) support the widespread usage of cars as we know them today. This may be one reason why the dominant design of cars has not changed fundamentally in nearly 100 years – four wheels, enclosed metal body, usually capable of carrying 2–7 people, powered by internal combustion engines. The multitude of 'touch points' between cars and the world in which they are used constrains both the speed and radicalness of product innovation, because of the sheer number of adjustments that a radically different approach would require in terms of user behaviour, infrastructure, etc.

A good example of this is propulsion technology. To move from a world in which vehicles are powered by internal combustion engines to one of pure electric vehicles requires the establishment of an entirely new infrastructure for re-charging batteries, comparable to the current infrastructure of petrol stations – a huge undertaking. 'Range anxiety', the fear of being stranded short of one's destination due to exhausted batteries, is currently a major barrier to the adoption of electric cars in that the existing settlement – in the broadest sense – between car makers and their customers is that cars should have a range of 300 miles (500 km) or more and plentiful refuelling points. Constraints such as these mean that the auto industry is characterized by firms who make products that are broadly similar in terms of fundamental configuration, and in which radical innovation is a risky strategy for competitive advantage.

Not only are the products of the car industry deeply embedded in the daily lives of their users, auto companies are usually highly embedded in the economies and communities in which they are located. This embeddedness means that large auto firms fall into the category of firms that are viewed as 'too big to fail', especially when the knock-on effect of closure on suppliers and other supporting firms is taken into account. Highly embedded firms are likely to enjoy greater stakeholder support than less embedded ones, and may therefore be able to obtain resources through non-commercial activities – i.e. other than through simply designing, producing and selling better products than their competitors. Being an 'embedded' enterprise means having settlements and relationships with many stakeholders (labour, unions, suppliers, governments) to whom the continued existence of the enterprise is important. The much-quoted comment by GM president Charles Wilson, made in 1953, 'For years I thought what was good for the country was good for General Motors and vice versa' is essentially an observation about GM's significance and embeddedness in the US economy and society.

However, embeddedness is a two-edged sword. On one hand it fosters support from stakeholders, support than can be particularly useful at times of crisis. On the other, it constrains on what can be done, or at least what can be done *easily*, because of the number of players who have interests in the outcome. And those with a strong enough interest in an outcome are more than likely to engage in political activity to protect their interests.

Returning to resilience, a central piece of our resilience story is that during times of difficulty or crisis, the ability to draw on the support of different stakeholders can make the difference between liquidation and survival. We suggest that embeddedness gives auto firms a remarkable degree of resilience, which is one of the reasons why the liquidation of an auto firm is relatively rare and why, when it does happen, it is more likely to be the culmination of a long period of decline rather than a 'sudden death'. The case of Rover, described in the next chapter, graphically illustrates this process – the final demise of Rover in 2005 was a culmination of a cycle of decline lasting 40 years or more. In the course of this long, slow decline Rover shrank from being one of the world's largest car makers, with hundreds of thousands of employees to a size at which its significance to most of its stakeholders (the exception being the few thousand employees who still remained in the company) had diminished greatly. Rover's closure, which was virtually unthinkable in the 1970s and 1980s created relatively little stir when the company finally closed its doors in 2005.

The third point is that patterns of settlements and the nature of relationships with stakeholders are shaped by national cultures and institutions (such as the tradition of close, long-term relationships between car makers and their suppliers in Japan, or the presence of labour on supervisory boards in Germany). These patterns are in turn important in defining the national character of different auto firms. This issue has been a major source of contention amongst academic commentators on the auto industry with some (such as members of the GERPISA academic network, writing largely from a sociological perspective) arguing that there is no one best way to organize and run an auto firm, but rather a variety of different national models, each of which can be effective. This perspective contrasts with that of those (such as Womack, Jones and Roos, authors of *The Machine That Changed the World*) who have claimed that certain universal operating principles, embodied in lean production and management practices, determine performance and hence an auto firm's ability to thrive and survive.

> We believe that the fundamental ideas of lean production are universal – applicable anywhere by anyone – and that many non-Japanese companies have already learned this ... We think it is in everyone's interest to introduce lean production everywhere, as soon as possible.[6]

In the section that follows we look in more depth at the operating principles of an effective auto company.

OPERATIONAL EFFECTIVENESS

In the previous section, we discussed the concept of embeddedness and argued that auto firms are highly embedded in their environments, and that this embeddedness, principally through the concept of settlements with stakeholders, can be a source of both support and constraint, which in turn influences survival, particularly at times of crisis.

In this section we explore the operational perspective on the survival and failure of auto firms. This perspective dominates much analysis of the auto industry and places the management of the firm and its operations centre stage.[7] Good auto companies are capable of designing, building and distributing good cars and this is the key to understanding competitiveness. The spotlight is on factors such as the quality, cost and other attributes of the cars themselves and the processes by which cars are designed and made. We are not the first to argue that this perspective has limitations. Williams et al. argued in 1994:

> An unconscious politics of managerialism runs through the text: at every stage [in *The Machine that Changed the World*] the company is the unit of analysis and the world is divided into good companies and bad companies with managers as the privileged agents of change who can turn bad companies into good companies.[8]

Much of our previous work has explored the relationship between the use of 'best practice' principles, particularly lean principles, and various measures of performance such as productivity, quality and so on. On the basis of this, we do not share the view of commentators such as Williams et al. who imply that managerial actions and choices are irrelevant to corporate performance. But we do believe that how operations are managed is certainly not the whole story when it comes to the success and survival of auto firms.

Car companies do much more than simply assemble cars, even though assembly is the most tangible part of vehicle production.

There are many processes involved in producing cars and orchestrating these effectively is a huge organizational challenge. A typical vehicle comprises around 30,000 individual parts and millions of units of the same model may be produced, often in several different factories around the world.

Hundreds, sometimes thousands, of people work in vehicle assembly plants. The core processes involve stamping steel body panels, welding these together to form the body shell (an operation largely performed by robots in most modern car plants), spray painting the body shells and then fitting the shells with engines, transmissions, and interior and exterior fittings as they pass along a moving assembly line, hundreds of metres long. Before a vehicle goes into production, hundreds of engineers will be involved in its design, development and testing. Development of new models typically takes 2–4 years. Auto firms spend enormous amounts on R&D. In 2013 the VW Group spent $11.4 billion on R&D, around 4.4 per cent of its revenues, followed by Toyota, GM, Honda and Daimler, who all spent $6–10 billion apiece, which on average represented 4–5 per cent of their annual revenue.[9]

The car makers themselves are only the tip of the iceberg. All round the world, thousands of suppliers provide parts and services to the car companies. Around 70 per cent of the cost of a vehicle typically comprises bought-in components. First-tier suppliers are often global mega-suppliers who undertake extensive development and proving work before producing and supplying components to the car makers. The largest suppliers, such as Bosch and Denso, are actually larger than many car makers. At the market end of the chain car makers have extensive distribution and dealer networks to look after parts supply, sales and support once the vehicles are out on the roads. It all adds up to a fiendishly complex system that has to be overseen and managed.

Apart from low-volume niche firms, most car companies have extensive ranges of models and many variants of each model. Hence they are constantly confronted with 'portfolio' decisions, such as where best to allocate resources amongst multiple and competing

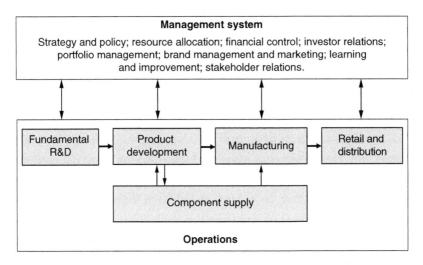

FIGURE 4.2 Core activities of a car company

demands. Sophisticated management and control systems are required in order to fulfil functions such as planning, technology development, financial control, management of product mix, marketing, production, distribution and brand management. Such systems must be able to provide coordination and direction across multiple market segments and many different territories across the globe.

Five core areas of activity for a car company are shown, in simplified form, in Figure 4.2. We shall describe each activity in turn, before considering how these activities are bound together via a *management system*.

Fundamental R&D

The development or acquisition of fundamental underlying technologies is a key requirement for a car company. Hence auto companies have centres and divisions whose role is to undertake research and development (R&D) and to acquire and develop fundamental technologies. Fundamental R&D is not usually undertaken with a specific model in mind. Technologies such as fuel cells, long-range battery storage for electric vehicles or autonomous vehicle technology may all be important in the future, but none are yet ready for the mass market. Fundamental R&D is not limited to the car makers – the larger and more sophisticated auto suppliers also undertake substantial R&D.

Fundamental R&D is distinguished from 'applications' engineering, the latter being the engineering of systems, subsystems and components for specific new model programmes. Too much emphasis on advanced engineering means that large sums of money may be spent on technologies that never find their way on to actual production vehicles. Too little, and a car maker falls behind in technology and its products may be judged as outdated and uninteresting by consumers. An image of technological sophistication can give cars, and the companies that make them, considerable cache and brand value and some car companies go to considerable lengths to emphasize this – Audi's slogan of 'Vorsprung durch Technik' being a good example of this.

The costs involved in R&D are so high that auto companies often collaborate with each other on long-term technology development in order to share the costs and risks, particularly for potentially generic technologies. For example, in 2013, Ford, Nissan and Mercedes agreed to collaborate on fuel cell technology; GM and Honda soon followed with an agreement of their own.

Fundamental R&D is not a major part of our story, but it is significant in the context of survival and failure, for a number of reasons. First, given that R&D (including the development of specific models, as well as fundamental R&D) consumes around 5 per cent of revenues of the leading car companies in the world, R&D is sensitive to the financial condition of a firm. Second, the outcomes of investments in R&D are uncertain and the results are only apparent in the long term. A car company under financial pressure may be tempted to defer expenditure on R&D and hence be forced to use older technology on its cars, probably also accompanied by long model replacement cycles, a reliance on face-lifts of existing models, re-use of designs and so on. At the extreme, this may even stretch to a car maker acquiring products from other car makers and simply rebadging them as their own (as Rover did with the CityRover in the last two years of its life, which was simply a rebadged version of the Tata Indica).

In the context of understanding the survival of auto companies, R&D also demonstrates the substantial lag that there can be between decisions being taken and the consequences of those decisions becoming apparent. Decisions which with the passage of time turn out to be crucial may hardly register as a flicker on the dial at the time. But they can set in train sequences of events whose importance only becomes apparent many years later. For this reason, reduced expenditure on R&D and new product development activities is often one of the first signs of the onset of strain and decline in an auto firm.

Product development

The relationship between basic research and product development in the auto industry may be likened to the relationship between a moving train and the stations at which it stops. Basic research and technology development are the 'train' – moving forward, often to very long timescale, exploring the technological frontiers in various domains – materials, electronics, engine technologies and so on. 'Product development' is the process of developing a specific, new vehicle and is the equivalent of a station stop, at which point a new model development project will take the technologies that are appropriate and mature (and sometimes those that are not!) and incorporate them into that model. The 'train' of fundamental R&D keeps on moving, developing and refining the basic technologies. Subsequent new model development projects will pull these off the train as they mature and are proven. Some technologies remain on the train and are never applied.

New vehicle development projects are formidable undertakings, typically taking anything from two to four years, involving hundreds of engineers in the car company (plus many more in the suppliers who will be supplying parts to the new vehicle) and costing, at 2014 prices, in the region of a billion US dollars, depending on the complexity and refinement of the vehicle and the carry-over of designs and components from the previous generation model. The process involves taking account of market requirements, target segments, competitor vehicles as well as environmental and regulatory constraints (such as safety and emissions legislation) and, working with suppliers, designing and developing a vehicle that will be competitive and compliant. Developing new products in the auto industry requires in-depth of knowledge of hundreds of specialist engineering disciplines (for example electronics, materials, mechanical engineering, quality, systems engineering), plus the commercial disciplines (marketing, finance, purchasing, logistics, legal, etc.) *and* the ability to integrate all this knowledge to produce competitive vehicles within the constraints imposed by time, cost, regulatory demands and the actions and offerings of competitors.

Product development processes are beset with uncertainty – initial product concepts and performance goals (e.g. weight, noise or fuel economy) may turn out to be too ambitious for a firm's development capabilities and resources. New products from competitors may move the goalposts within the target segment, requiring expensive adjustments during the development cycle. Trade-offs have to be made – between space and weight, or fuel economy and performance, or quality and cost. Failure to resolve these trade-offs, for example through insufficient testing and proving, runs the risk of costly problems once the cars are out in the market. Insufficient attention to ease-of-manufacture may mean that it is difficult for the factories to produce the vehicles to the right standards, leading to quality issues. Too much emphasis on ease of manufacture may compromise style, resulting in reliable, but bland products.[10]

A landmark study in automotive new product development appeared in the early 1990s.[11] Its authors, Clark and Fujimoto, found that Japanese automakers were able to develop new cars and bring them to market significantly more quickly than their American and European counterparts, with far fewer engineering hours and fewer defects when the vehicles were in production. They attributed this to the way the Japanese organized product development, in particular the use of relatively autonomous, co-located, development teams, under the direction of heavyweight project team leaders. The Japanese ran product development processes in parallel rather than sequentially, which significantly reduced lead times. They also made much greater use of the capabilities of their suppliers during the development process. Close, cooperative links between product and manufacturing engineers facilitated design-for-manufacture, with positive effects on productivity and quality in the factory.

The approach to new vehicle development described by Clark and Fujimoto was effective in bringing focus and coordination to new vehicle development projects, and became the accepted model of best industry practice for a number of years – and to a large extent still is. But as we described in Chapter 2, this approach came at a price in terms of the complexity of product portfolios, proliferation of parts and components and duplication of development effort. The same actions that delivered good coordination *within* specific new vehicle development projects (such as autonomous, co-located teams) also functioned to reduce coordination *across* projects. As the Japanese economy stagnated in the 1990s, the Japanese automakers faced strong pressure to reduce costs and so the pendulum swung away from autonomous teams and towards greater sharing of platforms and components across multiple models.[12]

In many ways this represents another manifestation of the market reach vs economies of scale and customization–standardization dilemma that we identified in Chapter 3. Focusing resources around the development of a specific model has many advantages, as Clark and Fujimoto showed, but can result in issues of duplication and excessive cost across the whole portfolio of models. However, a 'one size fits all' philosophy, with a high degree of commonality of designs and components between models, risks products that are not quite right for any particular market or segment. Whilst the holy grail of automotive product development may be maximum market reach with minimal variation (maximum commonality across products) this is a hard trick to pull off. In later chapters we shall see how both Saab and Rover struggled with this problem in different ways and will argue that the ability to master this trick is one of the key success factors in the contemporary auto industry.

Manufacturing

When many people think of car companies, they think of assembly plants, the huge factories from which the finished vehicles finally emerge. It is in the assembly plants that the vehicles assume their final form, as body panels are stamped from steel blanks, welded together to form the body, painted and then fitted with engines, transmissions, and other components. Assembly plants carry great symbolic value – the opening or closing of an assembly plant usually makes national, often international, headlines. A great deal of political activity may be triggered by the threat to close an assembly plant, as it is around decisions about where to establish new ones, with countries and regions fiercely competing with each other to attract the investment.

In reality, the image of final assembly as being the essence of a car company is quite misleading. Final assembly costs typically account for a relatively small proportion of total costs, around 12.5 per cent of a vehicle by value, as Figure 4.3 shows.

Some car companies actually contract other firms to carry out some assembly on their behalf. Both Toyota and Nissan do this in Japan, and in Europe Magna-Steyr, who did much of the development of the first generation BMW X3, as well as assembling it on BMW's behalf, provide contract vehicle assembly services to various auto firms. Small, contract assemblers are often used to assemble low-volume specialist models, such as cabriolets, on behalf of the volume car makers who seek to avoid the disruption to the flow of their high-volume assembly lines that such specials would cause. Contracting out specials, by the way, is another example of how volume car makers try and resolve the standardization–customization dilemma.

The high visibility of auto assembly relative to other activities (such as product development or component supply) means that it can be quite difficult to assess the fundamental strengths and capabilities

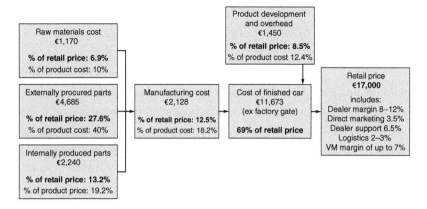

FIGURE 4.3 Vehicle cost structure.
Source: Holweg and Pil (2004)

of an auto firm from the outside as these are hidden behind the higher profile assembly operations. This means that as an auto firm declines, there may be a 'hollowing out' of capabilities over time (particularly those around R&D and product development) without this being particularly visible to the general public, as long as the current models keep rolling off the line. If a company has been subject to merger and acquisition (as both Saab and Rover were in the decades leading up to their demise) key functions may be taken on by other parts of parent firms, making it difficult to assess the subsidiary's real capacity for independent operation.

The extent of hollowing out tends to become apparent at times of stress, perhaps when it loses the support of an owner or partner on which it was reliant for key activities and functions. We will show later how Saab and Rover were largely 'zombie' companies by the ends of their lives, still alive (in that they were producing cars) but incapable of self-renewal and therefore living on borrowed time.

In Rover's case, the company's relative success during the latter part of the 1980s and into the 1990s rested heavily on its access to Honda designs and production technology. This was abruptly lost when BMW acquired Rover in 1994. BMW, apparently unaware of how much of Rover's success relied on support from Honda, initially adopted a hands-off approach. By the time BMW became fully aware of Rover's weaknesses a great deal of money had been already expended, with no end to the cash drain in sight. From the time of BMW's disposal of Rover in 2000 to Rover's final collapse in 2005, there was really very little left of Rover, apart from a single assembly plant producing outdated models. Although Rover may have looked like a normal car company from the outside, for the last five years of its life – and arguably even earlier – it had more or less lost the capacity to perform most functions apart from vehicle assembly and direct support to assembly.

The Saab story is somewhat similar. When GM disposed of Saab in 2010 it had owned Saab in whole or in part for over 20 years and many core functions (such as purchasing, product development and spare parts supply) had been integrated into those of GM. Moreover, GM controlled the licences for key designs and technologies of Saab vehicles and hence effectively had the power to veto tie-ups between Saab and other potential partners by withholding these licences.

The public visibility of car assembly within the entire car-making process is reflected in the attention that car assembly has received in analyses of management and competitiveness in car companies. These analyses have a long history, going back to the early years of the twentieth century when Henry Ford introduced standardization of parts, specialization of functions and the moving assembly line in order to reduce the time and cost of making cars. 'Fordism' even entered the vocabulary of social scientists as a term to denote mass production and the patterns of organization surrounding it.

However, the difficulties caused by the combination of relatively inflexible mass production methods in the factories and segmentation in the market were not difficult to see – inventories, waste and quality problems – mostly caused by a relatively inflexible production system attempting to grapple with a changing market that demanded greater and greater variety. (As we saw in Chapters 2 and 3, Henry Ford's answer to this of course, had been to pursue production efficiencies by ignoring the variety demanded by the market. His philosophy of 'You can have any colour you like as long as it's black' was emblematic of this.) With growing markets for cars in many parts of the world, especially in the decades following the Second World War it was not generally, the inefficiencies of mass production that received most attention, so much as the impact of the system on those who worked within it. Commentators typically focused on the de-humanizing effect of mass production, on worker boredom and alienation and on the difficult labour relations that characterized the auto industry from the 1960s onwards.[13]

Aside from some largely Swedish attempts to redesign car assembly plants to make them more worker-friendly, the dominant model of factory operation in the auto industry was mass production, albeit with some local variants in the light of national and market conditions, until the 1980s. Mass production may have had its drawbacks, but as long as everyone was doing it, it was possible to be competitive, particularly during the post-war boom years when demand and supply conditions for cars were favourable to the automakers.

The first real challenge to mass production in the auto industry came in the 1980s. By this time Japanese automakers had taken around 30 per cent of the global auto market. Accounts of how the Japanese car makers organized and managed their factories and their suppliers started to filter through to the rest of the world, and it became clear that here was a very different production philosophy to traditional mass production. This challenge culminated in the coining of the term 'lean production' to describe the Japanese approach, which in practice meant the Toyota Production System.[14]

As we described in Chapter 2, the term 'lean production' emerged out of the first phase of the International Motor Vehicle Programme (IMVP), a $5 million research project into competitiveness in the global auto industry which ran from 1985 to 1990 and involved 55 researchers worldwide. The programme compared the labour productivity and product quality of around 80 car assembly plants around the world. The main conclusion was that a distinct form of production organization and management, found in its purest form at Toyota, delivered far better productivity and quality than traditional mass production methods. The IMVP showed that Japanese vehicle assemblers had an almost 2:1 superiority over their US and

European counterparts in terms of labour hours to assemble a car, with considerably lower defect rates in their finished vehicles.

This performance superiority was attributed to 'lean production', an umbrella term covering the organization and management of assembly plants, design and development, supply chain management and retailing and distribution (with the first of these receiving by far the most coverage and the last of these the least). The core characteristics of lean practices are:

- Operations characterized by swift, even flows[15] through Just-in-Time (JIT) scheduling and production smoothing (*heijunka*) manifested by low inventories, small batches, mixed-model schedules and short lead times.
- *Kaizen* or continuous improvement of processes by using systematic methods to seek the root causes of quality and productivity problems; an emphasis on error prevention rather than detection and subsequent correction.
- High commitment human resource policies that foster a sense of shared destiny and community within auto firms as well as between auto firms and key stakeholders, in particular their suppliers. Lean production is characterized by close relations with a few suppliers rather than arm's length relations with many (note the significance of stakeholder relations in this model).
- Team-based work organization, with flexible, multi-skilled operators who take a high degree of responsibility for work within their areas, especially problem-solving, to support kaizen activities.
- Retailing and distribution channels that provide close links to the customer and permit a make-to-order strategy to operate (although admittedly this is one of the weakest areas for most car firms that have implemented lean[16]).

The proponents of lean production hailed it as a reversal of many of the principles of mass production: 'Lean production combines the best features of both craft production and mass production – the ability to reduce costs per unit and dramatically improve quality while at the same time providing an ever wider range of products and ever more challenging work.'[17] The IMVP research included a number of Japanese transplant factories in North America which had been established in the 1980s. The quality and productivity of the transplants was not as good as that of the parent plants in Japan, but it was not far behind, suggesting the Japanese superiority was not a function of features culturally specific to Japan that could not be replicated elsewhere:

> We've become convinced that the principles of lean production can be applied equally in every industry across the globe and that the conversion to lean production will have a profound effect on human society – it will truly change the world.[18]

This idea of a universal recipe for competitiveness in the auto industry and beyond did not go unchallenged, and the IMVP research was criticized on three main grounds.

The first of these was that the IMVP assembly plant productivity calculations exaggerated the Japanese superiority because they overlooked factors such as manufacturability (the ease with which the cars can be assembled) and capacity utilization (the extent to which the market is able to absorb the output a company is capable of producing). The second was that vehicle assembly, on which the productivity comparisons were made, is a relatively small part of the whole process of making cars; national level statistics that assess productivity by looking at total numbers of cars produced in relation to total employment in the auto industry in Japan and the USA do not show such marked differences in productivity, suggesting that efficiencies in car assembly plants may be offset by inefficiencies elsewhere in the supply chain. The third criticism was that lean production is only found in its purest form in the Toyota Production System (TPS), and represents methods which are 'a historical response to Toyota's dominance of the Japanese car market which [was] uniquely non-cyclical'.[19] In other words, the bundle of practices which the IMVP researchers labelled 'lean production' was something that emerged in a particular company, due to a unique set of circumstances and was not therefore a universal recipe for success.[20]

Such criticisms notwithstanding, *The Machine that Changed the World* went on to sell many millions of copies and lean production principles moved from being revolutionary, a paradigm shift in manufacturing, to accepted best practice. Subsequent studies of lean production and performance in the auto industry provided further confirmation of the link between lean practices and manufacturing and supply chain performance.[21] More or less all car companies around the world went through lean transformation programmes of one form or another during the 1980s and 1990s. US and European auto assemblers and suppliers, who had been shown to lag the Japanese on measures of inventory turns, a key measure of leanness,[22] caught up with the Japanese on this measure in 1997 and have matched them since then.[23]

Component supply

As we described earlier, a significant proportion of a finished vehicle – around 70 per cent by value – comprises bought-in components. The implication of this is clear – a very significant proportion of the cost and quality of a vehicle is attributable to the competence of the firms who supply parts to the car makers. Suppliers are therefore of critical importance to a car company.

Historically, auto supply networks in different countries and regions have developed in different ways. Different auto companies have displayed quite different trajectories in their relationships with suppliers. Ford, in its early days, emphasized vertical integration and in pursuit of control over its operations and good material flows chose to perform pretty much all activities involved in car making itself. General Motors was also relatively vertically integrated for much of the twentieth century. European car makers, partly due to the presence of an indigenous engineering industry that existed prior to the development of the car industry, partly due to lower volumes, tended to buy in a rather higher proportion of components than their US counterparts.

As the car industry in Europe and the USA developed, the norm was for car makers to multi-source components from a number of suppliers. This was partly to create price-based competition between suppliers and partly to guard against disruption to supply from industrial action, in particular during the 1960s and 1970s when industrial unrest was rife. During this period the relations between European and US car makers and their suppliers were characterized as arm's length, low-trust, transactional and adversarial with little appetite or opportunity for joint problem solving and improvement activities on the part of car makers or suppliers.[24]

As the US and European auto firms began to wake up to the advance of the Japanese producers, the weaknesses of the traditional (Western) model of buyer–supplier relations were vividly exposed. During the post-war period, the major Japanese car companies, Nissan and Toyota, had developed their own families of suppliers around them, known as the *keiretsu* system. Unlike the US and European adversarial model, relations between Japanese car makers and their suppliers were typically long term and collaborative in nature. Japanese car companies often held equity in their suppliers, and it was normal for personnel to rotate between car makers and suppliers within the same keiretsu. The IMVP research revealed the operational advantages in the Japanese system – better material flows between car makers and suppliers, joint problem solving and cost reduction activities and supplier involvement in design and development activities, all of which were commonplace amongst Japanese automakers and their suppliers.

The Japanese system also had some disadvantages. Close relations with a small number of suppliers restricted the ability of car makers to shop around for the latest technology from whichever suppliers might be able to provide it, and risk was relatively concentrated for both car makers (if a supplier got into difficulty) and suppliers (if things went wrong with their major customer). However, at the time, the competitive benefits that the Japanese model bestowed seemed overwhelming. Consequently many Western car makers began to emulate the Japanese system of suppliers, reducing the number of direct suppliers from the norm of around 1200 per car company to between 2–300. The espoused intention of the car

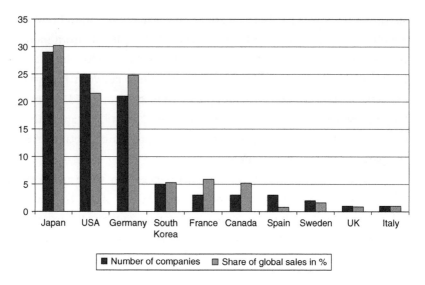

FIGURE 4.4 Top 100 global auto suppliers: nationality and share of global sales in 2012
Source: *Automotive News*. Nationality determined by location of headquarters.

companies was to develop deeper relationships with a smaller number of suppliers, and the emphasis was on cooperation rather than competition. This remains the orthodoxy today, although from the mid 1990s there has been considerable consolidation amongst component suppliers, with a number of huge global supplier groups, such as Denso and Bosch, emerging. As Figure 4.4 shows, the ownership of the major automotive suppliers is now concentrated in Japanese, US and German hands – together these three countries are HQ to 75 per cent of the world's top 100 suppliers, encouraging a much greater homogeneity of supplier quality that has been the case in the past.

Retail and distribution

Given the significance of retail, distribution and aftercare to the automotive industry it is remarkable that these features have received so little attention. In terms of the vehicle price that the customer sees, about one third relates to direct and indirect marketing costs, as well as incentives, rebates and stockholding and logistics costs. Also, given that the average life of a vehicle is in the region of twelve years (and rising) an enormous amount of the cost of ownership of a vehicle is bound up with aftercare activities. Although great attention has been paid to taking waste out of the manufacturing processes of vehicle assemblers and their suppliers, inventory levels of finished vehicles in automotive supply chains have stayed remarkably static for the last 20 years. Despite hopes of a world in which cars are built-to-order and the elimination of fields full of unsold cars, build-to-order remains the exception rather than the rule.[25]

There have been remarkably few innovations in the vehicle distribution system equivalent to those we have seen in the factories of auto assemblers and their suppliers. The general process of vehicle distribution is remarkably homogenous across the industry. The manufacturer 'sells' the vehicles it produces to its 'National Sales Companies', which in turn distribute the vehicles to captive, franchised dealerships. Sales volumes are tightly controlled by wholesale agreements, and financial incentives for dealers are strongly linked to the achievement of monthly sales quotas. If certain vehicles do not sell as expected, the manufacturer or the dealer may offer incentives to increase sales. These incentives come in many forms: price reductions, favourable finance and insurance options, better trade-in prices, and free servicing. Incentives tend to increase towards the end of a vehicle's model life, and generally are in the order of 10–20 per cent for retail customers, and up to 30–40 per cent for institutional buyers such as rental car companies.

In terms of the actual distribution process, the vehicles leave the assembly plant generally via rail or trucks towards national holding compounds. The actual pairing of the physical vehicle to a customer order can take a range of forms. The vehicle can be built to customer order ('build-to-order'); an existing vehicle in the planning pipeline may be amended to fit the customer order ('open order pipeline'); the vehicle may already have been built and be located in central stock, such as a national distribution centre; or it could be

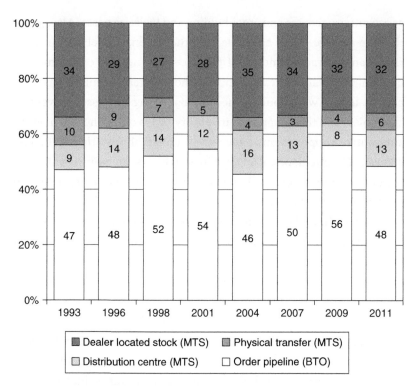

FIGURE 4.5 New vehicle sales sourcing in Europe.
Source: ICDP

located at a dealership. The actual mix of these order fulfilment modes varies across markets. Figure 4.5 shows the distribution in Europe over time. Other markets, such as the USA for example, tend to source sales predominantly from existing dealer stock.

Regardless of how orders are fulfilled, all distribution operations are driven by a shared fascination with market share and achieving volume targets. It is not uncommon for either manufacturers or dealers to compromise sales margins in order to achieve volume targets, which in turn contributes to the low profit margins common in the industry. At full retail price, the vehicle manufacturer should earn a 7 per cent profit margin in the volume car segment (excluding profit from financing and leasing). More common however is a marginal profit or a breakeven during the later stage of a vehicle's life cycle.

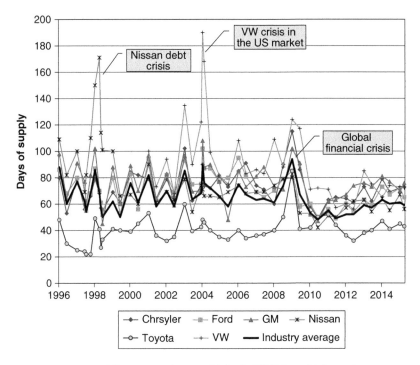

FIGURE 4.6 Inventory of new vehicles in US light vehicle market
Source: *Automotive News*

Levels of finished vehicle inventories in the market place, which are used to disconnect the factory from the variable demand experienced in most markets, can be considerable. Figure 4.6 shows the average inventory levels in terms of days of supply for the major US and foreign manufacturers. The industry average for complete cars has remained remarkably stable over time. Also interesting to note are Nissan's oversupply in 1999, which soaked up large amounts of working capital and contributed to the company's debt crisis, and the oversupply by VW in 2004, which led to a $1bn loss in the US market in that year.

JOINING IT UP: THE MANAGEMENT SYSTEM

In the preceding sections we looked at the key activity areas – the operational building blocks – of a competitive car company. To recap, these areas are:

1. Fundamental R&D – developing and acquiring competitive basic technology
2. Designing and developing new models
3. Selecting and working with appropriate suppliers
4. Manufacturing vehicles, efficiently, to the right quality standards, in the volume and variety mix required by the market
5. Establishing and operating adequate retail, distribution and service networks.

Companies do not necessarily have to be class-leading in every one of these areas in order to survive (design flair might compensate for shortcomings in reliability or vice versa, for example), but a company's position with respect to these five areas should enable it to be operationally competitive, in aggregate, with other auto firms.

Mastering any of these processes is an achievement in its own right, the orchestration and control of these constituent processes is arguably an even greater challenge, particularly because car companies are large, complex and operate in multiple territories around the world. Given its importance to corporate health, it is remarkable how little attention this orchestration has received. This is one of the key roles of what we term the 'management system', a concept borrowed from Stafford Beer's work on viable systems.[26]

Stafford Beer was a systems thinker and wrote about the viability of complex systems, viability being the capacity of a system (such as a company) to sustain itself in the long term. To Beer, viability not only requires effective subsystems, such as product development, manufacturing, retail and distribution in the case of an auto company, but also an effective system for coordination and control that sits over the various operational activities or subsystems. We shall refer to this higher-level system as 'the management system'. The term covers a broad set of people and processes – for example, those in strategy, coordination and oversight roles (managers, executives) as well as structures, systems and routines that supply and transmit information and decisions up, down and across the organization. The management system, to use another of Beer's expressions, is the 'brain of the firm'.

The management system serves several vital functions. One of these is to ensure coordination and coherence across the various units of an organization, for example, ensuring that the cars that are being developed are appropriate to the market; or that different models in a line-up are sufficiently consistent with the overall brand values of the marque; or avoiding product duplication and cannibalization of sales; ensuring control of costs and regulatory compliance and so on. This is primarily about effective execution, by ensuring that information flows between different sub units, divisions and functions as it should, that conflicts and trade-offs between competing requirements are resolved appropriately and generally making sure that the right hand knows what the left is doing. Fundamentally, this is an integration or coordination function and in large and complex firms it can be a significant challenge.

A second and crucial function of the management system is strategy and policy-making – not so much *how* things are done, but *what* is done. Many decisions crucial to an auto firm's long-term survival fall into this category, such as which geographical markets to target, which segments to pursue, the size and shape of the product portfolio, how much weight to give to ancillary activities such as vehicle financing, the brand image to cultivate and so on.

Execution is about designing, building and selling cars effectively. Strategy and policy decisions shape the long-term direction of the firm, for example the bases on which it chooses to compete (quality, cost, etc.); the markets in which it decides to play; and where it chooses to invest resources. Strategic choices also play out in the scope of an enterprise – its degree of vertical integration and whether to merge, acquire or divest activities. Strategy and policy are manifested in where resources are invested (or withheld) – for example, in particular products, activities and markets and not in others. Strategy typically involves trade-offs – specializing in one area or in one set of product attributes implies a firm is eschewing others, and not to do so risks creating confusion amongst customers who may be unclear about what the firm or the brand really stands for. Indeed, there is a view that the real indication of strategy is what a firm does NOT do, either by active choice or by default. Strategy also takes us back to the issues of stakeholders and constraints. Strategic choices are clearly shaped by the wishes and expectations of key stakeholders and executives do not have a blank slate of strategic choices, but face resource and other constraints that limit their feasible choices.[27]

Beer's perspective represents what is sometimes called an *information-processing* view of what makes an organization effective.[28] The essence of this perspective is that an organization's management system must be capable of absorbing, synthesizing and transmitting copious amounts of information both internally that is between an organization's constituent parts (to ensure common direction, control and coordination) and between the organization and its external environment (to understand and respond appropriately to opportunities and threats). The larger and more complex the organization, and the more uncertain and turbulent its environment, the more information must be processed and the greater the risk that the management system will be overwhelmed by this task. Symptoms of this include degradation in the quality of decision-making, missed targets, an inability to execute plans effectively and often crises of legitimacy in the eyes of external stakeholders. Large-scale mergers and acquisitions pose a particular challenge to management systems as they often involve a sudden step change in the variety and scale of operations to be overseen. As we shall argue in Chapter 5, the case of Rover graphically illustrates what happens when a management system is not up to the organizational and strategic challenges that a company faces.

An important point to remember is that the capacity of a management system is not synonymous with the abilities of the individuals who comprise it – when a management system is overwhelmed, even the most capable executives will find it very difficult to operate effectively. This phenomenon is widely known in systems and control engineering as Ashby's Law, which states that for a system to be in control, the capacity of a controller to process information needs to be greater than or equal to the information generated by the system that is being controlled.[29] In our context it means that even the most capable management system is bound to fail if the demands from its operations exceed its capacity to deal with them.

THE CONTEXT OF THE AUTO INDUSTRY

Much of what we have said so far in this chapter applies to the operation and management of any large company that operates on a global scale. However, the auto industry has a number of attributes that are particularly relevant in the context of crisis and resilience, and we shall conclude this chapter by briefly outlining these before presenting our analytical framework.

The first is the significance of the economic cycle to the auto industry. Cars are big-ticket, long-life items and the purchase of a car may be deferred when money is short, or brought forward when times are good. Hence the peaks and troughs of auto demand do not simply follow those of the economic cycle, but may amplify them. The auto industry has high fixed costs, which means that auto companies who are caught short of cash during a trough in the economic cycle do not have many remedial actions at their disposal to fix the problem quickly. Demand in most auto markets shows considerable cyclicality, as shown in Figures 4.7(a) and 4.7(b). The US market is particularly heavily driven by the economic cycle, which leads to considerable shifts in demand on a year-to-year basis.

To some extent this can be ameliorated by serving a spread of global markets, so when sales in one market are down (as has been the case in the European car market in the years following the 2007–8 global financial crisis) sales in others (such as China) can compensate. A car company that is dependent on a single region for most of its sales is clearly more vulnerable than one that serves more diverse markets. The impact of the economic cycle is clearly less of a problem if there are sufficient earnings in the good times to tide companies over the bad ones. But here a second attribute of the auto industry makes itself felt, namely *long-term overcapacity*.

(a)

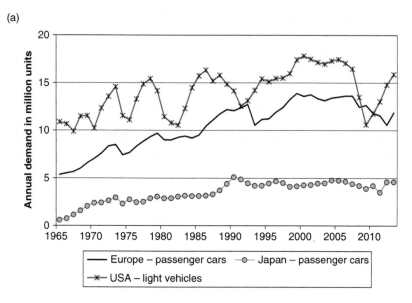

FIGURE 4.7(a) Cyclicality of demand. Annual demand in million units over time, selected markets.

(b)

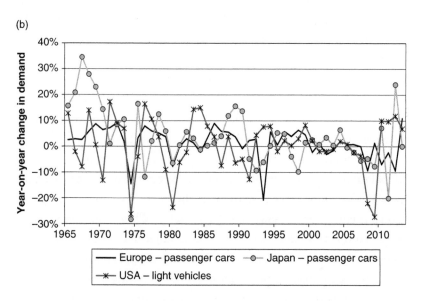

FIGURE 4.7(b) Cyclicality of demand. Year-on-year changes in %, selected markets
Source: World Motor Vehicle Data, various years.

There are a number of reasons for this overcapacity. There are powerful non-financial incentives for developing nations to build up their own car industries, just as there are for developed economies to retain theirs. These reasons include national pride in producing cars locally, as well as the creation and maintenance of relatively well-paid jobs, in car factories, in the factories of suppliers and in the many service and support activities that go along with these. Nations often compete fiercely for investments from global car makers. Vehicle assembly plants employ, on average 3–5,000 workers, and each of these can support between 3 and 10 further jobs in the supply chain (depending on the degrees of vertical integration and local content sourcing). Subsidies can take many forms, from training, tax breaks, to cheap leasing for buildings, to free infrastructure development. On average, subsidies of US$100,000 per worker employed are the norm.

Nations that are blessed with large potential markets can sometimes drive a hard bargain with global automakers, for example insisting on tie-ups with local firms and significant technology transfer as a condition of market access – as China has done, with considerable success.[30]

There are also strong disincentives for nations who have a history of car-making to lose it, for much the same reasons as there are for others to enter – the dent to national pride for a car plant closure, the economic impact of the loss of a large-scale industry closing, and so on. Hence a strong asymmetry develops, whereby it is much easier for car firms to add capacity in an upturn, than to remove it in response to a downturn or large-scale market shifts.

Taken together, these conditions have served to create and sustain long-term overcapacity in the auto industry. This means that in mature markets, in many market segments, several auto producers compete head to head with broadly comparable products. Whilst this is good for consumers who enjoy reduced prices, for auto producers it mostly means thin margins. On top of this is a set of commonly reported industry metrics that emphasize volume of sales and market share, both of which can serve to push margins into the background

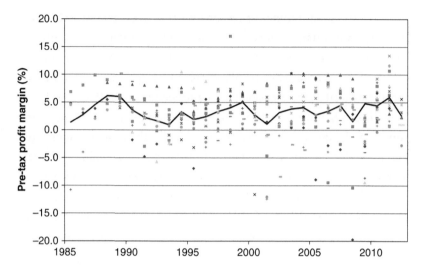

FIGURE 4.8 Average firm profitability in the global motor industry since 1985

Source: Thomson Reuters Datastream.

when it comes time to distribute shame and glory amongst executives. Consequently, most auto firms show relatively low returns on capital employed across the complete economic cycle – around 4–5 per cent,[31] and the weaker ones are prone to find themselves in serious distress in the troughs of economic and product life cycles – particularly those whose sales are concentrated in markets that are in recession. Figure 4.8 shows the pre-tax profit margins for a selection of major car companies over time, as well as an industry average, which illustrates the frequency in which major car firms report major losses when one or several of their major markets recede, as well as the rather low average profitability for the industry.

Thirdly, demand for particular models is linked to the model life cycle, with specific models typically enjoying a production life of 5–7 years. Demand tends be high when a model is relatively new and then falls as it ages. Interim 'facelifts', where the fundamentals of the car remain unaltered but cosmetic changes are made, may mitigate, but not eliminate this fall in demand. Thus, if an auto company finds itself with the wrong mix of models, either through its own misjudgement or a sudden switch in consumer tastes (due to, say, an oil shock), it can take years to put this right. It is therefore important in assessing resilience to view the strength or weakness of an auto firm across both the business and the product cycle, as it is easy to form an incorrect impression if one does not appreciate exactly where in the cycle the company and the industry actually are. A single high-profile hit model, especially when amplified by uncritical media coverage, can easily create the impression that the whole company is stronger than it is.

A fourth feature of the industry stems from the nature of the product itself. Cars are 'heavy, fast-moving objects operating in public space'.[32] The design, production and use of vehicles are therefore subject to extensive regulation in areas such as safety and environmental impact. Such regulation varies from territory to territory, and over time, so global automakers must deal with a multiplicity of regulatory regimes. As concerns over auto emissions and climate change have mounted over the last couple of decades, governments have introduced legislation and taxation designed to curb emissions. Auto companies have had to both engage with policy-making processes and work within the regulatory frameworks that have emerged from these. Increasingly, auto companies parade their green credentials in their mission statements and marketing collateral.

Across the board, regulation erodes auto companies' strategic room for manoeuvre, but also provides the potential for competitive advantage for those companies better placed to meet the requirements. Regulation also provides governments with a potential lever to tilt competition in favour of their home companies.

The final factor in this discussion of context concerns the nature of auto markets. This lays the foundation for one of the key attributes of our framework, which we shall call the 'market reach' of an auto company. We use the term 'market reach' to mean the quality of coverage that a company has in different segments of the market (luxury, mid-market, small cars, SUVs, etc.) and in different territories (Europe, USA, Asia, etc.). Quality coverage could be achieved by strong positions in particular niches, or by strong footholds in growing markets.

Market reach is significant because long-term overcapacity in the industry has created saturation and intense competition, particularly in mature markets. Auto companies which are dependent on stagnant markets and/or segments in which margins are low due to the presence of several producers in head-to-head competition risk underlying financial weakness due to low margins, weakness which is likely to be exposed by downturns in the business cycle.

The complexity of the global market for cars has increased enormously as the industry has developed and matured. We saw in Chapter 2 how as far back as the 1920s General Motors recognized the significance of segmentation in the US domestic auto market and developed cars and brands that reflected the aspirations and purchasing power of different groups of consumers. GM also pioneered the classic divisional corporate structure to support this strategy. In so doing, GM pushed Ford, a much more efficient producer of cars but with a much less differentiated line of products, off the top spot, a position that Ford has never been able to regain.

Car markets today are much more complex and sophisticated than 100 years ago, as can be seen in the proliferation of the different categories of cars that exist and in the multitude of different geographical markets, each with its own idiosyncrasies. In the USA, there are around 25 recognizable market segments in common use; in Europe the number is smaller, around 10, including mini cars, small cars, medium cars, large cars, executive cars, sports utility vehicles (SUVs) and multi-purpose vehicles (MPVs), roadsters and so on. Some of these categories have blurred in recent years with the emergence of cross-over products that straddle different segments. Examples of this are the high-roof derivatives of standard vehicles such as the Ford Focus C-Max or the Toyota Verso which combine the attributes of a traditional car with those of a multi-purpose vehicle. Also, whereas once luxury cars were, almost by definition, large cars, recent years have seen an explosion of demand for premium smaller cars, with the premium European brands all pushing aggressively into this space.

Increasing segmentation of mature markets means that sales volumes within each segment have fallen – gone are the days when a volume car maker could make sufficient sales off the three basic car types of small, medium and large. A proliferation of segments and hence of models to fill them, means spiralling R&D, manufacturing and support costs, whilst at the same time sales within each segment (from which these costs must be recouped) are lower. This presents a fundamental trade-off between economies of scale (which exert pressure for volumes of the same basic vehicles) and market coverage (which exerts a pressure for coverage of as many segments as possible). In the 1920s Ford's emphasis on standardization and economies of scale caused Ford to lose out to GM's more market-orientated approach. Managing this trade-off effectively continues to be a crucial determinant of competitiveness in the auto industry. A few strong-brand companies can thrive on limited market coverage and low volumes by commanding premium prices in particular niches – Porsche is a good example of this. Companies that do not have the brand advantages of Porsche and are unable to achieve the right combination of economies of scale and market reach are likely to find life hard, as we shall see with Saab.

Resource constraints mean that smaller auto companies have little choice but to restrict themselves to particular niches, and strive to develop strong reputations – and hopefully strong margins to match – within their chosen competitive spaces. Those that do not focus in this way run the risk of spreading their resources too thinly and producing cars that are not fully competitive with the class leaders. All car companies face tough choices in terms of the segments and territories of the market in which they choose to compete – it is simply much more acute for the smaller ones which have to support their infrastructures from lower volumes of sales. For this reason, *scale* is an important feature in understanding survival in the industry. There has been a considerable debate about the minimum viable scale for a car firm, with some arguing that a 1,000,000 units per annum threshold is the entry ticket to the volume car market. We agree that scale matters; however, to pinpoint a common threshold is too simplistic: luxury or niche segments command higher margins and thus require less scale to be profitable, for example. Equally, collaborating with other car firms on joint platforms or engines can also greatly reduce the need for scale.

Serendipity can play a part in market reach as well. As we recounted earlier, the 1974 oil crisis helped the Japanese auto producers establish market share in the United States, simply because when the crisis hit Japanese cars were small and fuel efficient at a time when US cars were not. The US automakers did very well in the late 1990s and early 2000s because of strong demand for SUVs which they were well placed to serve and which their (mainly Japanese) competitors were not. But such strokes of good luck and judgement aside, car companies rise or fall depending on their strategic decisions about market reach. If an auto company makes a major misjudgement about the model for a particular segment, it may be years before the error can be corrected due to the lead times involved in bringing a replacement to market.

The same applies to geographic regions. Once established, geographical auto markets rarely disappear, but they do mature. At some stage in their economic development, nations go through a period known as 'motorization', during which car ownership takes off and increases very rapidly, as it is in China, and to a lesser extent India, at the time of writing. After the period of motorization, growth in car sales slows considerably, eventually to replacement levels. A major challenge for car companies is to seek out and enter new, growing markets as existing ones mature. Early and aggressive movement into fast-growing markets whilst competition is still limited can therefore be an attractive option. However, market entry is a costly and often lengthy process, as the Japanese automakers discovered when they tried to enter the US market in the late 1950s and early 1960s. But with intense competition and overcapacity in mature markets, identifying markets that are growing and building a presence there, ideally ahead of the competition, is important to growth and profitability. The flood of automotive investment into China and India in the 1990s and 2000s is a manifestation of this.

Inward investment into China by auto companies is also an interesting illustration how context, operations and stakeholder issues interact. Historically it has been national and regional governments who are in the weaker bargaining position competing for investment from auto companies who hold most of the negotiating power. However, in China the state had initially insisted that tie-ups between foreign firms and indigenous auto firms a condition of market entry (along with undertakings to transfer technology to the Chinese partner). Desperate for access to potentially the largest auto market in the world, global auto firms went along with this and entered into joint ventures with indigenous Chinese firms, a process that has been dubbed 'obligated embeddedness'.[33] Competition between regions and ministries within China does of course persist and has proved a headache for the Chinese central government seeking to rationalize its auto industry.

AN INTEGRATED MODEL OF FIRM SURVIVAL AND FAILURE

We will now draw the threads of this chapter together and present the integrated model of resilience and failure in the auto industry shown in Figure 4.9. We then use these ideas to introduce the concept of the 'survival envelope' which conceives of the resilience of an auto company as a space whose area is bounded by the four features of stakeholder support, operational effectiveness, market reach and scale. We will then use this concept to guide our analysis of our two cases of failure – Rover and Saab – and our assessment of the prospects for current players in the auto industry.

We argue that these four features interact with the special conditions of the auto industry such as overcapacity (due, as we explained, to non-financial incentives for entry and barriers to exit), cyclicality and market complexity, in terms of both geographical territories and market segmentation.

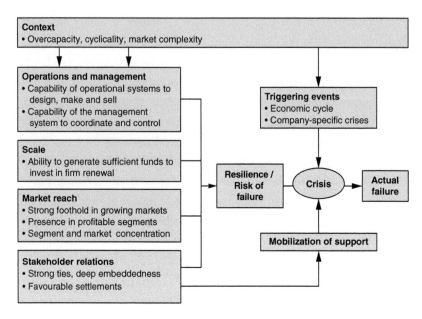

FIGURE 4.9 Integrated conceptual model

We suggest that the quality of organizations' relations with *stakeholders* is particularly important in industries that face a combination of cyclicality, high fixed costs and relatively long product development lead times, simply because the most obvious forms of adjustment to a downturn (reducing capacity, changing the product line-up, moving into new markets) are costly and take time to execute. Supportive stakeholders, however, can provide a reserve of resources that can help a firm through a crisis and hence provide flexibility and resilience. Firms that lack such support may be forced to make painful adjustments in order to weather the storm – if they can – or, in a worst case scenario, fail to make it through at all. Support can take the form of anything from the rapid provision of assistance in the aftermath of a disaster such as an earthquake,[34] a fire[35] or a terrorist act[36] through to being patient financiers, who place the long-term survival of the firm above their own immediate interests. An interesting implication of this is that auto firms that are located within societies that are strongly stakeholder-orientated (such as Japan and Germany) may be slower to adjust to changing conditions, but be less prone to fail than those in more liberal market economies such as the US and UK, where investors may be more likely to abandon ship in search of better returns. We shall discuss the implications of this for global patterns of ownership in the auto industry in our concluding chapter.

The concept of 'settlements' between firms and their various stakeholders – the implicit and explicit agreements about contributions, inducements and appropriate behaviour between organizations – is also significant in our model. An auto firm can have settlements that are more or less favourable to it – for example with respect to labour costs or flexibility; in the prices and services offered by suppliers; on the terms on which finance is provided; on the loyalty of its customers and so on. In aggregate, the favourableness or otherwise of these settlements can have a profound effect on a firm's competitiveness and may be part of a national pattern – for example, in terms of labour and inter-firm relations, norms for pay and benefits and relationships to financial markets. Over time, these settlements may become so deeply embedded in custom and practice that they are treated as insurmountable constraints by those who have to confront them day in and day out. Like a spider's web that traps an insect via contact with multiple threads, an organization's settlements with its stakeholders 'tether' it to a particular competitive position via a collection of settlements that are difficult to break, and that may constrain action on some occasions but provide support on others. We shall see in Chapter 5 that stakeholder constraint was one of several problems facing Rover for much of the 1970s and in the 1980s and that by the time the company was able to break out of its logjam, it had lost a great deal of ground in the market, ground that proved impossible to regain.

For firms in deep crisis, one of the few options for survival is to seek an extension of support from some stakeholders, probably in conjunction with breaking and renegotiating the settlements with others, in order to create slack and buy time for recovery. We see this pattern repeatedly in auto companies that have come back from the brink. In 2009 GM and Chrysler received reluctant bailouts from the US government (stakeholder support, in our terms) whilst radically renegotiating health care benefits with labour (breaking an existing settlement). Ford managed to achieve the same thing without government support but only by selling its luxury brands in Europe and taking on huge debt. When Nissan faced crisis in 1999 it was able to reduce its costs by dismantling its family of suppliers and engaging in much more price-based competition in its sourcing of parts. Doing so broke an existing set of settlements, this time with its suppliers, and required a strong outsider, in the form of Carlos Ghosn, to do it. This succeeded in driving down costs in the short to medium term.

The second category of factors concerns the effectiveness of the *operations* and *management system* of the enterprise. Operations have received the lion's share of attention in analyses of competitiveness in the auto industry and we are not denying the importance of effective operations to the health of an enterprise, for which the lean principles remain the dominant model. The ability to design, make and sell cars to competitive standards is clearly a critical success factor in the industry, as is the ability of an auto company's management system to provide coordination, control and strategic oversight – something which has to date received rather less attention than operations. The limitations of management systems are most likely to be exposed during periods of rapid growth, when the environment is turbulent or when a company faces some form of shock that requires a quick response. In all cases the amount of information that the management system must absorb, process and respond to can easily exceed its capacity to do so, leading to paralysis and/or poor decisions.

Taken together, the stakeholder and the operations perspectives go to the heart of one of the big debates on the auto industry – namely, whether there is a universal model of best practice and competitiveness that applies to all auto companies, everywhere (such as lean production), or whether there are a variety of different national models, each of which can yield competitiveness, but achieve it in a different way. Our model of survival and failure encompasses both of these positions. Of course, car companies must be capable of designing, making and distributing cars to competitive standards in terms of cost and quality and the operational practices necessary to do this are generally applicable, across companies and countries, albeit with some variations with respect to brand values and market segment. But to understand why some firms fail and some survive requires consideration of relationships and settlements with various stakeholders. Operational weaknesses may cause a firm to stumble, but supportive stakeholders mean that it does not have to fall.

The stakeholder and operations perspectives come from very different traditions and readers might think that they are separate – operations focused on efficiency and stakeholders on issues of support, particularly in a crisis. In fact the two come together in a number of ways. Long-term, high-trust relationships with suppliers support intense information exchange and collaboration during product development and facilitate the tight logistics inherent in lean systems. They also constrain rapid adjustment in a crisis. Cooperative, shared destiny relations with employees provide a foundation for flexible working and problem-solving, important for responding to changing demand and for quality improvement, just as antagonistic labour relations may be an impediment.

Market reach is important in understanding resilience in the auto industry for two reasons. Long-term overcapacity in the auto industry means fierce competition and hence low margins, particularly in territories where the market is flat and players are fighting to retain market share. This problem is particularly acute in certain segments, where there may be seven or eight car makers with products that directly compete with each other. A presence in markets and/or segments that are growing or where there are fewer serious contenders (such as some premium segments) is therefore highly advantageous to profitability and hence to resilience. Similarly, a product portfolio that covers a number of segments and territories limits exposure to risk from a slump in demand in a particular market. Thus a car maker such as VW, with a very strong presence in China, suffered much less in the aftermath of the 2007–8 crash than some of its European peers who were much more dependent on the depressed European market.

Finally, we turn to *scale*. Like many mass production industries, the auto industry is clearly an industry for which scale is important, in that, other things being equal, unit costs fall as production volumes increase due to classic economy-of-scale effects not only in production, but also distribution, sales after-market support and so on. However, there are some caveats to a very simplistic bigger-is-better view. Platform and component sharing between different models (as we described in Chapter 2) is a way of achieving economies of scale under the skin, whilst offering apparently varied products to different market segments. Joint development between different car makers can reduce the costs of product development for each partner, thereby reducing the production volumes necessary to recoup development costs. Off-the-shelf, or lightly customized systems, from major suppliers reduce the amount of development work that the car makers need to do. Thus, although greater market segmentation, with lower volumes of sales in each segment, might look like a reversal of the principles of economies of scale, often these now appear elsewhere in the system, at the level of the platform, module or component.

It is also worth noting that although scale is advantageous in driving down costs, some car makers, in some market segments, can command sufficiently high prices to yield good margins at modest volumes – Porsche being a good example of this. However, this is a trick that relatively few car companies can carry off and therefore for most scale remains significant.

The final aspect of Figure 4.9 is that it illustrates that although operational and stakeholder issues may create a vulnerability to failure or a propensity to survive, they do not necessarily determine precisely when the collapse will occur, or whether it is averted by the actions of powerful stakeholders. An imminent collapse usually requires a triggering event that tips an already precarious firm over the edge, which given the cyclicality of the industry is most likely to occur in a general downturn. Here, the cyclicality of the auto industry is significant. Just as it is with coastal erosion, or trees in a storm, it is the weaker entities which are most vulnerable to destruction in a storm, so it is with companies. Successive storms can progressively weaken the entity, until finally, in absence of a rescue from supportive stakeholders, it collapses.

THE 'SURVIVAL ENVELOPE'

The final part of our framework is the concept of 'survival envelope'. This concept integrates the various factors that we identified as significant to understanding resilience and failure. The idea is adapted from the notion of a performance 'envelope' that is found in a variety of settings. It is found in aviation in the notion of the 'flight envelope', a set of parameters which an aircraft must stay within if it is to continue to fly safely. The idea of 'limits' has also been applied to organizations to describe how surprises, often unwelcome ones, can occur when organizations try to operate beyond the limits of their capabilities.[37]

In the aviation example, determining the flight envelope for a particular aircraft is quite complex and involves many factors. However for the purposes of the analogy, it is only necessary to appreciate that for an aircraft to stay in the air, certain key parameters such as airspeed and altitude must remain within certain limits for any given configuration; for example, if airspeed is too low the wings will generate insufficient lift and the aircraft will stall. Equally, flying too fast can overstress the airframe. The limits of the envelope also vary with altitude and temperature. Higher altitude and warmer air temperature mean less lift at a given speed, thereby altering the flight envelope. Thus the envelope is dynamic – its limits and boundaries change according to a range of parameters.

Farjoun and Starbuck extend this argument to organizations, suggesting that all organizations have limits in terms of the range, amount, duration, and quality of things that they can successfully do within the constraints of their current capabilities. Once these are exceeded:

> even talented and intelligent people with plentiful resources and laudable goals can find themselves incompetent to deal with their challenges. Risks escalate, problems emerge, errors occur, errors are more likely to go undetected and uncorrected, solutions lag or lose their effectiveness, and threats become more ominous. Such consequences may be subtle – inefficiency, deviations from expected performance, unethical acts such as fraud, or employee burnout.[38]

Examples of limit violations include organizations taking on projects that they do not understand; operations evolving to levels of complexity that exceed the capabilities of the systems that exist to coordinate and control them; or performance promises being made that are unattainable. All these things can stretch organizations to new and creative solutions that may previously have been thought unattainable. But they can also result in disappointment and failure.

Although the concept of the envelope is most frequently found in treatments of performance, we believe the term is highly applicable to our analysis of resilience and survival. In the same way the boundaries of a performance envelope constrain what can and cannot be done, so, at the extreme, they determine whether an organization can continue to survive. The envelope determines the space within which one can safely navigate as a company. The smaller the area of the envelope, the less room for manoeuvre the company has.

In our model, the boundaries of the survival envelope are defined by four key elements of our conceptual model – prowess at operations and management, stakeholder support, market reach and

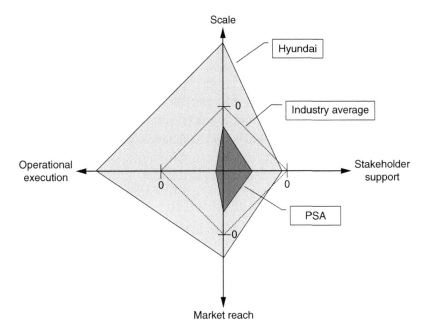

FIGURE 4.10 Survival envelope, with Hyundai and PSA as illustrative examples

scale. In combination, these four factors define the area of the survival envelope – the larger the area, the better the odds of survival and the lower the risk of failure.

In conceiving of the survival envelope as a space maintained by four attributes, as shown in Figure 4.10, we recognize that weaknesses in one area (for example operational execution) can be compensated for in others – for example scale or market reach. This is helpful in understanding the basic stability of the industry, both in terms of why failures are relatively rare and why companies that are admired in terms of their operational execution do not necessarily achieve positions of global dominance. Figure 4.10 shows the 'survival envelopes' of Hyundai and for PSA, which appeared in the highest and lowest positions respectively in our Resilience Index, which we present in Chapter 8.

Although general ideas and concepts are helpful in thinking about failure and survival up to a point, they are more potent when they can be used in conjunction with actual data to compare the survival prospects of different companies. We shall do this in the following chapters where we will use this framework to understand the prospects for resilience and failure of a cross section of auto firms. We look at two failures, Rover and Saab, and two survivors, Nissan and Chrysler.

5   Rover: Inside a failing car company

In this chapter we describe the evolution, decline and ultimate collapse of the Rover Car company, a UK auto firm that collapsed in 2005. Although the collapse occurred in 2005, Rover remains a very interesting example of crisis and resilience in the auto industry. The company, in various guises, had been around for a long time when it collapsed – over 100 years. At its peak it was large (producing around a million vehicles a year and employing approximately 200,000 people) and its decline occurred over a very long period – at least 40 years. Although there are many features of the story that are unique to Rover and the UK auto industry, there also many lessons from Rover's failure for other car companies.

Although the title of this chapter is 'Rover', 'Rover' or, strictly speaking, 'MG Rover' was in fact the brand name that was used on the company's vehicles only in the final years of its life, and before that was one of several brands offered by the company. The company was formed through a succession of acquisitions and mergers between smaller, independent producers, the last and most significant of which occurred in 1968 when the 'British Leyland Motor Corporation' (BLMC) was formed. BLMC was re-named a number of times over the years, with names that included British Leyland, BL, the Rover Group and eventually MG Rover. In the interests of simplicity we shall generally refer to the company as 'Rover', apart from when we are discussing specific events or periods in the company's history when we will use the name that applied at the time.

There have been several very comprehensive accounts of the history of Rover and the UK auto industry more generally. It is not our intention to replicate these here, but interested readers may wish to consult Williams et al. (1987), Church (1994) and Pilkington (1996).[1]

We shall refer to various sources as we recount the Rover story, but we will draw most heavily on around 45 interviews that the authors personally conducted, along with Mike Carver, with key participants in the Rover story, a number of whom were CEOs of the company at various points in its history. We do so because we feel that this gives a unique picture of the internal dynamics within a large, struggling company and of the choices (and in some instances the lack of room for manoeuvre) that those in the midst of crisis perceived themselves to have. We conducted most of these interviews after the collapse of Rover, so in many cases we were asking interviewees to recall events that had taken place many years previously. We are aware that selective memory and post-hoc reconstruction are part and parcel of being human and this is always a risk of this approach, but we were struck by how deeply, and self-critically, many interviewees had thought about events at Rover, and about the part they had played in it. Consequently, we tell much of this story through the words of those who were directly involved.

The structure of this chapter is as follows. First, we present a brief overview of the evolution and decline of Rover. We then trace events in more detail, period by period, from the creation of the conglomerate in 1968 until the present day. Finally, we use the ideas contained in our resilience model, which we introduced in Chapter 4, to understand how Rover stayed afloat for so long, and why it eventually failed.

HISTORICAL OVERVIEW

The early decades of the Rover story in many ways reflect the classic pattern of industry proliferation and consolidation described by Utterback (1994). In the UK, as in many other countries, at the end of the nineteenth and the beginning of the twentieth century many firms entered the nascent auto industry, often having been first established in other light engineering fields, such as bicycle or motorcycle manufacturing. Thus, Rover had not one, but many different starting points. Rover itself was established as a bicycle manufacturer in

1878 and produced its first car in 1904. Other companies that were later to become part of Rover such as Triumph, Austin and Morris were all established between 1885 and 1915. As in other countries, many of the UK's early auto companies failed, merged or were acquired as the auto industry grew and consolidated. In 1920 there were 90 car makers in the UK; by 1929 this had shrunk to 41 and by 1946 to 32. However, set against the USA, the UK auto industry was small and fragmented. In the years just before the Second World War, the USA produced 10 times as many cars as the UK, with just three producers responsible for nearly 90 per cent of total US output (Allen 1970). The issue of industry fragmentation and the attempts to address it will loom large in the Rover story.

After the Second World War, the UK's auto industry was still relatively modest in terms of its aggregate output at around 300–400,000 units, split roughly one third between the domestic market and two thirds for export. The high proportion of exports was partly a consequence of explicit government pressure to prioritize exports, and one side effect of this was to drive UK auto firms towards captive empire markets. The industry remained rather fragmented in its ownership and production organization, although there were further mergers as explicit effort was made to build a British auto industry with sufficient scale and concentration to be internationally competitive. Although there had been consolidation before WWII, this began in earnest with the merger of Austin and Morris in 1952 to create the British Motor Corporation (BMC). However, this merger was largely defensive. Considerable rivalry and animosity existed between the two companies prior to merger and this continued afterwards, impeding efforts to build a single company. This rivalry lingered on for years – indeed, for decades. In spite of this, BMC pioneered a number of influential innovations, such as the Mini, launched in 1959 and designed by Alec Issigonis, who had also designed the 1948 Morris Minor. The Mini was to stay in production for over 40 years, until 2000, by which time over five million Minis had been produced.

Jaguar Cars joined BMC in 1966 and the company became British Motor Holdings (BMH). In parallel, in 1960 Standard-Triumph became part of Leyland Motors as did Rover, in 1967. These two groups, British Motor Holdings and what was by then called the Leyland Motor Corporation, joined together to form the British Leyland Motor Corporation (BMLC) in 1968. Thus, as Figure 5.1 shows, over a

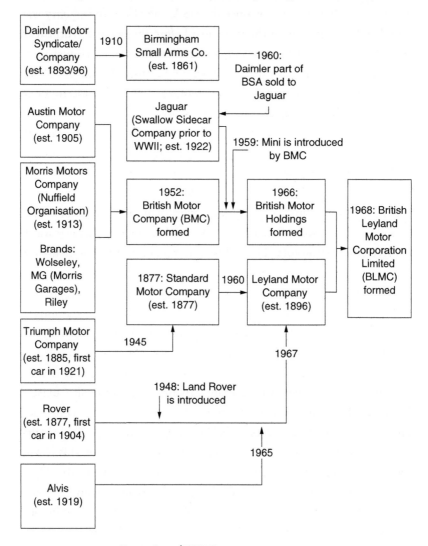

FIGURE 5.1 Formation of BLMC

period of about 60 years, around a dozen car companies came together to form BLMC. By 1968 the company was a very large, diversified conglomerate, which in addition to cars, also produced products such as trucks, armoured vehicles, earth moving and refrigeration equipment and had its own parts and logistics operations.

In the two or three years immediately following the formation of BLMC, the combined company enjoyed production volumes of close to one million vehicles and was one of the largest car companies in the world. However, BLMC executives had inherited a diverse, sprawling collection of activities, a number of which had been financially weak and suffering problems of one sort or another prior to the merger. Consolidating and integrating these into a coherent whole was a major challenge. Consolidation occurred, eventually, but the integration upon which the success of the consolidation depended, took much longer. Aging models, increasing competition from overseas car makers, the loss of production due to industrial disputes, and the oil crisis of the early 1970s, plus a variety of operational difficulties, combined together in a toxic mix. To make things even worse, the first cars developed under the BLMC umbrella, the Morris Marina (1971) and the Austin Allegro (1973), were not well received and fell well short of their projected sales targets. Losses began to mount and the company turned to the Government for support.

With worsening finances, BLMC was nationalized in 1975 and renamed British Leyland. It received a £2 billion government cash injection to modernize its plants and its products (about £18.2 billion in 2015 prices, putting it in the same league as the UK Government's bailout of the Royal Bank of Scotland in 2008). However, matters continued to worsen. Michael Edwardes was brought in as CEO in 1977, renaming the company 'BL Ltd' in 1978. Desperately in need of new models and with limited capacity to develop them on its own, the company searched for a partner, entering into collaboration with Honda in 1979, which at the time was a much smaller, and still relatively young car company. In 1979 Honda granted BL the right to produce one of its models, the Ballade, to be sold as the Triumph

Acclaim. BL subsequently produced other Honda designs for sale as Rovers and also produced some vehicles on Honda's behalf which were badged and sold as Hondas. Subsequently the two companies took cross-shareholdings in each other with Honda taking a 20 per cent stake in BL Cars (Land Rover was excluded), and BL taking a 20 per cent stake in Honda's European manufacturing operation.

In 1979 Margaret Thatcher's strongly pro-market Conservative government came to power. The Conservatives were committed to the primacy of market mechanisms, and to promote this via privatization of state-owned enterprises, rolling back the influence of the state and curtailing the power of organized labour. For a company in BL's position – ailing, state-owned and with conflictual labour relations – this was very significant, because within the prevailing political climate events at BL took on enormous political and symbolic as well as commercial significance. One manifestation of this was Edwardes' campaign to restore what was described at the time as management's 'right to manage' by rolling back the influence of the unions on the company. Another was a string of privatizations of parts of BL, beginning with Alvis (armoured vehicles) in 1981, followed, over the next six years, by units such as Leyland Tractors, Jaguar, Leyland Trucks, Istel (the IT services arm of BL) and Unipart, the parts and logistics operation. All of these played strongly to the Government's privatization agenda. Multiple plant closures and the elimination of various brands also occurred during this period.

The main steps in this process of consolidation and disintegration post 1968 are summarized in Figure 5.2.

Edwardes left the company in 1982 but the process of consolidation continued. From 1981 the mass market cars division of BL traded under the name of the Austin-Rover Group, and three new 'home' developed cars, the Metro, Maestro and Montego, were launched in 1980, 1983 and 1984 respectively. The Honda-designed Rover 200 launched in 1984.

In 1986 Graham Day, who had overseen the privatization of the British Shipbuilders Corporation between 1983 and 1986, was made

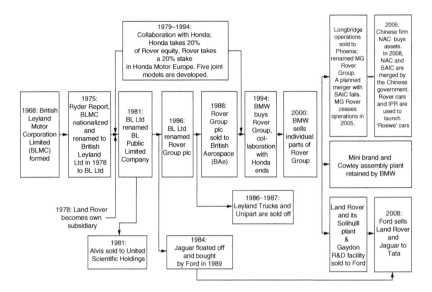

FIGURE 5.2 Divestment after 1975

CEO and the company was renamed 'the Rover Group'. Following a number of divestments, the company had now slimmed down to comprise the Austin Rover Group which produced volume cars, the Land Rover Group, the parts operation, Unipart, and Leyland Trucks. The last of these incorporated Freight Rover, which produced vans. In 1987 Leyland Trucks was sold to DAF and Unipart was spun off via a management buyout.

By this time the output of volume cars had more or less halved since the creation of the conglomerate, dropping most steeply between 1970 and 1980, a fall from a peak of around 900,000 units to around 400,000 in 1980 (Figure 5.3). Output stabilized at this level for nearly 20 years, until it went into a steep decline with the withdrawal of the Metro in 1997. However, whilst output may have stabilized, UK market share did not, and this shows a more or less continuous decline from 1968 to 2005, as Figure 5.4 shows.

The Conservative Government's objective had always been to rid itself of BL as soon as was practical and in 1988 the company, by this time calling itself the Rover Group, was sold to the aerospace and

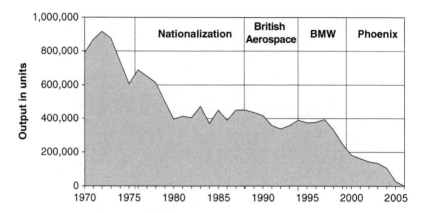

FIGURE 5.3 Car production at BL/Rover, 1970–2005 (excludes Jaguar, Land Rover and New Mini)

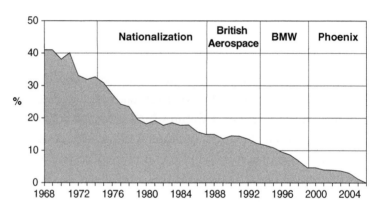

FIGURE 5.4 BLMC/Rover's UK market share, 1968–2005

defence firm British Aerospace (BAe). Honda retained its 20 per cent share. Rover remained under BAe's ownership for six years, continuing to work closely with Honda, and producing cars that were largely designed by Honda, although there was some genuine joint development for the Rover 800/ Honda Legend model.

In 1991–2 BAe ran short of cash and in 1993 put Rover up for sale as part of a move to raise cash and to focus on their core aerospace business; Rover was sold to BMW in early 1994. The sale was controversial, with many observers inside and outside Rover prefer-ring a sale to Honda, which had by then been Rover's loyal partner for nearly 15 years. Despite strenuous attempts to convince Honda to increase its stake from 20 per cent, Honda refused to do this offering only to increase its stake in Rover to just under 50 per cent. This was not sufficient for BAe, and Rover passed to BMW for £800 million in cash, equivalent to £1.7 billion when Rover's debts were taken into account.

As we described in Chapter 2, the 1990s were marked by significant merger and acquisition activity in the auto industry, as volume makers sought to acquire premium brands (such as GM with Saab and Ford with Jaguar, Volvo and later Land Rover) and smaller automakers sought greater scale. The BMW acquisition should be seen in this context. There was concern within BMW that it was too small to survive in an industry where scale and critical mass were seen as increasingly important. At the time of the acquisition BMW was producing around half a million units a year and had no presence in the 4×4 market. Some within BMW felt that chasing greater volumes by moving into segments of smaller vehicles risked dilution of the BMW brand, so buying Rover appeared to offer greater volumes without risk to the core brand, and with the added bonus of Land Rover and its 4×4 products. However, it soon emerged that there were differences of opinion within BMW, particularly between CEO Bernd Pischetsrieder and his number two, Wolfgang Rietzle, concerning the viability of the Rover cars operation and whether cars should be cut back and development effort focused on Land Rover.[2]

With the sale to BMW, Honda declared that it would not provide further support to Rover, other than allowing the designs already in production to be produced under licence. At this time Rover had a number of models. There was the aging Metro, by then 14 years in production, the Maestro and the Montego, the last two of these in their final few months of production. In the late 1980s BAe had refused to invest in a replacement to the Metro, so there was no like-for-like replacement in the pipeline. In the middle of the range there was the Honda-based 200/400 series, due for replacement in 1995 by a smaller version, intended to also serve as a replacement for the Metro by occupying two market segments or categories with one offering. Further upmarket was the 600, based on the Honda Accord, and the 800, jointly developed by Rover and Honda and also selling as the Honda Legend. There was also the profitable Land Rover division.

Notwithstanding the support that many felt for Honda, and concern that the sale represented a betrayal of a long-term partner, the fact that BMW, a well-resourced, successful, upmarket car maker had bought Rover meant that, on paper, the future looked bright. However, things spiralled downwards surprisingly quickly. Aware of the sympathy for Honda, including in British Government circles, BMW sought to avoid actions that could have been seen as heavy-handed and initially adopted a largely hands-off approach. However, by 1995 concerns were mounting – about the quality of Land Rover products, about falling sales of Rover cars, which declined by 12.7 per cent in the first seven months of 1995[3] and about the development of the new Rover 75, which was to replace the Rover 600. Bizarrely, BMW chose to prioritize replacement of the 600, the newest of Rover's existing models, located in a segment which BMW occupied, and unlikely to achieve high volumes of sales. The high volume Metro, which was the model most desperately in need of replacement, was ignored.

From 1996 BMW began to manage Rover much more actively. Wolfgang Rietzle, a critic of Rover's volume cars operation, was made chairman of Rover and John Towers, who had been retained by BMW as CEO of Rover, left the company in April 1996. He was replaced by Walter Hasselkus, a long-term BMW executive. Rover was facing strong headwinds – the pound appreciated significantly against other major currencies in the late 1990s, hurting Rover's competitiveness. BMW was publicly critical of the UK Government (which from 1997 was a Labour government, after 18 years of Conservative rule) for, as it saw it, allowing the pound to appreciate which hurt Rover's competitiveness. This fuelled BMW's determination to pursue a contribution to its planned investments to replace Rover's mid-range models from the British Government, as other car makers had done. BMW was partially, but not completely, successful in getting agreement to this. Amid heavy losses, in the latter part of 1999, BMW began to look for an exit from Rover.

This exit happened in May 2000 when BMW broke up the Rover Group and separately sold Land Rover and the volume Rover cars business. One of the would-be buyers for the cars business was a group of venture capitalists, Alchemy Partners. Alchemy proposed to convert Rover into a low-volume sports car company, focusing on MG-branded cars. This route was initially favoured by the UK Government, but there was widespread resistance to Alchemy from the trade union movement and elsewhere because of the immediate prospect of substantial job losses. An alternative to Alchemy was the Phoenix consortium, headed by former Rover CEO John Towers, who had left the company in 1996. Partly as a consequence of political pressure, Phoenix triumphed and bought Rover for £10. They pledged to maintain employment and claimed to be able to return the company to profit within two years. The company was renamed 'MG Rover' and received a 49-year loan of £470m from BMW and a licence to use the Rover brand.

However, two parts of the Rover Group did not go to Phoenix. BMW sold Land Rover to Ford for £1.8bn, which included the Gaydon R&D facility and the Solihull assembly plant. Thus Phoenix inherited neither the profitable Land Rover operation, nor the R&D facility – essentially it got the Rover 75, then two years in the market, the MG F sports car and the Rover 25/45, a face-lifted version of the already-fading 200/400 series that had been launched in 1995. BMW retained the new Mini, which was under development at the time of the sale and the facilities to build it at Cowley, near Oxford. The new Mini launched in 2001.

Following the sale, Rover 75 tooling and production was moved to the Longbridge facility. The company, renamed MG Rover, still produced the 25, 45 and 75, but was now deprived of two of its key brands (Mini and Land Rover), and to all intents and purposes had no R&D capability. In terms of the core capabilities framework in Figure 4.2, Rover was no longer a complete car company, lacking as it did both basic research and product development capabilities, and therefore the ability, not to mention the resources, to renew itself. In one sense, this was nothing new; Rover had been reliant on Honda for the development of new models in the mid-range volume car business since the early 1980s. But this reality was now very visibly exposed. The intention of the consortium was to find another car maker to provide a platform for Rover to adapt, much as Honda had done previously, but this proved impossible.

From 2000 onwards the decline continued. In the first eight months of 2001, operating losses of £254m were reported. Amidst the acquisition of the Italian sports car maker Qvale (which led to the creation of the SV sports car, of which a total of 25 were sold by April 2005), the company announced an alliance with the Chinese group China Brilliance, to help fund investment in new models. However, this deal was not completed, despite an initial cash injection by the Chinese company.

Desperate for a new small car, in 2003 MG Rover launched the CityRover. This was a vehicle produced by Tata in India and sold there as the Tata Indica. MG Rover essentially made some minor cosmetic changes and rebadged the vehicle, which was not well received by the market. MG Rover reported losses of £77m in 2003 and output fell further, as Figure 5.3 shows. In an effort to raise cash, the Longbridge site was sold for £45 million, and leased back. In November 2004 a plan for a £1bn joint venture with the Shanghai Automotive Industrial Corporation (SAIC) was announced, and the rights for the 25, 75 models and the K-series engines were sold to SAIC for £67m. However the plan for the joint venture stalled.

By March 2005 sales had continued to fall, and fearful of Rover's increasingly fragile financial position some suppliers began to demand cash payment upon delivery of components. In April 2005 an attempt to save the SAIC deal failed, although a bridging loan of £100m by the British Government was offered in order for MG Rover and SAIC to reach a deal. At this point, some suppliers halted deliveries of components. On 15 April 2005, a century of car production at Rover's Longbridge plant came to a halt and approximately 5,000 Longbridge workers faced redundancy.

In July 2005 Rover's remaining assets were sold to Nanjing Automotive, who dismantled the majority of the production equipment and shipped it to China. In 2006 Nanjing leased around a quarter of the Longbridge site from the property company to which MG Rover had sold it in 2003–4.[4] In 2007, MG sports cars began rolling off newly established production lines in China.[5] Some limited production took place at Longbridge from kits imported from China between 2008 and 2011. Nanjing merged with SAIC in 2007, which subsequently moved their European Technical Centre on to the Longbridge site. The Chinese government-supported merger reunited the IP and production assets needed to build the previous Rover models and engines in China.

One thing which did not follow Rover's tooling and remaining intellectual property to China was the right to use the Rover name, which BMW had retained when it sold the company in 2000. This was purchased by Ford in 2006, largely to protect the Land Rover brand, and passed to Tata Motors when Ford sold Land Rover to them in 2008. Consequently, Nanjing-SAIC established the Rover-sounding 'Roewe' brand under which to sell their Rover-based cars complete with a logo strongly resembling the old Rover badge. A number of Roewe models are in production, the most recent, the Roewe 950, based not on old Rover technology but on GM's Epsilon platform – SAIC has a long-running partnership with GM.

Not all was lost for the UK, though, as 'Leyland's children' – Mini, Jaguar and Land Rover – all flourished under new ownership. As Figure 5.5 shows, the combined output of these former subsidies of the Rover car company now account for more production volume than the combined enterprise produced at any time since the late

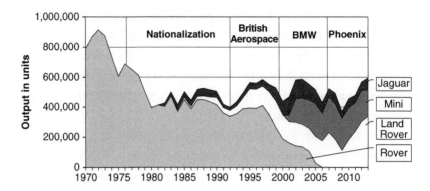

FIGURE 5.5 Production of Rovers, Land Rovers and Minis in the UK,
1970–2013
Source: SMMT, annual reports

1970s. Figure 5.5 shows only UK production of Mini and Jaguar Land
Rover, and excludes overseas production in Austria and Holland, and
Brazil, respectively.

As will be clear from this brief overview of Rover's history, the
Rover story spans a long period – upwards of 40 years – and has many
twists and turns to it. In the rest of this chapter, we shall pick out a
number of themes and lessons, loosely organized around the four
main elements of operations, market reach, scale and stakeholders.
Our aim in this chapter is not to duplicate the comprehensive
accounts of the Rover/Leyland story that are available elsewhere,
but rather to paint a picture of the internal dynamics of the company
as it formed and declined, based on the extensive interviews that we
conducted with senior executives of the company.

1968–1975: THE EARLY YEARS OF THE
CONGLOMERATE

As we have described, the company was formed in 1968 out of a
disparate set of previously independent companies, some of them
themselves formed from previous amalgamations. For the first
15 years of its existence the conglomerate produced much more than
just cars – trucks, buses, construction equipment, commercial
refrigeration equipment and a miscellany of other products were all

included in the portfolio. This wide range of products greatly compli-cated the overall management task and reduced the focus and resources available for the development of the car business.

In the 1960s there was concern that the UK car industry was not growing as fast as American, French and German competitors, which in turn was linked to a declining share of imperial markets, which had been a major destination for UK exports. The rapid growth of the continental European market benefited the French and German producers in particular, and created pressure for developments in products and processes to which UK producers, who were still primar-ily focused on domestic and imperial markets, were less exposed. It may be overstating the case to say that the expansion of the European market in the 1950s and 1960s was analogous to the growth of the Chinese market from the 1990s onwards, but the growth of the European market was certainly advantageous to those companies well placed to exploit it, in much the same way that China's has been more recently.

The cross-trading of cars between European countries was one consequence of this, enabled by the Common Market and falling import tariffs. Tariffs on cars imported to the UK, which had been 30% in the 1950s had declined to 15% by 1970 and disappeared completely during the 1970s following the UK's (late) entry to the common market. Import penetration of cars in the UK climbed from a mere 2.2% in 1955 to 56.7% by 1980 (Owen 1999).

In the 1960s economic planning was in favour with govern-ments on both the left and right of the political spectrum. The Labour Government that took power in 1964 favoured the creation of large companies through mergers as a means of improving the competitiveness of British companies and the creation of BLMC sat squarely in this tradition. In an interview that we conducted in 2007, Tony Benn, who was Minister of Technology at the time of the BLMC formation, explained how he saw his role: 'Deindustrialisa-tion was the political issue ... when I was the Minister, which I was for 11 years in one form or another, my job was to try and stop the deindustrialisation and see that the Government assisted the best it could with the development of our industry.' If the government agenda in the creation of BLMC was 'competitiveness through scale', how did the car makers see this? And why, given the obvious challenges of executing a merger, did they go along with this? Lord Stokes, the first CEO of the merged enterprise, who we interviewed in 2006, described it as follows:

> The fact is that the government can put tremendous pressure on you in every direction they want, and there's no doubt about it – you can't ignore it. They tried, Tony Benn tried very hard, for instance, to get us to take over the Chrysler plant, that was one; we refused that, we were quite sure that was a dead duck. Hillman – we knew it was beyond redemption, in a way, but in the end, the pressure was that BMC was going to go bust, as far as we could see, if we didn't agree to a merger, and there was a lot of pressure put on from every possible direction – from the Government, City sources and everything else, who thought that it was possible to achieve something. We eventually came to an agreement, and reached a price, and we took them over. It was a merger, I suppose is the way you'd put it. It was very difficult, because when we got access to BMC's books – we did have some access to the books, obviously, before we took it over, but you never get true access ... they'd got no programme to develop the future vehicles and the place was in a mess.

Many car companies have grown through a process of relatively strong, large companies acquiring relatively weaker, smaller ones. There have of course also been examples of mergers of relatively equal companies such as Renault and Nissan and Chrysler and Mercedes-Benz, but these are unusual. In the case of BLMC, what effectively occurred was the simultaneous amalgamation of previously independent brands and companies, some themselves only partially integrated from previous mergers. Some had strengths in niche positions (such as Rover, Jaguar, Land Rover and Triumph) but were now combined with the volume business of Austin-Morris which was a much weaker proposition. As George Simpson, CEO of Rover from 1989 to 1994 put it:

> When I joined in '69 I joined a sprawling, fragmented, disparate entity called BLMC, which had just been formed. Looking back, Donald Stokes [the first CEO] had been handed an impossible restructuring task ... It was the mother of all integration projects ... Lord Stokes was faced with a task, in industrial terms, probably as big as anybody had faced in the western world. It was an impossible task ... there wasn't the strength of management, people with the ability to tackle that size of task ... I never saw a very clear strategy, that wasn't communicated to me. Within where I worked there were always targets to work to but we never felt it was a clear strategy. There was no constancy of purpose, things changed very frequently so the priorities were a priority one day and the next it was something else.

When companies grow organically, they gradually develop the capabilities necessary to manage scale and complexity. These are what in Chapter 4 we termed the 'management system', that is, the techniques and processes of financial control, costing, budgeting, marketing and portfolio management necessary to cope with greater scale and complexity. In simple terms, the key principle is that for an organization to operate effectively the capacity and sophistication of its management system – its policy making, coordinating and control mechanisms – must be commensurate with the variety and complexity of operations that have to be coordinated. This need is heightened dramatically at times of crisis and externally induced change, when more active piloting is required and the organization cannot survive by simply reproducing routines and patterns that may have worked in the past.

Yet BLMC was essentially a collection of relatively small owner-managed enterprises (in ethos, if not necessarily legally so), many of which individually lacked these capabilities. Stokes again:

[BMC] was a very typical Midlands tin-bashing outfit, which had grown and grown and grown. We had factories all over the place, making bits of motor cars, and you were transporting bodies from one place to another, engines from another place, transport costs were absolutely fantastic, and also, they never really got integrated. I think one of the troubles was that we lacked any hard core of trained management – including myself, actually. I was brought up to run a factory with under 1000 people, and with no staff at all apart from a few odds and sods. The whole thing was just 'whoosh', like that.

Essentially these issues were now compounded by the fact the newly created BLMC became, more or less overnight, a highly diversified enterprise employing around 200,000 people. Moreover, some of the constituent parts were themselves in a very weak condition, so it was not as if they could be left to their own devices whilst the larger management issues were resolved. With hindsight, many interviewees observed that the pursuit of scale at any cost had made the problems worse, not better. Sir John Egan, who was later to become CEO of Jaguar described it to us as follows:

You had all of these currents running through the BL story of how they didn't know how to design new products, poor industrial relations, a poor rationalisation program, really quite anarchic in terms of managerial process. You had government programs going on like regionalisation and stop-go, which didn't give them much of a chance either, and a relatively ill-educated management team. You add it all up and the chance that possibly they had was frittered away between 1970 and 1974. There was no coherence in anything.

Ironically, the picture of a portfolio of brands targeted at different segments of the market, a model used successfully by companies such as VW today, existed at the outset for BLMC. Stokes:

We were trying to brand it into Jaguar as the top end of the grade, and coming down to Rover as the next slot. Then you've got – we hoped, then – to have BMC middle-range products, and come down to the Minis and so on. We got all this beautifully done on paper. Putting it into practice was difficult.

Goffrey Robinson, Financial Controller of BLMC in 1970, observed:

> What should have happened – at the beginning, if it had happened, it would have been good – we should have had a Specialist Car Division, Jaguar-Rover-Triumph, together with Land Rover, which was added on to Range Rover, together with the sports cars, the Triumph and the Jaguar which were there, and that could have been a great company and, I believe, a profitable company if it had been done properly from the beginning.

Table 5.1 shows the extensive and chaotic product portfolio that BLMC inherited in comparison to those of the major continental European car producers at the time.

Part of the problem for BLMC, in addition to a lack of managers and executives with experience of running an enterprise of this scale, was that there were profound differences in view of what the under-lying model of the new company should be. There were two main camps: those who believed that the company should concentrate on

Table 5.1 *Brands, models and production volumes in 1968. Source: Adapted from Carver et al. (2015).*

	BLMC	VW	Ford	Renault	Citroën	Opel
Brands	11	2	1	1	1	1
Model lines	21	7	5	4	3	3
Volumes per annum	762,000	1,089,000	441,000	707,000	419,000	540,000
Average production volume per model	36,286	155,570	88,200	176,750	139,667	180,000

the stronger, premium brands, and be organized as a relatively loose federation and those who argued that the best way forward was as an integrated whole. The latter position was reinforced by one of the actions taken to redress shortfalls in the management system, namely significant recruitment from Ford, particularly in the areas of finance and product planning. The Ford people were seen as intruders by many of the incumbents and were widely seen as attempting to impose Ford-style practices on an environment to which they were ill-suited. Several interviewees also reported that many of those recruited from Ford with its centralized, process-driven culture struggled to be effective in the much looser, ad-hoc, BLMC environment.

> We got people in from Ford, and all they wanted to do was draw maps or graphs with titles of people on jobs they should be doing, irrespective of whether they were capable of doing them.
>
> *(Lord Stokes, interview, 2006)*

> There were quite a lot of people from Ford came into BL over the years and it was said, quite rightly, that these guys had grown up on the back of processes, they could work within the processes, but when they were put into the British motor industry they were lost, because they hadn't introduced those processes. Therefore, when they were working in chaos they couldn't deal with it. Chaos involved quick-witted sidestepping, in rugby terms. There was never control of the processes.
>
> *(Industrial engineer from that period, interviewed 2005)*

> There was a total lack of clarity about whether the Group should be run as some sort of Ford-like centralised structure, or as a federation of independent companies, and Donald Stokes could never make up his mind which way he wanted to go, with John Barber arguing one line and the ex-Leyland people arguing another line ... It was hopeless, it was an uneasy mixture of Ford who'd grown up with Ford's manuals and all that sort of stuff, and the old-style Leyland people who were entrepreneurs, 50 orders for

buses from Castro one week, and so on. It was a total mess.
I often thought that Alfred Sloan couldn't have done it, it was
just impossible.

(ex-Personnel Director, BLMC, interviewed 2005)

A central staff was established early on but was very small – only
around 20 people at first, for a very large and diverse organization.

Overlaid with the issues of new-found size and complexity were
some of the shortcomings in fundamental processes, particularly in
engineering and new product development – basic capabilities of a car
company, as we saw in Chapter 4. These shortcomings manifested
themselves in different ways in different parts of the company, but
had a number of common threads.

The first was a history of strong *concept* engineering, which
stemmed from a history of exceptional individual designers, such as
Alec Issigonis, who designed very successful models such as the Morris
Minor, the Mini and the Austin-Morris 1100/1300 series, (and also the
much less successful BMC 1800, cruelly nicknamed the 'land crab'
because of its unattractive styling, and Austin Maxi). Spen King, chief
designer of the Range Rover was in a similar tradition. Nick Seale, one
of our interviewees from Product Planning, described it as follows:
'The epitome of that was the heritage you got from Issigonis, because
he was the epitome of saying, "I will do it." Two fingers to anybody
outside the engineer, including the designer and the stylist, and you can
see it.' This sentiment was echoed by John Bacchus, who held a variety
of executive roles in the company and who joined BLMC having
worked in Chrysler and Ford:

> the ultimate on ownership was Alec Issigonis, but of course, in
> some ways that could be a very negative influence, because that
> ownership was, 'It's mine, personally, and I will dictate exactly
> what is done to every bit of it' . . . It was a shambles. It was a fiefdom
> of little barons who ran it totally autocratically, and it was, 'Go
> away, when it's ready, we'll tell you', or 'When it's ready you can
> get on and make it.'

Issigonis resisted evolutionary changes to his original design, even though market analysis indicated that these would increase the vehicles' appeal. However, this was not an isolated example. Stokes had similar perceptions of Bill Lyons, Jaguar's co-founder and Managing Director, before and after incorporation into Leyland:

> [Lyons] kept Jaguar as a sort of private fiefdom under his control, because he designed all the new Jaguar cars, nobody else – no committee designed Bill Lyons' cars, he produced one and so, that's what it is. Most of them were quite good, except he couldn't build them properly, but as a concept they were extremely good cars.
>
> *(Lord Stokes)*

A side effect of such behaviour was an emphasis on what might be termed 'intuitive engineering' and a consequent lack of process and discipline. This had at least three effects. First, with increasing complexity and sophistication, of products, processes and markets, intuitive approaches to engineering were progressively less able to deliver the consistency, thoroughness and follow-through necessary to produce well-engineered vehicles.

Secondly, the presence of a small number of outstanding engineers generated and perpetuated a myth that engineering competence was actually higher than in fact it was – previous strength in what was essentially concept engineering was over-generalized to other aspects of the company's operations. This is quite a subtle process, and hinged on the existence of high-profile examples that run counter to a general trend, therefore allowing participants to believe that criticism of vehicle design and quality was less warranted than it actually was. In Rover's case this perpetuated a belief than things were much better than they actually were in terms of basic standards of engineering and manufacturing. John Bacchus described his surprise on first encountering the engineering standards of BLMC:

> [A colleague] came into our office one morning and said, 'You'll never believe it – they've just run the first 1750 E-Series prototype'. This was the Maxi facelift, it started with a 1500 and went to a

1750, pre-production or something. I said, 'Oh, good – everything all right?' and he said, 'You will never believe it. The crankshaft's fouling the transmission.' I honestly said to him, 'Don't be stupid, Peter, things like that don't happen!' ... That incident was my first sight of the very superficial nature of this engineering excellence that they'd had the reputation for, which was actually based on enormously talented individuals.

Thirdly, 'hero-engineers' felt a strong sense of ownership of their concepts and were resistant to subsequent changes to the products that were the embodiment of these, even if this was clearly what the market was demanding. For example, Issigonis resisted the replacement of his original sliding windows with wind-down windows on the Mini, and King was reluctant to add a four-door model to the Range Rover series (his original design had only two doors) for many years.

A final issue relates to the significance of rapidly strengthening competition – the burgeoning European market, and the associated rise of the German, French and Italian producers; the loss of advantage in the old imperial markets; and falling tariff barriers and increasing penetration of the UK market by imports. Comments from our interviewees suggest that there was remarkably little recognition of these forces across the company:

I think it's probably fair to say that, despite the fact
that they sold all over the place, in terms of international
outlook, for Austin-Morris, export started outside the West
Midlands, and for Rover they started outside the borough of
Solihull, notwithstanding the Land Rover ... There was, I found,
a frightening lack of awareness, and appreciation, and
understanding, of what was happening in the industry outside the
UK ... That was the frightening thing, this insularity – terrible
insularity, particularly on the part of the engineering
organisation.

(John Bacchus)

This insularity seemed to be aggravated by the internal competitive dynamics of the merged corporation as individuals and departments struggled to defend established positions. Time and energy was directed inwards, toward internal organizational-political issues and away from external, market-facing matters:

> The engineer was held as a bit of an idol, not only in the company, but outside as well. It was really critical, so if anybody challenged their territory it was a matter of life and death, almost. A lot of the energy of the company was actually involved in this internal positioning, rather than saying, 'the Japanese are producing some interesting things, Fiat has got some stuff, VW are producing the Golf'. These things were going on outside, but a lot of the energy was about how to hold on to your territory, and create things in your part of the company.
>
> *(Nick Seale, Product Planning)*

Even before the creation of BLMC, Austin-Morris had been generating insufficient funds for model renewal, and the amalgamation created another layer of problems and complexity with which the corporation was ill-equipped to deal. Between 1968 and 1973 BLMC's pre-tax profit margin averaged just 2.9 per cent. In 1974 there was no profit and in 1975 the company dipped into significant loss.

In addition to dealing with shortfalls in basic capabilities and the challenges posed by post-merger scale and complexity BLMC also faced a number of other formidable challenges. The UK as a whole faced turbulent labour relations, and BLMC was afflicted as badly as anybody by these, and worse than many. Industrial disputes cost valuable production due to frequent stoppages. The company faced challenges from its environment – stronger competitors, the removal of tariffs on vehicle imports into the UK and the first oil shock. In combination with the company's weaknesses in design and production quality, these factors led to a catastrophic fall in output, from around 900,000 units a year in 1971 to just 600,000 in 1976. The oil shock hit all car producers of course and output dipped across the industry. However, for most producers output recovered, but for BLMC it did not, apart from a brief uplift in 1976, as can be seen in Figure 5.3. In 1974 the company ran out of money, the banks refused to provide more loans and so BLMC was forced to seek government assistance (Owen 1999).

1975–1987: STATE OWNERSHIP

The choice facing the UK Government was stark. A private sector turnaround would have required swift and radical surgery which in turn would have meant rationalization and redundancies. Not only was this unpalatable to the recently re-elected Labour Government, but in a curious twist of continuity, the Prime Minister and Secretary of State for Industry were none other than Harold Wilson and Tony Benn, the two people who had overseen the creation of BLMC seven years previously. The Government opted instead to underwrite BLMC's debts and set up a committee headed by Don Ryder to investigate the options for the company. The findings appeared in 1975 in the form of the Ryder Report, which essentially recommended that the company continue to compete in all segments of the market and that the state inject £900 million (£8.2 billion in 2015 terms) to support 'product-led recovery'. The Ryder Report was widely seen as wildly optimistic. Not everyone, including some within BLMC itself, agreed that maintaining a presence in the mass car market was wise, arguing that a more specialist set of offerings, at lower volumes but higher margins, was a more feasible route.[6] However these views did not prevail and BLMC was nationalized and renamed 'British Leyland'.

The injection of resources by the state addressed the immediate issue of BLMC's shortage of funds to develop new products, but as we saw in the previous section, this was only part of the problem – the *capability* to develop competitive products was still seriously lacking and the company's sales and market share continued to fall rapidly (see Figures 5.3 and 5.4). It was also the UK's poster child for poor industrial relations.

In 1977, Michael Edwardes was brought in as CEO. He later published an autobiographical account of his time at British Leyland – see Edwardes 1983.[7] Edwardes took reform of industrial relations, specifically as he saw it, 'restoring the right of management to manage' as a major plank in his recovery strategy for the company. Talking to us in 2005, Edwardes described the situation he faced as follows:

> We'd had 32 million man-hours of strikes in '77, before I came in. By the time that had happened to a company that was in deep trouble anyway, that was not cost competitive with the Japanese, by that time I think the die was cast. What one had to do at that point was slim down the company to its competitive position, which meant a lot of people going, and then you'd got to slim down to the point when there wasn't the volume, and so it went on ...
> I think that I was doing a mopping-up job when I came in.

Edwardes is widely credited with subduing the turbulent, combative labour relations at Leyland and in doing so provided a model for many other sectors of UK industry to follow. However, Edwardes freely acknowledged that the emphasis on industrial relations had a toxic side effect – a diversion of attention away from other matters that required urgent attention: 'We got distracted. Where the Germans were spending 80% of their time on product, I was spending 80% of my time on industrial relations, so that was a total waste.' Edwardes reported other challenges as well, again symptomatic of a management system that was still not up to the task of coordinating and controlling an entity the size and complexity of Leyland: 'For 10 years there were no product profit and loss accounts. It took us into '78, I went in in November, we got our first stab at product profitability in the first half of '78. I couldn't believe it. For 10 years they were flying blind.'

Output fell sharply during the Edwardes era, before stabilizing at around 400,000 cars per annum in 1980. Share of the UK market, which has been at around 40 per cent in 1971, had more than halved, to about 18 per cent. However, industrial relations had greatly improved, due to Edwardes' efforts to break the power of the more militant trade unions on the shopfloor. The company had been rationalized considerably. Although cutting costs was one reason for the rationalization, easing the load on the management system caused by the scope and complexity of the conglomerate was also a factor:

> We were making refrigerators, earth-moving equipment, it was madness. Once you put all this lot together, everything was there except one thing – and that was management. If there's one thing you do to bad management is you don't add things for it to do, you take things away.
>
> *(Edwardes)*

There was now an integrated programme of new model development in the form of the Metro, Maestro and Montego developments. There was considerably more coherence than there had been 10 years before. However, the sales of current models were falling, and the larger cars (the Princess, launched in 1975 and the Rover SD1, launched in 1977) were beset with quality problems and failed to meet their sales targets. This followed the flop of the Allegro (the small to mid-sized car that had replaced the 1100/1300 series) and the TR7 (a two-seater sports car). Noting the difficulty of integrating the diverse engineering organizations John Egan, former CEO of Jaguar commented: 'The only cars [BL] had that were any good had been produced by the earlier companies, before they merged … I cannot think of any car that was produced by the merged process that was successful.' Recognizing the product development shortfalls in the company, and the acute need for a model to plug the mid-range gap until the Maestro was due to come on stream in 1983, BL sought a partner that could provide it with a new model. An alliance was struck with Honda of Japan in 1979 initially to provide the Honda Ballade for BL to build, sell and distribute as the Triumph Acclaim. Over a period of years Honda would go on to provide a number of models for BL-Rover.

At the time, BL was actually by far the larger car company, a sign of the stark contrast between Honda's growth and BL's decline in the years that followed the alliance. Honda was to remain a partner to BL-Rover for 15 years, and provided Rover with a number of successful new models throughout the 1980s and early 1990s, until Rover's then owner, BAe, sold Rover to BMW in 1994. The Honda collaboration is an interesting piece of our story for a number of reasons. In addition to providing a much-needed medium-sized model to fill a gap in BL's product pipeline, it provided a golden (and early) opportunity for BL to learn from another very capable car company – more than a decade before *The Machine that Changed the World* was published and well before many Western auto companies had had much exposure to their Japanese counterparts. Although BL clearly did learn a great deal from Honda, this was at times a painful process for both parties, and proceeded in the face of resistance from many at BL. There was, at best, ambivalence on the part of some very senior people at Rover towards the Honda relationship, and a continuing reluctance to accept and act upon Honda's advice:

> I was aware that there wasn't wholehearted support, among quite a lot of senior Rover people, for the relationship. I think that the position broadly was that people didn't like the relationship very much; they didn't necessarily want to work very closely with Honda, but they did see – a lot of them saw – that it was necessary.
> *(Honda interviewee 2006)*

However, on the assembly lines, production line operators quickly noticed the difference. John Bacchus describes how he was accosted by an assembly line worker during a walk through the Cowley assembly plant about a month after BL had started to build the Acclaim: '[The assembly line operator asked] "Why don't we design cars like this?" I said, "Why, what do you mean?" He said, "Because this is designed so that the only way you can build it wrong is to do it deliberately, and ours aren't like that."' Honda executives were very aware of the differences between manufacturing efficiencies and quality standards at Rover compared to their own quality standards. Indeed, quality was a particular area of tension because as the partnership developed Rover built Honda-badged cars on Honda's behalf. As one of our Honda interviewees commented:

> We found that on average each Rover-produced car had well over 100 faults. Many of these faults were very small, but Honda standards were high and our attitude was that in order to maintain our standards, every fault however small, had to be dealt with … Of course we reported to Rover what we had found. Their response was one of disbelief. They said that, in general, their customers were finding few faults in the Rover versions of the cars in question and they could not accept the Honda results. There was a lot of discussion between the two companies and we explained the Honda attitude and tried to demonstrate the faults.

Observations from Honda interviewees about conditions at Rover provide an interesting insight into the reasons behind the different performance levels of the two companies:

> [High quality] will require detailed liaison between those responsible for the design of the model and those responsible for the production facilities in the first place and a thorough awareness of the operating processes on the production line. Changes have to be made all through and to get the right balance requires very close liaison between all departments concerned. In my opinion, the liaison between departments in Rover did not work properly.

The consequence of these different approaches was graphically illustrated by the reception of the Honda Legend and Rover 800 (Sterling) in the USA. This was a joint development between the two firms, and was the model that was supposed to re-launch Rover in the US market. The underlying design of the two derivatives was essentially the same, yet the Honda version was virtually at the top of the JD Power quality index whilst the Rover version was close to the bottom of the same ranking. Analysis of the failures revealed that it was largely the Rover-designed or Rover-modified parts that were the source of these problems. George Simpson, CEO from 1989 to 1994 explained:

> I cannot under-estimate, and under-communicate to you the importance of Honda to the company, particularly the designs. The difference I made was I stopped arguing with Honda. When I became Chief Executive, XXX [a senior figure in the Cars division] had left a legacy of people fighting Honda every inch of the way, as if they were on another side ... and when they suggested something, instead of saying, 'These guys are some of the best car manufacturers in the world, why don't we just accept this component that they've designed,' XXX would send these engineers off and come to the next meeting with a drawing to compete with it.

Notwithstanding these tensions and issues, by building Honda-based products and under Honda's influence in manufacturing, Rover's products and reputation improved considerably and throughout the 1980s output remained reasonably stable at around 400,000 units. Honda won converts amongst senior executives who at first had been reluctant to acknowledge Honda's superiority over Rover in many aspects of car making. One of our Rover interviewees, a senior product planner, recounted what he described as a 'road to Damascus' moment for one sceptical senior Rover executive. The incident occurred late in the development process for the Honda Legend/Rover 800 which was jointly developed by Rover and Honda and concerned the door window sealing system, which is significant for both wind noise and aerodynamic drag. Early on in the development process, and against the advice of Honda, Rover engineers had opted for a state-of-the-art, but unproven, sealing system. As the production date approached, it emerged that there were serious issues with this system. This would have been a disaster for the programme, but the Rover engineers took the problem to Honda, who agreed that Rover could use their sealing system – that is, the system that they had advocated all along. Our interviewee described the review meeting at which this emerged:

Everybody, all his Board, we all sat there around the table waiting for [the sceptical senior Rover executive] to go straight through the ceiling. I thought, here we go, but to my utter amazement he was quiet, controlled, and he said, 'Gentlemen, I'm only going to say one thing: I have sat here over the past four years, as we've gone through this programme, and I've listened to you all saying, 'f***ing Honda this', and 'f***ing Honda that' – and I've joined in. But I've just sat and listened to this tale of woe and all I'm going to say to you is, thank God for the Honda Motor Company'. With that, he got his papers together and walked out and went back into his office.

Under Honda's influence things were improving, albeit slowly and sometimes painfully, in terms of Rover's core capabilities. However, the company was still in state ownership with, since 1979, a strongly pro-market, Conservative government in the driving seat. This was the situation for eight years, from the election in 1979 until Rover's sale to British Aerospace in 1987. Michael Edwardes, appointed in 1977, had been in post for two years when the Conservative government came to power and was one of the first people on the 'front line' between the company and those now representing its state owner. Reflecting on the situation when interviewed in 2006 Edwardes was clear about his options at that time:

EDWARDES: 'Given the constraints on time, because of constraints on the labour market, given the lack of money, I don't think I would have made any major decision differently. All I could do was cut it down, and try to save jobs by selling off. That was all that could be done.'

INTERVIEWER: Save what you could, basically?

EDWARDES: 'That's right, and to do it in a way which was acceptable to the public. I had to do things in a political way ... When Walters [the Prime Minister's Chief Economic Advisor] worked for Mrs Thatcher

> he advised her to close BL. We lunched with him, four
> of us, and he said "We need to give this country a
> massive shock, if we close BL it will give it a massive
> shock and everything will come right." I was against
> that, what I was doing was what everyone understood,
> I was cutting, I was closing the business slowly
> instead of closing it with a great crash.'

Although Walters' advice to use BL as a means to shock the country was not followed, political influence on the affairs of the company was clear to see. For the Conservatives, the temptation was to use BL as a demonstration of free market economics, sending messages of 'survival of the fittest'. During the Labour years, influence took the form of alignment with organized labour and a reluctance to downsize via plant closures and redundancies, necessary as these may have been to the long-term interests of the business. A senior advisor in the company, who had previously also been a senior civil servant explained: 'It was a salvage operation, because every time you tried to shut a factory there was a whole host of MPs who would get up and say, "That's our constituency, we can't possibly agree to that." During the Conservative years the influence was just as strong, but the emphasis was in the opposite direction – BL became symbolic of a re-assertion of managerial prerogatives, of curbing trade union power and of course of the supremacy of market as a means of discipline and resource allocation. Sir John Mayhew-Sanders, a member of the BL Board for several years from the late 1970s onwards, described the situation thus:

> I was aware that the company would not survive as an independent
> company, and could not survive as an independent company,
> from the very first minute I talked to Keith Joseph, and then to
> Michael Edwardes, about becoming a member of the Board, because
> by then it was clear what Government's policy was. Obviously it
> was going to be broken up, because no-one would have bought
> the whole thing, you could see that.

> The other thing that BL, or the Rover Group suffered from, was
> government interference ... The instances were hugely large in
> number, where the intervention of Government in our affairs was
> a hideous and obviously detrimental thing for the company. One of
> the problems was, the people interfering were politicians, they tried
> to be part time leaders of a major, or a significant automotive
> company, and they were laying down the law ... I increasingly
> became disillusioned with what we could do. The strategic
> decisions being taken by, or over-influenced by, Government, made
> any serious industrial discussion and participation in decisions
> really almost pointless...

This situation clearly shaped the nature and form that discussions at
the Board took, as second-guessing what the Government might wish,
and delivering this, became secondary to the traditional function of a
Board of looking after the long-term health of the enterprise:

> The Rover [BL] Board meetings were far more contrived, and
> artificially structured, than most Boards are. In the Boards I've sat
> on, where they need to be, it's not difficult for one Director, or the
> Chairman, or the body of opinion in the Board, to switch, if you
> like, from the formal, contrived and procedural meeting, to a down
> to earth, real discussion about what the right thing to do is. Now,
> the BL Board was never a Board like that.

Without government support in mid 1975, BLMC would have gone
out of business. In practice, this would have meant administration,
and most probably the selling off of those parts for which buyers could
be found and the closure and liquidation of what remained. Yet this
support clearly came at a price, in that the company was, through
virtue of being owned by the state, much more at the mercy of
political currents than might otherwise have been the case. Just as
Edwardes' time and energy had been drawn into dealing with labour
issues, so time and energy went into managing the relationships with
government, who continued, with great reluctance, to provide

financial support to the company until an exit could be found. Yet even this process was not without its twists and turns. In the mid 1980s, Ford was interested in buying an improving BL in its entirety; GM was interested in Land Rover. Ray Horrocks, then Head of the Cars division, opposed the idea of a sale to Ford and was forced to leave the company when the Government sent in Graham Day as Chairman and CEO: Horrocks:

> My problem, essentially, was that there was this initiative to sell the business, lock, stock and barrel, to Ford – this is the Cars business – and I did not believe that was the right way forward, as I've said before. I think there would have been significant hurt as far as the employees were concerned. I understood the position of the major shareholder [the Government], and as I said to a Commons Select Committee, 'If any director goes against the wishes of the major shareholder, he will get what he deserves.' I got what I deserved – very simply.

As it turned out, neither Ford nor GM's interest in BL came to fruition. Sensitivities about foreign takeovers of British engineering firms were running high at this time. The possible acquisition of Westland Helicopters by an American firm caused a row in Cabinet which spilled into the public domain and resulted in the resignations of the Minister for Defence, Michael Heseltine and the Minister for Trade and Industry, Leon Britten. A side effect of this was that selling BL (and particularly Land Rover, a bastion of Britishness) to a non-British buyer became politically risky.

However, as Figure 5.2 shows, selective divestment did occur, most vigorously in the period 1984–1987, and the search for a British buyer for the main Group continued. A senior figure in the company put it as follows:

> We'd been very much focused on looking for someone in the vehicle business, but the solution had to be wider. If you accept the political vetoes, then what was acceptable had to be a major British

conglomerate, to whom the cash flows of BL were OK, who understood long product cycles, and – without saying BAe – had to be BAe, or something that was a major engineering or manufacturing company.

British Aerospace bought the company in 1987. As with many other decisions concerning BL, this one attracted a mix of views. Margaret Thatcher expressed her delight at BAe as a buyer for Rover, later writing in her memoirs 'And best of all [BAe] was British.'

1987–1994: PRIVATIZATION AND BAE

Following the termination of discussions with Ford and GM, Graham Day was brought in to head up Rover. The company was renamed 'The Rover Group' and under his leadership serious attention was given to image and branding. The period was known as the 'Roverization' period and all non-4×4 models were badged as Rover, the MG brand being later revived in the mid 1990s with the MGF sports car. The aim of Roverization was to position Rover as an upmarket, premium brand, clearly differentiated from mass market offerings of competitors such as Ford and GM and some of the continental European manufacturers. It was against this backcloth that British Aerospace appeared as a suitor. BAe was itself recently privatized and its Chairman, Roland Smith, was a firm believer in diversification. Smith believed that there would be great benefits from bringing together two large engineering companies.[8]

However, many members of Rover's Board were not convinced of this. John Mayhew-Sanders, still a Board member at the time, described it as follows:

> I think most of us, certainly I, thought this was an appalling deal to do ... [But] anyway, that was the position. It was the pressure of Government, obviously, for its political purposes – getting rid of the company, and appearing as Rover's saviour and describing it as a 'wonderful deal'. But I think, with hindsight, we can see that it was absolute nonsense, and it resulted in the collapse, basically, of the company ... I think I knew it was doomed after, or during, the BAe

negotiations. You could see the strategic objectives defined by Government were so absurd that they obviously couldn't survive ...

... the motives for the deal were the wrong ones. They were to rid the government of BL; they were to hand the company, in each range of markets, over to a company which had no experience, or even any particular interest in running it, they didn't know how to run a volume and a specialist, car company ... but we agreed to it because of the pressure of Government – because they were the major shareholder.

Despite some rhetoric about synergies between BAe's aerospace operation and Rover's car operations, by all accounts BAe was 'a hands-off' owner. George Simpson, who took over as CEO of the Rover Group in 1989 (Graham Day remaining as Chairman) described the Group's priorities:

We had 5 or 6 key things: premium pricing, go upmarket, get into Europe, major quality push, very active model development program [...] During that 4 or 5 years we did new Range Rover, we did the Freelander, although it was launched after I left, we introduced back the MG into the market place, we did 200, 400, 600 with Honda, so there was an intense period of model development, we treated people as our greatest asset instead of our greatest liability, so Rover learning business was created, we did a new deal with the unions, I never lost a day in the 5 years I was Chief Executive, which was a bit different from 200 strikes a day.

Simpson, who had a seat on the BAe Board, described one of his main tasks during this period as being to seek funds from BAe to support the above activities, in particular new model development. He was often successful in this, but after a while describes encountering resistance from BAe to support Rover's appetite for funds for investment. One manifestation of this was BAe's refusal to support development of a replacement for the Metro, by that time already more than 10 years in production. Although Rover had improved enormously on many measures, Simpson still felt there was a long way to go in terms of brand and positioning:

> We got everybody saying, 'We have to be more like a BMW', and in my 5 years that kind of characterised what we tried to do. The cars got better, the pricing got better, our reputation and the brand got better, but there was still miles to go, there was a huge gap between us and BMW, and more importantly, our volume and premium pricing position was kind of in no-man's-land. It wasn't at BMW's level and we certainly weren't at Ford or at GM's. So I always felt that yes, we could run faster and we could do better, but there had to be another solution for Rover.

However, by 1991 BAe itself was in financial difficulties. Its share price was falling and in September that year it had a rights issue to try to raise extra cash, which failed. There was a Boardroom coup and Smith was ousted. There were large-scale redundancies in BAe, mainly in the regional jets division. Against this background a sell-off of non-core activities began, and this meant Rover was again up for sale. Simpson now had a new task: to quietly find a buyer. In the latter part of 1993, there were two main candidates in play: Honda, Rover's long-time alliance partner, and BMW.

Honda was the first port of call, and for most people in and around Rover, the favoured candidate to buy out BAe. However, there was a problem, which was that Honda did not want its stake in Rover to exceed 50 per cent, whilst BAe sought to maximize the amount of cash that they would receive from the deal and were seeking a clean exit. BMW initially indicated an interest only in Land Rover. Simpson, aware of the underlying economics of the Rover Group, knew he had to hold out for a sale of the whole Group. Simpson describes the preliminary discussions with BMW which began in earnest in August 1993:

> [BMW] said, 'We're very interested in acquiring Land Rover from you.' I said, 'Well, that's very interesting, I'm very interested in acquiring Land Rover from me as well but nobody will allow me to

do that!' The reason we had to do a [package] deal was that although I sometimes made £100m and sometimes lost £100m in my time here, let's say £100m profit was £400m from Land Rover and £300m losses from Cars (don't take these numbers literally because I can't remember them) – was that the Cars business, even after all the work that Edwardes had done, then Graham had done, then I had done, even a whole lot of work, it was still fundamentally a loss-making business. Because of its positioning, because it wasn't a volume player, because it didn't command high enough premiums, it was still a loss-maker so it was a dichotomy. So taking the good bit away was obviously not a really good outcome for anybody.

In October BMW indicated that they would be prepared to take the whole Group, putting Simpson in a very awkward position. As he explained:

The most difficult thing was trying to explain that to Honda. When I went to the [BAe] board, it happened in December, on a Thursday morning, I made a presentation and said, 'This is very hard for me because I've spent 5 years of my life cultivating this relationship [with Honda] and these guys are good for the company and make no mistake, the withdrawal will make big problems for BMW (which it subsequently did) but this is what you get.' And the Board, having listened to what I'd said, said, 'Look, we would prefer to do a deal with Honda, given what you've said, and it will allow you to keep face and keep your integrity. Why don't you jump on a plane and go out and see [Honda] and without giving away confidences, do a deal that matches the deal we've got on our hands?' So I flew off to Tokyo on Thursday afternoon and got there Friday morning. I got a bollocking from the British Ambassador in Japan because the government at this stage were pro-Honda, they were very strong supporters of Honda through the period Michael Heseltine was Trade and Industry Secretary, and he was saying, 'Over my dead body are you going to do this to Honda.'

However, Honda would not budge and so, in January 1994, the Rover Group was sold to BMW. BMW paid £800 million, but there was also £900 million of debt, so the true price was £1.7 billion (approximately £3 billion at 2015 prices). Simpson estimates that BAe cleared around £1.2 billion (at 1994 prices) on the deal.

1994–2000: BMW

For many observers, one of the great mysteries in the Rover story is why things went so wrong during the BMW period. Although sympathies towards Honda were strong and widespread, the fact that BMW, a successful, well-resourced and upmarket car company with a reputation for engineering excellence, had bought Rover boded well for the future. The fact that it went so spectacularly wrong gives a number of insights into why mergers and acquisitions, particularly in car companies, can be so problematic.

What was BMW's thinking in buying Rover? Walter Hasselkus, who was CEO of Rover from 1996 to 1998, who we interviewed in 2008, explained it thus:

> When Bernd Pischetsrieder informed us about the acquisition of Rover we found it a fantastic idea. The general feeling was that it was a really great idea and a great coup ... the Board had wrestled with the question, where do we go, what has to happen? And the opinion was or the consensus was we need higher volumes ... Then obviously the next question came up, how do we achieve it and one idea was to have a 1 Series or 2 Series BMW, but as I understand it and if I remember correctly we almost all agreed at the time that it would not be a good idea to launch and design and sell a model below the 3 Series. The reason being that it was felt and we more or less all agreed that what was called the centre of gravity, so the brand value, the brand image, the centre of gravity, would be lowered by a smaller model which by its nature would have meant fairly high volume. Therefore when that had been decided the question was 'How do we achieve higher volumes?' And then Rover

came up and Rover had good heritage – well, the name was probably a little bit old fashioned but nevertheless – and that's the reason why.

BMW's thinking thus very much reflects the thinking of that period, when smaller companies were concerned about scale, and in BMW's case, how to achieve scale without compromising a very strong, distinctive brand.

Why did things go wrong? The first factor seems to be that BMW appeared to simply overestimate Rover's basic capabilities when they took them over. BMW also seem to have assumed that the Rover–Honda relationship would continue as before following BMW's purchase of Rover, something which Honda was not prepared to do. As a Honda Board member from that period explained to us:

> a lot of people have asked why Honda was willing to work with Rover, but not with BMW. The official position was that we were willing to help a British company with the aim of that company becoming a self-sustaining, independent entity. We had no desire to own the company. BMW was a German company with no need of help. The circumstances were different. In reality, we did not want to work with BMW. It was a big, successful company and we did not see where getting involved would lead.

Honda continued to allow Rover to use Honda designs for a fee (something which they were legally under no obligation to do), but the relationship and the associated support that Honda had previously provided ended at the point of sale.

A second issue, perhaps as a consequence of the speed and secrecy of the acquisition, was that BMW had undertaken remarkably little planning as to how they would handle Rover after the acquisition. Hasslekus again:

> But what we did not do from my point of view is before the decision was taken or at least immediately afterwards, sit down and really think about how are we going to structure the business, what cars do we want to be built, do we want Rover to be run as a more or less

independent entity, obviously within BMW but with authority in Britain, or do we want to maximise synergy effects? At the end of the day my feeling is we wanted a little bit of everything. Bernd Pischetsrieder said and quite rightly so, if we introduce all the BMW systems and methods and quality or whatever it is, Rover will inevitably become quite expensive and we can't afford that. But at the same time the systems should be the same and, as I said, all the synergies should be achieved. And it was not really clear and decided from my point of view how to run Rover within the BMW world.

In the absence of such planning, BMW defaulted to a very 'hands-off' mode in the first couple of years, partly due to concerns about cultural sensitivities. This was noticed by observers in both Rover and in BMW. As a senior Rover product planner described to us:

> [BMW] were extremely professional, to the extent that they'd all had their British cultural training, and they understood that we liked to start all meetings with a joke, so we would get a standard joke at the beginning of every meeting, which was embarrassing to the extreme ... but the real reason is, I don't think they could countenance coming in to a company, and coming in with jackboots. They would be so unpopular, and culturally it would be bad karma, whatever, for them. They couldn't do it, so they let us carry on, trying to influence us, almost like they would only come in if we really failed. It was a disaster. They should have come in, they should have come in and really shaken us up, really been critical, but they didn't. They'd left the management as was, left the plan as was...

From the vantage point of BMW, Walter Hasselkus had rather similar observations: 'BMW, and particularly Bernd Pischetsrieder, didn't want to be seen as coming in like the stormtroopers and waves of German tanks and so on, these kinds of things, like Boris Becker coming onto the tennis court.'

Whatever the reasons behind it, BMW's initial distance from Rover contrasted markedly with the situation during the alliance with Honda. Although Honda was not in a position of ownership and authority, the close working relationships between Honda and Rover meant that there was constant pressure on Rover to improve. With Honda it was a 'drip, drip, drip' pressure. As one Rover interviewee put it to us:

> Maybe the honeymoon period was too long, whatever, it did nothing much, and even worse it actually allowed us to fall back, Without Honda driving you and having this comparison all the time, and Honda engineers there saying, 'Why don't you do this?' – you fell back, and you were allowed to fall back as well. It slipped.

The BMW acquisition injected resources, but the initial hands-off approach removed many of the routines that had been a source of discipline and a spur to improvement. One of Rover's problems in the past had been operations whose scale, variety and complexity were too great for its management system to handle. The operations were now much slimmed down, but BMW did not fully understand them, and in the early days at least, was reluctant to intervene for social and cultural reasons.

Differences within BMW about Rover eventually led to the resignations of both Pischetsrieder, the main supporter of BMW's relationship with Rover and Reitzler, the number two, who was opposed to it. BMW began to look for ways to rid itself of Rover, and entered into negotiations with Alchemy, an equity capital firm specializing in turnarounds. This revealed that Rover's management systems, such a source of weakness for so many years, still posed major problems. As Jon Moulton, Alchemy's CEO described to us:

> By the time we [Alchemy] got to it with BMW, the patient was terribly ill, the volumes were far too low, but still the financial control was as bad as it had ever been. BMW were unable to tell us, during negotiations, anything about the management accounts of Rover. We didn't believe them, we thought they were just hiding it.

The only figures they could give us were the amount of money they were putting in each month, they gave us some numbers on the numbers of cars being sold by Rover; those numbers, unfortunately – as reported to the BMW senior management – were not actually the numbers of cars they were selling, they were the numbers on the spreadsheet out of the five year plan. And that's the honest truth. So the senior management of BMW didn't even know what volume of cars Rover were producing.

Alchemy's bid to buy Rover soon encountered union opposition as it would have meant an immediate and drastic downsizing and consequent loss of jobs. The Government, who had initially supported Alchemy, wavered in the face of pressure and switched its support to the Phoenix consortium headed by John Towers, former CEO of Rover. As described previously, the Phoenix plan was to try to retain the volume cars business, whereas Alchemy would have focused on low volume MG-badged sports cars. Tony Woodley, later the General Secretary of the Unite union, played a prominent part in the pro-Phoenix campaign. Recognizing that it was a long shot, some years later during interview he reflected on his support for Phoenix:

> Somebody said, in 2000, 'Tony, you've got a failed ex-Chief
> Executive of Rover, and two second-hand car salesmen; do you
> think this is going anywhere?' My answer was, 'When you're in the
> middle of the Atlantic Ocean without a lifeboat, and a lifebelt, and a
> lifeboat comes along, you don't ask if there are any holes in it – you
> get in the * * * thing!'

The Alchemy vs Phoenix question demonstrates a tension that is repeatedly visible in the history of Rover. Until the reforms in the late 1970s, the union agenda of protecting employment (in the short term) impeded reforms and factory closures that may otherwise have occurred on the basis of purely commercial criteria. It is arguable whether creating a successful car company was ever particularly high on British Aerospace's agenda, given their focus on short-term financial issues. The sale to Phoenix promised fewer job losses in the short term, but it was never clear how the company could attain viability. Yet there was hostility to Alchemy's more radical proposal to create a significantly smaller, but possibly longer-lived, business.

The Alchemy bid, which would have meant downsizing the company to a small-scale niche sports car maker under the MG brand, would nonetheless have been a much more sustainable option. However, this would have meant immediate redundancies at Longbridge of at least 4,500 workers, most likely even more. Under Phoenix, the 9,060 Longbridge workers of the total 32,070 Rover employees all kept their jobs in the first instance (Rover Task Force Report, 2000). Under Phoenix the Rover workforce at Longbridge reduced to 5,100 by 2005. Hence, Phoenix cushioned redundancies from a projected 9,060 in 2000 to 5,100 in 2005.

Land Rover was sold to Ford for £1.8 billion, while BMW retained the Cowley plant to produce the New Mini, which became part of the BMW Group as an independent brand. Rover, now comprising only the volume cars operation, the weakest part of the business, and without even limited product development capability (because this had gone to Ford along with Land Rover), underwent its third change of ownership in 12 years.

2000–2005: PHOENIX

When Phoenix bought Rover in 2000 it was already obvious to many observers that the company could not survive, unless a joint venture partner could soon be found. Towers was always very clear about this, and remained so, up to and beyond the time that Rover went into administration in April 2005. Interviewed on the BBC a few days after the crash he said:

> I've got to be practical about this: we can't do it alone. We do need a joint venture process ... We've gone through five years, five years when people said it would be impossible – they gave us 14 months, basically – but going through that process, we always knew that we

needed to get more international, we needed that JV, and my
energy, and my focus, is still very, very much associated with trying
to get that process back in place. We need to do that to get the
economies of scale, and the global capability that we didn't have as
a stand-alone business.

In terms of our capabilities framework, Rover was no longer a fully
capable car company, and by 2005 had not been for some time. In
retrospect, one could criticize the Phoenix directors for portraying the
illusion that MG Rover was viable enough to survive, but given their
need to secure a partner, this was perhaps the only line that they could
take. By 2000 the merger wave that the auto industry had seen
throughout the 1990s had subsided, and it became clear that many
mergers such as the one between Daimler and Chrysler had not
yielded the hoped-for benefits.

Overcapacity, then as now, was a key concern in the industry.
As a consequence there was little rationale for any established player
to buy Rover, which by this time offered little other than some aging
models and assembly capacity of average quality in a region with little
prospect for growth in sales. The only hope for Rover was a partner in
a market that showed real growth, in which the MG and Rover brands
might have some value, such as China. Chinese manufacturers, while
plentiful in number, were short on technology. Interest in Rover by
Brilliance in 2002 and SAIC in 2004 was therefore primarily geared
towards getting access to Rover's technology (which was still market-
able in China and other developing regions), and possibly its brands for
use in the Chinese domestic market.

As we write this in 2015, the main traces of Rover's volume car
business are some increasingly elderly vehicles that are still on the
roads around the world. In China, a number of models continue to be
built to Rover designs, sometimes using tooling transported from
Longbridge. And some of 'Leyland's children' – Jaguar and Land Rover
(now owned by Tata Motors) and Mini (retained by BMW) – continue
to exist and produce cars in respectable volumes: in total, around

600,000 units in 2014. Ironically, the vision that some people had for BLMC in the mid 1960s, of a handful of specialist brands, operating at the premium end of the market, has come to pass – but by a very circuitous route that few could ever have imagined.

ANALYSIS

The Rover story is a fascinating illustration of how processes of crisis and resilience impact on auto firms. In this section we draw out a number of the themes from the story and discuss these in relation to the resilience and survival framework that we introduced in the preceding chapter. We argue that Rover's failure is an example of the 'Swiss cheese' mode of failure,[9] an alignment of many conditions, over a period, that those responsible for managing Rover were unable to overcome and, in some instances, actively contributed to. We shall also see that the four key factors of markets, scale, operations and management and stakeholder relations can interact in complex and self-fulfilling ways.

Market reach and scale

Although we have focused on the period from 1968 onwards, it is clear that the seeds of many of the issues that we have described were sown long before then.

Relative to auto industries in other countries (the USA being the most extreme example) the UK's auto industry was relatively slow to consolidate. The nature of the UK car market during the early decades of the industry, being small and varied relative to the US market, was reflected in the nature and structure of the car producers, with really only Austin and Morris as British-owned volume producers. Following the Second World War, Government-led pressure on British manufacturers to export had the side effect of pushing auto companies to pursue the low hanging fruit of soft, imperial markets. This in turn had further knock-on effects. It meant that UK producers were inadequately prepared to capitalize on the rapid growth in the continental European market. Their competitors in Germany and France and to some extent Italy had little choice but to sell to their neighbours at an early stage in the market's development and hence acquired the awareness and capability to produce vehicles targeted at the continental European market. For UK producers the gravity of this developing situation was partially obscured by tariff barriers on imports which existed until the 1970s. By the time the tariff barriers fell away, the continental producers were some distance ahead, and an already weak BLMC was exposed to the full force of their competition.

The UK's late entry into the Common Market meant that the UK's domestic market was shielded from continental European competition at the same time reducing the attractiveness of the European market to UK producers. Rather than responding by engineering their products so that they had a wider appeal, the early response to this was the establishment of overseas factories to locally assemble kits, in order to get round the tariff barriers. At one point BLMC had factories in Belgium, Spain and Italy as well as in Australia. In the terms of our survival model, in the post-war years UK auto firms were facing issues that would, within a decade or two give them problems with both market reach and with scale. The industry was relatively fragmented and rivalrous; it was poorly positioned to take advantage of the European market, which was set for a period of rapid growth; and the severity of these issues was obscured by a combination of tariff barriers to imports and a concentration on imperial markets, in which the UK's relative advantage was about to decline rapidly as the British Empire faded into history.

Of these various issues, the one that seemed to most captivate policy-makers was the issue of scale, and it was this that primarily motivated the UK Government to promote the creation of BLMC through the merger of BMH and Leyland, with a view to creating a national champion able to compete globally with the US giants such as Ford and GM. As we have seen, the reality did not work out like that. Again, there were a number of reasons for this, but what is clear is that scale was only one piece of the picture – the position of BLMC in relation to potential markets and competitors were very significant factors also. So, it turned out, were shortfalls in operational capabilities and management systems, which were aggravated, not improved by the merger.

Operations and management systems

Our interviewees vividly portrayed some of the operational and managerial shortcomings of the merged enterprise. Many of these centred on shortfalls in the core capabilities of a car company that we identified in Chapter 4, particularly the processes of designing, developing and manufacturing the vehicles themselves. Here it is apparent that a number of factors were at work, and that the picture is not as straightforward as 'the cars simply weren't good enough'. A theme that ran through several accounts was that many of Rover's cars were based on strong and in some cases very innovative product concepts. Examples of this abound – the original Mini, and its larger sibling the 1100/1300 series, both of which were conceived in the days of BMC, were breakthroughs in their day, as was the original Range Rover, which pre-dated the huge growth in the luxury SUV sector by more than two decades. However, these strengths in conception were not matched by capabilities in execution and had a couple of additional downsides. One of these was that they encouraged a cult of the hero-engineer who felt a large degree of ownership over 'his' vehicle (the lead engineers were all male in that period) and who could be very resistant to changes and suggestions that challenged the original design and conception. This meant that a rather personal, intuitive approach to engineering pervaded the company, at a time when increasing product and process complexity mean that more specialist knowledge, more process and more discipline were becoming mandatory. Designing for ease of manufacturing was a particular casualty of this situation and something which those working on the assembly lines noticed as the Honda designed cars began to arrive ('Why don't we design cars like this?' as a Cowley assembly line worker remarked).

A second consequence was more insidious. Because the company had produced innovative models in the past, this fostered complacency and a belief that its current capabilities were higher than they actually were, impeding change. This came through strongly during the period of the Honda collaboration, when resistance to accepting advice and guidance from Honda remained significant for many years into the alliance. Honda's analysis of the fundamental problem is telling: 'the liaison between departments in Rover did not work properly'.

Turning to the management system, that is, the apparatus for setting strategy, coordinating and controlling the operating units and managing finances, external relations and so on, it is clear that there were significant shortcomings before the merger, particularly with respect to the volume cars business of Austin-Morris (BMC). The fact that analyses by Ford revealed that the Mini made little or no profit, despite strong demand, is a sign of failure to 'join up' the various strands of design, production, marketing and product costing. Yet if the management systems of some of the constituent parts of BLMC were weak before the merger, they were completely overwhelmed by what followed. For perhaps 10 years or more, it was never clear that the company had a management system with the sophistication and capacity to handle the task that it faced. Part of the problem was an overnight step change in complexity, but this was only part of the problem. Many of the constituent parts of the new conglomerate were themselves financially weak, had aging models and over-stretched engineering and other functions facing a world that they were ill equipped to deal with. On top of this was a major task in terms of integration and rationalization in an environment characterized by rivalrous, independent units, defending their patches of turf. It was, as George Simpson put it, 'the mother of all integration jobs'.

That a large, complex and difficult-to-manage organization was created without an adequate management system was one part of the problem. However, in the case of Rover, several other factors hit at the same time, putting additional load on the already over-pressed centre. The company was running out of cash at the time of the merger, and was not generating sufficient funds to resource its own product development; the UK's entry into the Common Market exposed the firm to the full force of foreign competition at a time when it was weak; Michael Edwardes reports how he was preoccupied with labour relations issues to the neglect of engineering reform; and so on.

A management system must have the capacity and capability to process the inputs that it receives from its own operating units as well as other sources; overload, selective attention and key tasks that are not properly executed are the inevitable consequences of a mismatch in capacity and load.[10] The 'management system' is really a shorthand term for a whole series of capabilities – in financial control, portfolio management, marketing and so on – that Rover lacked. The end would certainly have come much sooner had it not been for the partnership with Honda, who essentially plugged Rover's gaps in design, product development and to some extent manufacturing expertise. Some within Rover recognized the importance of Honda early on; others took longer to do so. In the 15 years of partnership with Honda, Rover learned a great deal, but it is sobering to see that BMW's takeover revealed that this had not been enough to restore Rover to a fully capable car company.

Stakeholders

We argued in Chapter 4 that car companies are embedded enterprises, and as such are clearly much more than just commercial enterprises. Rover graphically illustrates this issue. The company had, at various times in its life, to reconcile the wishes of multiple stakeholders with very different agendas, something which has been identified as a threat to a system's viability.[11] From a commercial perspective, in the mid 1970s reform was delayed because of the politically unpalatable consequences of job losses. In the late 1970s the company became emblematic of a struggle by a right-of-centre government's drive to curb union power and promote a pro-market agenda. In the 1980s, Rover became an instrument to take a privatization agenda forward, leading to some decisions that were not necessarily optimal from a commercial point of view. Even in 2000, shorter-term considerations of employment protection may have outweighed longer-term commercial ones. So the Rover case both illustrates the support stakeholders can provide – for example the bailout and subsequent financial support – but also the sometimes profoundly constraining forces of stakeholders as well.

We shall return to these issues in Chapter 8.

6   The failure of Saab Automobile

As this book goes to press in 2015, Saab Automobile is not producing cars and has not done so in significant volume for four years. The company declared bankruptcy in December 2011. Its main assets were acquired by a Chinese consortium, National Electric Vehicles Sweden (NEVS) in June 2012 and for a few months in the latter part of 2013 and early 2014 a small number of vehicles were actually produced, before NEVS filed for bankruptcy in August 2014. In late 2014, Indian Auto Group Mahindra & Mahindra was rumoured to be considering buying the remnants of the company.

In this chapter we trace the history of Saab Automobile from its establishment in the 1940s to the present day. We analyse the underlying reasons for Saab's failure, and set these in the context of the contemporary global automotive industry and in terms of the conceptual framework that we introduced in Chapter 4.

Saab (Svenska Aeroplan Aktie Bolag) was started in 1937 to produce military aircraft. Its formation was a government initiative, a response to the increasing likelihood of war in Europe. The company was started with private capital and built a new factory to the north of Trollhättan, which built Saab cars until 2014.

The company initially built a version of the German Junkers Ju-86 medium bomber under licence, adding a light fighter-bomber (the American Northrop B5) soon afterwards. Production of various other aircraft followed. However, as the Second World War drew to a close, it was clear that demand for military production would fall and that other activities would be needed to keep the Saab workforce employed. A number of alternative avenues were explored, including spinning reels and prefabricated sheet steel warehouses. Two were selected for further development – civil aviation and car manufacture.[1]

173

EARLY CAR PRODUCTION

The German auto producer DKW provided an example for Saab to follow, building relatively inexpensive cars powered by two-stroke engines. Ironically perhaps, DKW was later assimilated into what became Audi, one of Saab's strongest competitors. After the war, Saab began work on a front-wheel drive vehicle, powered by a two-stroke engine. Saab applied its expertise in aerodynamics from its aircraft operations to the vehicle, the Saab 92, and in 1949 produced a car with an astonishingly low drag coefficient for the time of 0.30.

The Saab 92 went through successive evolutionary changes throughout the 1950s, becoming the Saab 93 at the end of 1955. This evolved into the Saab 95 estate car (in 1959) and the Saab 96 saloon (in 1960). Both remained in production for nearly 20 years with over half a million 96s produced in total. In the early 1960s Saabs driven by Eric Carlsson enjoyed rally success, winning the British RAC rally three times in a row and victories in two Monte Carlo rallies. This rally success was to have a positive effect on the Saab brand for many years.

Alongside auto production, Saab's aviation activities continued to expand. The company produced both military and civil aircraft and also moved into combat aircraft systems, avionics and missiles. For a period, Saab even designed and produced mainframe computers. Production facilities expanded, and aircraft production moved from Trollhättan to Linkoping in 1960. A new car plant opened at Trollhättan in 1960 with a capacity of 30–40,000 units a year and this remained Saab's main production base until its recent demise. By the mid 1960s Saab as a whole employed 11,500 people across eight plants in Sweden. Saab also established a joint venture with Finnish automotive company Valmet in the late 1960s and production of Saab vehicles took place at the plant in Uusikaupunki until 2003. Saab, by that stage 50 per cent owned by GM, withdrew from the joint venture in 1992.

The two-stroke engine, up until then one of Saab's hallmarks, was dropped in 1967, to be replaced with a V4 four-stroke engine designed and produced by Ford. Henrik Gustavsson, Saab's Technical Director, defended the decision to source an engine externally: 'As an extremely small automaker in international terms, Saab cannot afford to make mistakes. Therefore it is vital that our product development work be properly directed, and that every modification, every improvement should be fully justified – and preferably of an innovative nature.'[2] The brand values that were to define Saab cars for the next three to four decades were already recognizable. US *Car and Driver* magazine, commenting on the new Saab 99 model that was unveiled in 1967, remarked: 'Saab does not make cars – it makes Saabs – models offering a highly distinctive and particularly logical solution to at least one of man's transport problems.' The Saab 99 originally utilized a 1700cc Triumph engine – another example of Saab's limited resources necessitating the external sourcing of a key technology. British-made engines were used in the 99 for about five years, but eventually reliability issues caused Saab to bring engine production in-house. The launch of the 99 signalled a clear move upmarket for Saab. Like the 96, the 99 was to have had a long production life, of around 20 years.

In 1968 Saab announced its intention to merge with Scania-Vabis, a Swedish producer of trucks and diesel engines. The merger took place in 1969. In addition to production facilities in Sweden itself, Scania operated plants in Brazil and the Netherlands. By the 1970s, the company was a fully fledged technology conglomerate with a product division structure, comprising four main divisions: Aerospace, Scania Trucks, Cars and Nordarmatur (which produced valves and pipes).

Like many companies, Saab's car division was hit by the recession that followed the oil shock of the early 1970s and car production fell. As we described in Chapter 2, most nations have been through extensive rationalization and consolidation of their motor industries and policy-makers and auto industry executives in many countries were concerned that their car companies lacked the scale to be globally competitive. The auto industry in Sweden, represented by Saab and Volvo, faced similar pressures to achieve greater scale. In 1977, the Boards of Volvo and Saab-Scania proposed merger of the two companies, in large part because new model development was becoming prohibitively expensive for small auto producers, which was of course one of the reasons for the very long model lives of Saab and Volvo products. However, these merger proposals came to nothing. The reasons for this included differences between the two companies in design philosophy and Saab's fears that its identity would be lost given Volvo's greater size. Both companies were also concerned that the other would cannibalize their existing share of the trucks market.[3]

SAAB CARS IN THE 1970S AND 1980S

Following the unsuccessful talks with Volvo, Saab's car division took a different route to controlling development costs, based on joint development with other car makers. Saab entered into an agreement with Italy's Lancia (a rather unlikely bedfellow, in brand terms) which resulted in the co-development of the 'Type Four' platform on which the Saab 9000, the 1985–96 Fiat Croma, the 1987–98 Alfa Romeo 164 and the 1984–94 Lancia Thema were all based. The Saab 9000, launched in 1984, symbolized Saab's serious arrival into the European luxury segment. Incredibly, this was only Saab's third all-new model launch in nearly 40 years of car manufacturing.

In 1978 Saab saw a major innovation with the introduction of a turbo-charged version of the Saab 99, one of the first mainstream turbo-charged production cars in the world. Turbo-charging became one of Saab's signature attributes during the 1980s and reinforced the Saab brand as innovative and technologically advanced whilst adding 'power' and 'performance' to the mix. This complemented the marque's earlier rallying success. Also in 1978, the Saab 900, a major evolution of the 99 was launched, although the 99 continued in production up until 1984, by which time nearly 600,000 had been produced.

In Germany, Audi, which had been part of the VW Group from the mid 1960s, was pursuing a somewhat similar brand strategy.

In the 1980s Audi successfully repositioned itself from being a worthy but dull brand, the kind of car that bank managers drive, to a car that young, aspiring and relatively wealthy buyers might want, using technological innovation as the means. Audi's advertising slogan 'Vorsprung durch Technik' – 'progress through technology' – epitomized this.[4] Audi used innovations such as sleek aerodynamics and four-wheel drive to promote an image of technological sophistication. Aerodynamics were represented in a TV commercial showing an Audi 100 towing a series of parachutes along salt flats, with a voice-over proclaiming it as the most aerodynamic production car in the world. Four-wheel drive was conveyed in a commercial in which a woman chased her man (who was flying a glider) up twisty mountain roads in an Audi Quattro to tell him his mother was calling him on his car phone. In the space of a few years the average age of an Audi driver in the UK fell from 52 to 38 years.[5] The success of Audi's strategy was to spell trouble for Saab in the future.

In some markets, such as the UK, Saab's advertising during the 1980s emphasized the aeronautical credentials of the parent company. A series of commercials showed images of Saab cars interspersed with those of Saab fighter jets, culminating in punchlines such as 'Saab – Nothing on earth comes close' and 'Only one aircraft manufacturer makes cars … sierra, alpha, alpha bravo … SAAB'.

Whatever the contradictions between the link to military aircraft and other attributes such as safety and durability, in the mid 1980s Saab sales grew and exceeded 100,000 units a year for six straight years. In 1985, *Fortune* Magazine published a piece analysing the appeal of the Saab brand:

> The Swedish carmaker has more than doubled U.S. sales in six years, to 33,000 last year, by going after what might be called the Big Chill factor: ex-hippies who, now affluent, retain a bothersome social conscience and are somewhat reluctant consumers. The Saab of the Sixties was the automotive equivalent of the Earth Shoe – an oddly shaped, rock-solid car that puttered along on a three-cylinder,

two-cycle engine. It's a far plusher and racier car now, but the company wants to keep the same sensible image. So Saab's promotional literature apologizes for the luxury features of the 900 series: 'The only reason for making a car this comfortable is that it makes you a better driver.' And ads for the new 16-valve intercooled Saab Turbo editorialize, 'In any other car, this much power would be irresponsible.'[6]

In 1987 Saab's production reached an all-time high of 134,000 units. Although substantial for Saab, this was tiny in comparison to US giants such as Ford and General Motors or Europe's Volkswagen-Audi Group which by then measured their output in multiple millions of units. Following this peak, Saab's sales declined steeply and as the 1980s drew to an end the Cars Division of Saab was losing money.[7] Of Saab's two models, the 900 had been in the market for more than 10 years and the 9000 for 5, so new models were needed. The problem was how to finance new model development whilst ensuring a satisfactory return on investment given Saab's modest volumes.

The influential Swedish Wallenberg family, through their investment company Investor AB, had been major shareholders in Saab for many years. Marcus Wallenberg had been on the Board of Saab from 1939 to 1980, and Chairman of the Board from 1968 until 1980, when he retired. Investor AB held, and continues to hold, equity in many major Swedish companies. This concentration of ownership in Swedish enterprises – Investor's holdings accounted for about a third of the Swedish economy in the late 1980s – posed considerable risks, particularly as Sweden seemed on the verge of joining the European Community, which would have meant the elimination of protectionist policies that had shielded Swedish companies from global competition and foreign takeover.[8]

Concerned by the threat of hostile foreign takeover of Saab-Scania, Investor increased its stake in the company and took full control. Given the financial difficulties of the Saab Cars Division, the Wallenburgs sought a partner for the cars business and moved to enter a partnership with Fiat. Discussions also took place with Japan's Mazda, but did not proceed.[9]

As we saw in Chapter 2, in the late 1980s the auto industry was entering a period of intense merger and acquisition activity. Smaller auto companies were struggling with product development costs. Because these firms had lower production volumes they were not able to spread their development costs over so many units, painting them into a corner of painful trade-offs between higher prices per car (which the market might not bear), lower margins and less frequent model replacements.

At the same time, larger auto companies were seeking to add premium brands to their portfolios, either by developing these themselves (as Toyota, Honda and Nissan did with their Lexus, Acura and Infiniti brands) or by acquisition. Consequently there was considerable activity in buying and selling smaller auto firms (and some larger ones as well) for a period of about 20 years. This particularly affected the European premium and semi-premium brands. Alfa Romeo was acquired by Fiat in 1986; Chrysler bought Lamborghini in 1987, selling it on to a Malaysian investment group in 1994, who in turn sold it on to the VW Group in 1998. Lotus was bought by GM in 1986, sold to a Luxembourg-based holding company in 1993 and then sold on to Proton in 1996. In 1994 Aston Martin was bought by Ford, who held it until 2007. As we saw in Chapter 5, Rover was bought by BMW in 1994 which held it until 2000. Ford acquired Jaguar in 1990, Land Rover in 2000 and Volvo in 2000. Ford sold Jaguar and Land Rover to Tata of India in 2008 and Volvo to Geely of China in 2010.

Merger and acquisition (M&A) activity in the auto industry was not confined to the acquisition of specialist brands by the larger auto firms. In 1998 Daimler and Chrysler merged, an arrangement which came to an end in 2007 when Chrysler was sold to private equity firm Cerberus Capital Management. Chrysler was later taken over by Fiat. In 1999 Renault and Nissan embarked on their strategic alliance, in which the two separate brands were retained but in the context of considerable integration below the surface.

The significance of this M&A activity is that it makes it clear that Saab's story of a small auto producer which by the late 1980s found the going tough is not of itself particularly unusual. What is unusual is how the story ended, around 20 years later, with Saab Automobile more or less ceasing to exist. It is to this part of the Saab story that we now turn.

ENTER GENERAL MOTORS

In 1989 GM had been negotiating to buy a half share of Jaguar, but lost the deal to Ford, who bought the whole company outright for $2.6 billion.[10] GM then moved in on Saab, ousting Fiat who were also suitors, and paid $600 million for 50 per cent ownership of Saab, with an option on the other 50 per cent. Under the terms of the agreement GM had management responsibility for the joint venture, which was established as Saab Automobile AB. At the time GM said that its intention was for Saab's facilities to eventually make products both for GM and Saab, although the phase-in of GM products was predicted to be gradual. GM also stated that there would be some sharing of components and engineering and the joint venture would have access to GM's worldwide technology and supplier networks.[11] In 1990, Saab Automobile recorded a loss of US$848 million in 1990, a loss of US$9,200 on each car sold.[12]

GM's strategy for Saab had a number of strands, covering both products and production. GM's target sales for Saab were stated as 250,000 units per year – approximately double anything that Saab had achieved in the past. (At the time Ford had similar aspirations for its recently acquired Jaguar.) GM also made changes to the production process in order to improve efficiencies. In 1990, Saab took around 100 labour hours to produce a car, but this had been cut by nearly 50 per cent by 1992.[13]

An immediate priority was to develop a replacement for the Saab 900, which had already been in production for 12 years when

GM arrived on the scene. The new 900 was launched in 1994 and was based on GM's midsize GM2900 platform. This platform had gone into production in 1988 and was the basis for the Opel Vectra, the Vauxhall Cavalier/Vectra and a variety of other GM models. However, a conflict between realizing economies of scale through platform sharing and Saab's distinctive brand identity soon became apparent – a conflict that remained an issue throughout GM's stewardship of Saab.

Even in the mid-market for which it was designed, the cars based on the GM2900 were not especially well received. In the case of the Vectra, for example, successive surveys of owners by *Which?* Magazine (a UK consumer magazine) revealed it to be one of the least-liked vehicles in its class and found it to be 'dogged with reliability problems'.[14] The Saab 900 model which shared this platform was also not well received by the market when it was launched in 1994. 'It handled clumsily, suffered alarming quality lapses and was later reported to have done poorly in Swedish crash testing'.[15] These are problems for any vehicle, but especially for one in the European premium segment, let alone for a brand such as Saab which competed with brands such as Audi and BMW.

Such issues notwithstanding, the launch of the new 900 provided a sales boost. In 1993, Saab's total sales, globally, were down to around 71,000 units, comprising around 35,000 sales of the 'classic' 900, by then 15 years old. The company sold around the same number of 9000s, then nine years in production and with only the benefit of a minor facelift in 1991. The new 900 sold around 60,000 units in its first year and over 100,000 in 1997. Saab was even able to post a small profit in 1994, its first since the GM acquisition. However, the aging 9000 required replacement and Saab was not generating much cash to support this.

In 1996 GM and Investor agreed to invest US$524 million into Saab to support a five-year recovery plan, which involved replacement of the 9000 and 900 with two new models. It was also clear that sales volumes, which had stubbornly refused to rise much above 100,000 units per annum, would need to increase, which implied that the company needed a more mainstream image in order to broaden its customer base. Saabs had a reputation for being 'quirky', and were particularly liked by those in the creative professions, academics and the like. GM seemed to recognize and respect this. Richard Wagoner Jr, then GM's president said of Saab: 'The brand attracts a very different consumer than we normally see in General Motors showrooms. We want to keep that brand very distinctive and very unique.'

The 9000 replacement, the 9-5, was introduced in 1997 and used the same GM2900 platform as the 1994 900. Economics may have dictated the need to share technology with other GM products, but like the 1994 Saab 900 before it, this did not necessarily help the reputation of the 9-5. The perception amongst purists was that the new models were not 'real' Saabs and lacked the strength and body stiffness of earlier generation Saabs – important attributes of the Saab brand. 'Saabness' was increasingly seen as cosmetic, conveyed by minor details such as the location of the ignition key by the gear stick, the dashboard display and other identity items. The 2003 Saab 9-3 took this further, being designed mainly by GM's European subsidiary Opel and, like the 9-5, continuing the move away from Saab's distinctive and practical large hatchback configuration that had characterized its products since the late 1970s.

Notwithstanding the grumbles of Saab purists, sales continued to increase and were sustained at 120–130,000 units from the late 1990s until 2008, when they declined sharply. Unfortunately, increased volume did not bring profitability. In 2000 Investor AB exited completely, selling its 50 per cent stake to GM for $125 million – a quarter of what GM had paid for its initial 50 per cent, 10 years previously.

In 2003 Saab's engineering department was merged with GM's European operations at Russelsheim in Germany. This meant the loss of 1,300 engineers and designers at Saab and effectively signalled the end of Saab's ability to develop its own products (contrary to claims that would be made later by Spyker, who bought Saab from GM in

2010). Sales and marketing for Saab in Europe were also integrated into GM's operation in 2004.[16]

As Saab's integration with GM proceeded, there were signs of tension between Saab and its parent. As the *Economist* was later to observe:

> GM once saw Saab as a potential rival to BMW. But whereas BMWs became the default choice of striving young professionals in the 1990s, buying a Saab was a statement of eccentric individualism – something utterly alien to GM's corporate culture. GM constantly tried to force its often stodgily conventional engineering on Saab in an effort to save money, while Saab, just as stubbornly, attempted to preserve what was different about its cars, such as putting the ignition on the floor by the gearbox. Not surprisingly, the results pleased neither GM's bean counters nor Saab enthusiasts.[17]

BMW was not the only problem for Saab. Other German premium car brands, such as Audi, advanced steadily during the 1990s, capturing a large slice of the growing European premium segment that better-executed Saab vehicles might otherwise have occupied. Volvo, with a somewhat similar brand and market position to Saab, extended its model range and introduced high-performance models such as the turbo-charged T5 that played more on 'heart values', extending its traditional safe-and-solid, family-car image. By the 2000s, Volvo's sales were in excess of 400,000 units per year, still small by global standards, but quadruple those of Saab. Due in part to the successful manoeuvres of its competitors, Saab ended up in the uncomfortable position in terms of both operations and marketing, of making around 120,000 not-quite-premium cars a year.[18]

The European premium makers were moving into the segments in which traditionally they had not had a presence. Audi, BMW, Mercedes and Volvo were all expanding their ranges – between 1997 and 2002, for example, Mercedes, BMW and Volvo all introduced four-wheel drive sport-utility vehicles. Saab meanwhile had only two models, both of them in the large car segment, both front wheel drive. Lacking a smaller vehicle and an SUV in the Saab range, GM succumbed to 'badge engineering', that is, the application of one marque's brand to another company's products. This took the form of the Saab 9-2X and the Saab 9-7X, both of which were sold only in the USA. The 9-2X was a re-badged and lightly modified Subaru Impreza, produced in Japan. The 9-7X was a Chevrolet Trailblazer built in Ohio and sporting a very un-Saab-like eight cylinder engine. The 9-2X was quickly and disparagingly dubbed a 'Saabaru'.[19]

THE GLOBAL FINANCIAL CRISIS

GM enjoyed a boom period in the early 2000s, driven largely by buoyant demand for profitable SUVs and light trucks (pick-ups) in the US market. This demand benefited the US producers in particular because their main competitors, notably the Japanese makers, were not particularly well placed to meet this. However, the boom concealed a number of long-term, difficult issues facing the US producers, such as high health care and pension obligations, ailing brands and unreformed working practices, not to mention the continued loss of market share to the Japanese producers in many segments, apart from SUVs. At this point GM was producing no fewer than eight brands – Chevrolet, Pontiac, Buick, Cadillac, GMC, Saturn, Hummer and Saab. Concerned about the longer-term situation, some of GM's major shareholders started applying pressure for reform, summarized in a 14-page memo in 2005 which argued that:

> General Motors was in a heap of trouble ... but it also had enough cash to mount a turnaround effort. The key would be management's willingness to act urgently by eliminating dozens of near-duplicate models, dumping unneeded brands, making realistic sales assumptions and negotiating a better union contract.[20]

The memo concluded that GM was likely to run out of cash in 2008 unless action was taken and it recommended the disposal of Saab and Hummer. However, no action was taken and it took the global financial crisis of 2008 to provide the trigger for these (and other) actions at GM.

As the 2007 global financial crisis took hold, many governments provided support for banks to prevent a collapse of the global financial system. Car sales around the world fell dramatically, exposing the underlying weaknesses of many companies, including GM. In the first quarter of 2008 GM lost $3.25 billion. In 2008 Ford, who had acquired Jaguar at about the same time as GM had acquired Saab and had later bought Land Rover, sold both of them to Tata Motors of India in order to raise cash. In 2009, Ford sold Volvo to Geely of China.

In the second quarter of 2008, GM's losses were even worse than in the first quarter, at $15.5 billion. In June, GM announced a range of measures to cut costs, including four plant closures in the USA. In late 2008, the US government agreed to a $17.4 billion package of support for Chrysler and GM, subject to them submitting viability plans in February 2009. In December 2008 GM put Saab on 'strategic review'.

In Saab, the financial crisis began to bite. In 2008, sales fell nearly 30 per cent on 2007, dropping from 125,000 units to 90,000. Jan-Åke Jonsson, the CEO of Saab Cars from 2005 to 2011, who we interviewed in 2012, described it thus:

> In 2008 you can say there were two impacts that had a major
> influence on Saab, one was of course that in the middle of a year,
> and I would say relatively immediately, volume started to drop.
> And it wasn't only in the US, it was the same in Europe and also the
> Asia-Pacific market started to slow down. But for us we were very,
> very small in markets like China, non-existent in India, Brazil or
> any other developing countries. So that meant that what happened
> in Europe and North America immediately impacted us from a
> volume side.
>
> And it's unusual that you have both North America and Europe
> happening at the same time, but that was basically what happened
> at this time. And it came relatively sudden I would say, there were
> no real huge signs that demand was suddenly dropping. GM started,

it was about 25% lower than 2007, so we were predicting about 100,000 from our point of view for 2008. That then came down another 10% during the course of the year; I think we did just over 90,000 in 2008. When we then looked at 2009 we predicted a carry over volume, that the market would basically be carried over from 2008, but I would say nobody knew at that time because it came very fast and it went down very, very quickly and in particular markets like the US, which was extremely important for us, you know it came from a high of 17.5 million new cars down to around 10 ... And as we were not so strong in Asia we had nothing where we could recover this volume.

Thus, Saab's dependency on the USA and Western European markets and their absence of a truly global sales footprint proved very damaging.

In February 2009 GM submitted the viability plan required by the US Government as a condition for a rescue. The plan proposed the loss of 46,000 jobs (20,000 of which were in the USA), the closure of five factories in addition to those previously announced, the elimination of the Saab, Hummer and Saturn brands and closure of a number of dealerships in the USA. The company stated that in the US market it would focus on the Chevrolet, Cadillac, Buick and GMC brands. Saab was put up for sale immediately, with a deadline for it to be sold by the end of the year or closed.[21] Saab CEO Jonsson had his own views on the reasons for the sale:

it wasn't because we were a drain on them, but it was more political gain, that they were looking to get money from the US Government and in order to do so they had to demonstrate that they gave priority to the US market and US employment and if they could show that we were unloading or shutting down activities outside the US that is of course strategically okay. And you could say the same was the discussion with Opel where they were to sell Opel, which was also nice music for the US Government at that time.

GM announced the winding up of Hummer in February 2010.

However, Saab was only the tip of the iceberg. GM's plan identified the need to make $1.2 billion in savings in its European operations. In addition to Saab, GM announced its intention to sell its Opel plants at Bochum in Germany, and Antwerp in Belgium and Vauxhall at Ellesmere Port in the UK. The Chairman of GM's European Employees Forum said:

> The current plan could include, for the Opel/Vauxhall brand and the GM/Opel/Vauxhall subsidiaries, mass dismissals and probably several plant closures. This would have disastrous consequences for the GM brands and companies in Europe ... The spin-off of Opel/ Vauxhall and the spin-off of Saab is the only reasonable and feasible option for General Motors which would not destroy the European operations and its European assets. There is no future with GM. We can only see any prospects with a divestment.[22]

In the case of Opel-Vauxhall, discussions took place over several months with various governments and potential buyers, and GM received a firm bid from Canada's Magna International. However, in November 2009 GM withdrew from negotiations and announced that it intended to retain Opel-Vauxhall.

GM itself entered Chapter 11 (a status which permits reorganization under the bankruptcy laws of the United States) in the USA for four weeks in June and July 2009.

GM's decision to dispose of Saab led to a frenzy of activity. The company quickly applied to the Swedish courts for, and was granted, protection from creditors, to give it time to restructure and seek a buyer. However, the business plan submitted to the court as part of this process was seen as overly optimistic. Saab responded by substantially revising sales projections downwards. Saab's business plan called for the company to sell 65,000 to 70,000 cars in 2009, down from 94,000 in 2008, but from then on sales volumes were forecast to rise to 150,000 units in three to four years.[23]

It was estimated that approximately 15,000 jobs in Sweden in Saab and its suppliers were dependent on the survival of the company, along with those in around 1,000 dealers worldwide.[24] Any potential new owner for Saab would face the challenge of Saab's debts which in May 2009 were estimated at US$ 1.2bn to GM, US$ 42.1 million to the Swedish government and US$ 80 million to other creditors.[25]

By mid April 2009, 27 parties had indicated an interest in buying the firm and by May it was reported that 10 parties were 'seriously' interested. By mid May this was down to three, and Saab applied for, and was granted, another three months protection from creditors.

In June 2009, Koenigsegg, a tiny Swedish manufacturer of sports cars, was confirmed as a bidder for Saab, backed by a consortium of Norwegian investors with unspecified support from a Chinese backer, variously reported to be the First Auto Works and Beijing Automotive Industry Holdings (BAIC). A loan from the European Investment Bank, backed by the Swedish government, formed part of the deal.

In November 2009 Koenigsegg withdrew from the deal and Saab was left without a buyer and facing imminent closure.

SPYKER

At this point, Dutch sports car maker Spyker appeared on the scene. Spyker CEO Victor Muller, a 50-year-old Dutch businessman, started the process with a simple email to GM director Bob Lutz. Muller later recounted: 'Eight minutes later, I got a reply and next thing we know we're on a rollercoaster ride that will take 93 days, working 20-hours a day.'[26] The two companies were a world apart. Saab was capable of making in excess of 100,000 vehicles a year. Spyker had produced just 43 in the previous year. Muller comments:

> I had no idea. Not a clue what it would entail. I only knew Saab was for sale, and GM was threatening to shut it down. I didn't know how much money it would cost, or what the business model was like – I was an outsider. But I thought it was obscene that this brand might go down.[27]

As the saga moved into December, GM announced their intention to wind down Saab – somewhat ironically, as a new 9-5 model was now virtually ready for launch. However, last-ditch efforts to broker a deal with Spyker continued. BAIC were still on the scene, but only as a buyer of tooling of the old 9-3 and outgoing 9-5 model. In January 2010 the CEO and entire Board of Saab were replaced with two 'wind-down' supervisors, labelled as 'executioners' in one news report.[28]

The rollercoaster continued throughout January 2010. Specula-tion alternated with a sense of resignation about the future of the company. Then, on 26 January, it was announced that the sale of Saab to Spyker had been agreed. Under the agreement Spyker agreed to buy Saab from GM for US$74 million in cash and US$326 million in preferred shares. The new company was to be called Saab Spyker Automobiles. Saab's supporters were jubilant. IHS Global Insight analyst Tim Urquhart commented:

> [Saab] is a really brilliant brand. It's probably one of the biggest brand mismanagement stories in the history of the automotive industry. Saab could have been the 'Swedish Audi' if it had been taken on in the right way 20 years ago. It's been completely mismanaged, underinvested in by people who don't understand what the brand means, and what it has the potential to mean.

In a comment that captured the contradictory pressures between, on the one hand, huge loyalty and enthusiasm for the brand amongst the Saab faithful and on the other, a tough competitive environment, Edmunds.com analyst Michelle Krebs observed:

> While many around the globe, especially in Sweden, will be thrilled to see the quirky but much-loved Saab brand saved, the new owners have their work cut out for them. It will not be an easy road to keep the tiny company going and growing in the intensely competitive world market.[29]

Saab had been thrown a lifeline, but the underlying issues that had led to its difficulties remained. However, a brand new model, the new 9-5, was ready for launch – could this be the model to revive the com-pany's fortunes?

What was Spyker starting with in January 2010? There were two models on the books – the Saab 9-3, which was already seven years old, but scheduled for replacement in 2012. There was the outgoing Saab 9-5, a 12-year-old model that was at the end of its production life, but about to be replaced later that year by the all-new 9-5, based on GM's Epsilon platform. The Epsilon platform had entered production in 2003 and supported a wide range of models sold under the Buick, Cadillac, Chevrolet and Opel brands, amongst others. Also in the pipeline was a sport utility vehicle, to be badged as the Saab 9-4X, which shared a platform with the GM's Cadillac SR-X. This model was to be produced at a GM facility in Mexico.

Spyker declared its intention to position Saab as an 'independent performance-oriented niche car company with an industry-leading environmental strategy ... Saab's brand DNA is unique and rooted in its aeronautical heritage, innovative and independent thinking and its Swedish origins.'[30]

The theme of restoring Saab's brand and DNA recurred repeatedly: at the final signing of the deal in February 2010, Victor Muller declared:

> We need to give our customers the clear message, that Saabs will be Saabs again. The company has lost its DNA over the past years and that has caused its customers to turn its back on it ... We are not looking for new customers, we're just looking for getting our own customers back.[31]

Saab's new owner planned to restore Saab's production and sales volumes to pre-crisis levels of 100,000–125,000 vehicles per year, including the 9-4X to be produced by GM in Mexico. Given that many of Saab's functions were integrated with those of GM, there was a significant amount of unpicking to do, particularly with respect to sales and marketing. The Spyker plan also involved establishing new sales and distribution channels in markets where Saab had not historically been strong.

Spyker claimed that Trollhättan had the full capability to develop complete vehicles and would continue to do so, but this seems improbable, given the design and engineering downsizing reported to have taken place in 2003[32] and the substantial contribution of GM to Saab's new models. Indeed, it was the very scale of GM's engineering contribution that was seen as the reason for Saab's loss of distinctiveness, and this was one of the areas where Saab and GM were most integrated. Jonsson commented:

> Whereas Saab was not integrated into GM everywhere in some of the major areas it definitely was. And I would say one of the key items that impacts any car company is product development, you know the whole engineering side was integrated fully into General Motors.
>
> On the sales and marketing side you can say that it was a split situation where in some countries we utilised the GM national sales organisation, like call it GM Italy. GM Italy sold Saab, Chevrolet, Cadillac, Opels, GM Spain the same. But you know in some other markets like Belgium, Holland, we had our own importers and that was more you could say a traditional historical aspect that we had importer agreements with these countries since a long time.
>
> On the dealer side there were actually few dealers that were common between other GM brands and Saab. Typically we had one third that were only selling Saabs, we had one third that were selling Saab and other GM products and we had one third that sold Saabs together with anybody else, VW or Subaru or whoever it was. So that was the setup.

The January 2010 business plan envisaged a maximum need for cash of US$1 billion before Saab returned to profitability, which was forecast to be in 2012. This amount was to be made up from various sources, including:

- GM, through $326m redeemable preference shares
- Favourable terms for parts and services from GM to Saab, plus deferred payments
- A €400 million (US$544 million) loan from the European Investment Bank, backed by the Swedish Government, mainly for R&D projects at Saab.[33]

On paper, it looked as if Saab had a chance, albeit a long shot. There was a brand new model ready for launch. There was finance from a number of sources to cover the estimated US$1 billion required before sales and production volumes built up to breakeven levels. There were high levels of goodwill towards the brand.

However, the obstacles to be overcome were daunting. The Trollhättan plant, which had ceased production as part of the GM wind-down, had to be restarted; the now tarnished Saab brand had to support a huge upswing in production and sales from 2008 and 2009 levels; customer confidence in the company had to be restored; and activities that were integrated with GM had to be unpicked and re-established on a free-standing basis.

More or less everything would hinge on how the new 9-5 was received. Although the model would be launched by a newly independent Saab, it had been designed and conceived under GM's stewardship, the very thing which many commentators blamed for the alleged erosion of Saab products' distinct identity. Saab as a company might be independent of GM, but its products would bear GM's legacy for many years.

In March 2010 the company declared a sales goal of 50–60,000 units in 2010 (of which 20,000 were expected to be new 9-5s[34]), 70–80,000 in 2011 and 100,000 in 2012. Historically, Saab's sales had been heavily concentrated in just three markets – its home market of Sweden and the USA and UK, which accounted for 60 per cent of its sales. Finding and penetrating new markets was clearly essential.[35]

At the March 2010 Geneva Motor Show, Muller shared ideas for Saab's future product portfolio with an enthusiasm that clearly infected some of the motoring journalists present. One of these ideas was for a smaller retro-style vehicle based on the old Saab 96, hoping to reproduce the success that BMW had enjoyed with the Mini One and Fiat with the new 500. Muller enthused: 'Where can you find an iconic design like [the 96] which hasn't been put back into production in a modern way? I think we can easily sell 30-50,000 a year'. Muller argued that the BMW Mini provided a glimpse of what was possible with Saab: 'They sell twice as many as they thought they would. They sold 230,000 last year – how well does the Mini contribute to the bottom line of BMW?'

On 22 March 2010 the production lines at the Trollhättan Plant started rolling again after several weeks' cessation. The first car off the line was the new 9-5 model. In May the company proceeded to purchase Saab's three sales companies in the UK, US and Sweden from GM.[36]

In June 2010, Muller reported that Saab had used US$165 million of its US$544 million loan from the EIB. He emphasized the importance of strategic alliances with other car makers for new product development, and was upbeat about the prospects for this. With all car companies under pressure, technology sharing, he argued, was an effective method of bringing breakeven points down.[37] In July 2010, the company made a final cash payment of US$24 million to General Motors, thereby completing the sale.

June also saw the launch of the new Saab 9-5. The success of this model was going to be absolutely crucial to the turnaround of the company as it was this that would generate the cash to propel the company forward. The car received a positive, but somewhat luke-warm reception from the motoring press:

> As good as the German rivals? The Saab is certainly a lot more interesting and, to my eyes, rather better looking. I also like the idea of supporting the underdog at this vital time. (Don't worry, the dealer chain is fully intact.) Given a choice of an A6, a 5-series, an E-class or a Saab 9-5, I'd take the Saab and enjoy the difference.[38]

> Is the new 9-5 going to rip up the rulebook? Hardly. Saab has a mountain to climb to persuade buyers to take it seriously again. They should. This is the best resolved big Saab ever, but many customers will be wary after the bankruptcy and may well be perfectly happy with their A6s, 5-series and E-classes.[39]

The 9-5 has plenty of notable qualities. All it really lacks is a distinctive style. It wears the insignia of Saab well enough to suggest that it could establish itself alongside the BMWs and Audis. But what it hasn't quite shaken off is the insignia of Vauxhall.[40]

In August 2010, the company appointed a new importer for Japan, PCI, who took over the task of marketing, sales and distribution in Japan from GM Japan.[41] Saab also pushed into South America, seeking new importers for Mexico, Brazil and Argentina.[42]

However, the earlier sales estimate of 50-60,000 units in the first year was soon scaled back to 45,000 units – an ominous sign. Combined sales in Saab's three major markets were running at under 3,000 units a month, suggesting that even this revised estimate was overly optimistic.[43] September brought news of an agreement with BMW to supply engines. Details were scarce, but the arrangement pertained to a 1.6 turbo charged petrol engine, with supply to start from 2012.[44]

More warning signs appeared in late October 2010, with a second downgrading of production forecasts, this time to 30–35,000 units, which sent the value of Spyker's shares tumbling. This forecast was more in line with actual monthly sales, but only about half the forecast of six months before. It was beginning to look as if the Saab 9-5, the car on which the company's future depended, was not achieving the necessary sales volumes. Saab cited issues due to recovery from the plant shutdown earlier in the year and delays with suppliers as reasons for this: 'You will not sell product that's not on the showroom floor. It's been a tremendous fight to fill the pipeline. This is now finally starting to happen.'[45] In early January 2011, the confirmed sales and production figures for 2010 were released. In 2010 Saab had produced just 32,048 cars. This was little more than half of what had been forecast at the start of the year, although it was an improvement on 2009 when just over 20,000 units had been produced. Victor Muller explained the figures thus:

One of the largest challenges in 2010 was to restock our dealers around the world to normal levels again, especially in a market like the United States, where you need dealer stock in order to be able to sell cars. For instance, when we acquired the company in February 2010, there were a mere 500 cars left on the ground in the United States. Normal inventory levels in this market should be at 6,000–7,000 units.

In 2009, Saab Automobile sold 39,800 cars, but built only 21,000. As a result, inventory levels were depleted by almost 19,000 units. In 2010, we only filled the pipeline with less than 4,000 units. All in all, with all the accomplishments made so far, I am very confident that the foundations for delivering on our business plan are in place.[46]

This explanation sat uncomfortably with an announcement that came less than a week later, namely that Saab was reducing output from 39 cars per hour to 28 per hour as part of a normal 'winter slowdown'. The union representative for IF Metall, Håkan Skött, pointed out on Swedish local radio that 28 cars an hour was insufficient for Saab to meet its 2011 output target of 80,000 cars.[47]

In February 2011 the first 9-4X came off the assembly line in Mexico, for the planned launch in the USA in May 2011. Sales of the 9-4X in Europe and the rest of the world were to follow in August 2011. But by late February there were more signs that things were going awry, with an announcement that Spyker was to sell its original sports car business to Russian investor Vladimir Antonov for US$12 million in order to raise cash to support Saab's operation.[48]

At the end of March, Saab's President and CEO Jan-Åke Jonsson, unexpectedly[49] announced his retirement. Jonsson had been with Saab for 40 years, and had been at its head for nearly six years. Victor Muller took on both roles, ostensibly until a successor could be found. New distribution deals for Saab in Russia and China were also announced.

On 29 March Saab was forced to stop production due to a dispute with a supplier, International Automotive Components (IAC), over payments for parts supplied.[50] Production restarted, but stopped twice more in the following week. The Swedish National Debt Office also sought assurances from Muller regarding its guarantees for the EIB loan. Rather bizarrely, given the company's situation, Muller commented:

> I have compared Saab often to a beautiful lion who grew up in captivity ... One day that lion is loaded on to a truck and released in the vast savannahs of Africa. That mighty animal has to learn how to hunt for its own prey and support himself. Being used to receiving his meals in a stainless bowl, that lion has some serious challenges adapting to his new-found freedom.[51]

In early April Muller was making reassuring noises about Saab's finances, a position that elicited the headline 'Rent Skitsnack' ('Bullshit') from *Dagens Industri*, a major Swedish newspaper. By mid April an increasing number of suppliers had stopped deliveries to Saab. On 7 April production stopped, with no date given for a re-start.

Saab was now facing chronic liquidity problems and embarked on an increasingly desperate set of measures to raise cash. Vladimir Antonov, the purchaser of the Spyker sports car business (who in 2009 had been refused permission to invest in Saab amidst unsubstantiated rumours of involvement in money laundering and organized crime[52]) re-iterated his desire to take up to a 30 per cent stake in the company. Saab also entered into discussions to sell its Trollhättan properties, which since have been partly sold and leased back.

The situation was becoming increasingly critical and was showing signs of spiralling out of control. Anders Borg, the Swedish Finance Minister, went on Swedish TV stating that more clarity was needed about Saab's control structures. Lars Holmqvist, the CEO of the European Association of Automotive Suppliers commented:

> With a very unclear ownership structure and no financial muscle, it seems [Saab] are into a very negative spiral. The reason they are stopping is they have not paid their bills and will not get components. They are not selling cars and are making very big losses ...

If it is right what is being reported, it means Antonov would go in immediately with SEK270m (US$43.2m) – that is not [enough] even to cover the debt owing to the suppliers ... It would not even help starting. It could release some components, but that is of course not [the] major problem.[53]

The 'unclear control structure' with which Saab now found itself was causing problems. The EIB, the Swedish state (as guarantor of the loan) and GM all had a stake in any outcome, and their approval was necessary for the sale of facilities and fresh investment by Antonov. Late April brought approval of Antonov as an investor from the Swedish National Debt Office, but the position of the other stakeholders on this was not clear.

On 3 May there was another twist – Saab announced it had signed a US$223 million deal with China's Hawtai to produce and sell Saab cars in China. This too would require approval from Saab's multiple stakeholders and by the end of the first week of May fingers were being pointed at the EIB for holding up approval of Antonov and Hawtai as investors. Days later the goalposts moved again when it emerged, on 12 May, that Hawtai had apparently failed to get the necessary regulatory approvals in China.

Muller was out in China, seeking another partner and within four days came an announcement – a memorandum of understanding (MoU) had been signed with Pang Da Automobile Trade company, China's largest public auto distributor, with 1,100 dealerships worldwide. Under the agreement Pang Da was to make a €30 million payment for (yet-to-be-produced) Saab cars with another €15 million for more within 30 days.[54] The agreement also made provision for a joint venture operation to manufacture Saabs in China, with a manufacturing partner to be identified and appointed. The purchase of the cars themselves did not require government approval, but a joint venture for a manufacturing operation did. Obtaining such approval was not a straightforward matter. The Chinese government had been working hard for many years to rationalize China's fragmented auto industry, in order to ensure a limited number of high-volume, globally competitive car companies, and limiting tie-ups with foreign auto-makers was one way of achieving this.

However, the news of the Pang Da deal and the modest liquidity it injected into Saab was sufficient to restart vehicle production at Saab on 27 May. By 8 June the line stopped again, due to supply issues. On 13 June it was announced that a Chinese manufacturing partner, the third leg of the stool along with Saab and Pang Da, had been identified and that a Memorandum of Understanding had been signed with Zhejiang Youngman Lotus Automobile. Under this agreement, Youngman would produce Saab cars in China – subject to various approvals. At this point, most observers assumed that the main hurdle would be Chinese regulatory approval, but as events unfolded, the significance of GM would become very clear.

Problems continued to snowball for Saab. Production remained stopped. There were delays in the payment of salaries to Saab staff in June and July, and at the end of July the EIB refused to approve Antonov as an investor in Saab. Anotonov was subsequently arrested in London and questioned over allegations of fraud.[55] In 2014 a UK court ruled that Antonov should be deported to Lithuania and at the time of writing an appeal against this was pending.

All went quiet with Pang Da and Youngman during August 2011, although in early September Youngman expressed confidence that regulatory approval for the proposed arrangements would be forthcoming.

In early September Saab employees had still not been paid for August. On 7 September Saab filed for bankruptcy protection, requesting time to embark on a voluntary reorganization. The company stated:

> Following court approval, the voluntary reorganisation will be executed over an initial period of three months. If required, the reorganisation period can be extended by another three months, up to a maximum of twelve months. Swan and Saab Automobile are

confident that they will secure additional short-term funding for the reorganisation period and are currently in negotiations with several parties about obtaining such funding.

Funding for Saab Automobile to exit reorganisation has been secured through binding agreements with Pang Da and Youngman as announced on 4 July, which agreements are, however, subject to obtaining certain approvals.[56]

On 8 September this request was denied by the Vänersborg District Court on the grounds of insufficient evidence that a successful restructuring was feasible. At this point it looked as if this was the end of the road for Saab. Far from giving up, Victor Muller proclaimed 'We are not dead yet' and appealed against the court decision to refuse the reconstruction of Saab on 8 September, arguing that there was 'money on the horizon waiting to come into the country'.[57] This marked the starting point of a three-month-long rollercoaster ride for Saab and its employees.

Although Muller had been insisting that there was 'cash to pay salaries', on 10 September he made a U-turn, admitting that Saab was unable to pay outstanding salaries. On 12 September, Unionen, and Ledarna, a white collar union, filed a request to force troubled automaker Saab into bankruptcy, which would enable them to protect some of their lost earnings. A third union, IF Metall, followed suit on 21 September. Even though their salaries were on the line, many union members were unhappy about sending Saab into bankruptcy and this move was undertaken reluctantly.

In the meantime, Victor Muller launched a press campaign stating that 'Swedish Automobile N.V. (SWAN) ... entered into a memorandum of understanding with Pang Da and Youngman for the sale and purchase of 100% of the shares of Saab Automobile AB (Saab Automobile) and Saab Great Britain Ltd. (Saab GB).' Given this announcement and the prospect of a bridging loan, on 21 September the Appeals Court upheld Saab's appeal. This reversed the District Court's ruling of 8 September, giving Saab time to restructure and allowing the State to cover employee salaries until 21 October.

Early October brought a flurry of rumours that Geely, the Chinese owner of Volvo, had an interest in acquiring Saab, but these were quickly denied.

During October, negotiations continued with Youngman and Pang Da, but by 20 October the deal had apparently collapsed and only a small portion of a promised bridging funding had been transferred to Saab. The court-appointed administrator, Guy Lofalk, filed a petition to abandon the reorganization of Saab, arguing that there was insufficient cash to complete the reorganization and suggesting that one solution was to let the Chinese companies buy the company outright. Pang Da and Youngman did indeed offer to buy Saab outright for US$30.4 million (200 million SEK). In an interview with Reuters, Muller responded: 'The token offer was unacceptable because it would trigger every conceivable change-of-control clause and that would possibly mean the end of Saab.' At the time, some commentators accused Muller of risking the future of Saab by trying to retain too much personal control, but with hindsight it seems more likely that this reflected concern over GM's position over complete Chinese ownership. For some days, it looked as if any deal with Youngman and Pang Da was off.

Then, on 28 October, a deal in which SWAN sold Saab to Pang Da and Youngman for US$134 million (€100 million) was announced. Under the deal (which was actually only ever a memorandum of understanding) the two Chinese companies pledged to inject US$855 million into Saab in a bid to revitalize the company. For some days, the headlines proclaimed that Saab had been saved. Ambitious projections of output (e.g. 35–55,000 cars in 2012, 75–85,000 in 2013 and a long term projection of 185–205,000 units) were made. The Administrator's application for Saab to exit reorganization protection was withdrawn. On 28 October, Victor Muller declared:

> After the better part of seven months of agony for the company, we have come to a point where we can proudly say that we made it.
>
> I have had no life in the past two years ... My job was to save the company. I think I achieved it ... [I feel] great relief about the deal.

> We can be comfortable that the business plan that the company had made will now be executed and that the funding will be provided.

The jubilation turned out to be short-lived. By 4 November, there were indications from GM that they would not approve the sale. The Pang Da-Youngman acquisition required approval from several parties, most notably GM, Chinese authorities, the European Investment Bank and the Swedish Debt Office.

On 8 November, GM issued a statement that the proposed deal would harm its interests in China, and that it could not support it: 'GM would not be able to support a change in the ownership of Saab which could negatively impact GM's existing relationships in China or otherwise adversely affect GM's interests worldwide.' Commenting on GM's rejection, Muller remained bullish, saying 'There is always Plan B.' However, even he seemed to be losing faith: in an interview from 30 November, he stated:

> But right now I do not understand on the other hand why the Chinese continue to pump money into the company. As the situation is, it means that they put their money into a black hole, without getting anything back ...
>
> Should I slumber for a moment, SAAB would disappear in a heartbeat.[58]

For GM, the problem with the sale of Saab to a Chinese company was GM's joint venture with Shanghai Automotive Industry Association (SAIC), China's largest car maker. As we have described, the new Saab 9-5 was based on GM's Epsilon platform, which also formed the basis of a Buick model produced by SAIC. Thus, a significant amount of the GM technology and know-how that was embedded in Saab vehicles also went into SAIC products. Thus, by sanctioning the sale of Saab to a Chinese company, GM would effectively have been supporting a competitor to its major partner in the fastest growing auto market in the world. SAIC made no secret of their unhappiness at the prospect of the sale of Saab to another Chinese company, and this was widely reported in the Chinese media.

To try to get round this, Muller tried to bring in a Chinese bank, thereby only 'selling' a minority stake in Saab (49.9 per cent) to Youngman and Pang Da. However, on 8 December GM stated it would not support a proposed ownership structure for Saab that included a Chinese bank:[59] 'We have reviewed Saab's proposed changes regarding the sale of the company. Nothing in the proposal changes GM's position. We are unable to support the transaction.'[60] This prompted the Administrator to submit an application to the district court to reinstate the bankruptcy, arguing that: 'we are at the end of the road. We would have been happy if we would have had an option, but it is purely mathematical, we're out of money.'[61] In response, Victor Muller was quoted on Swedish TV criticizing the Administrator for being 'incompetent to handle SAAB as a company, the partners involved in SAAB and the complex process'.[62]

As the end approached, it was clear that Muller's attempts to get round GM's opposition to the deal were not working. On 18 December a GM spokesman stated:

> Saab's various new alternative proposals are not meaningfully
> different from what was originally proposed to General
> Motors and rejected. Each proposal results either directly or
> indirectly in the transfer of control and/or ownership of the
> company in a manner that would be detrimental to GM and its
> shareholders. As such, GM cannot support any of these
> proposed alternatives.

On 19 December, Saab itself petitioned for bankruptcy, closing the curtain on a seven-month drama and on the prospects for continuing employment for most of Saab's 3,600 workers. Victor Muller announced this saying: 'This is the darkest day in my career, probably in the history of Saab. But we had no other alternatives.'

POST BANKRUPTCY: NEVS

At this point, it seemed that the Saab Automobile story would end here. The receivers estimated that the company had debts of $1.9 billion, offset by assets of just $532 million. And yet, against all odds and most rational analyses, as this book goes to press more than three years later the Saab story still goes on. How can this be?

In the weeks following the December 2011 bankruptcy, there were reports in the business and automotive press of indications of interest in Saab's assets from a number of parties. These included India's Mahindra and Mahindra, a major manufacturer of SUVs who had a taken a 70 per cent stake in South Korea's Ssangyong Motor Company earlier in 2011, Turkey's Brightwell Holdings (a private investment company) and China's Dongfeng Group. Youngman was also reported to still be interested.

However, the prospects for finding a buyer for Saab looked bleak. In the run-up to the bankruptcy declaration, GM had made it clear that it would exercise its right to withhold access to the technology on which Saab was heavily dependent if it felt its interests would be compromised. The consequences of this had already been seen with Youngman and the Chinese market. Without GM's willingness to license its technology, huge financial backing would be needed, at a time when the world was still feeling the effects of the 2007–8 crash. Joe Phillippi, president of AutoTrends Consulting of New Jersey, observed: 'GM doesn't want to put another competitor in business ... To me, it sounds like liquidation. Who wants a relatively small car factory in Europe right now? I don't know of anybody.'[63] Even with GM's technology, there were doubts that Saab was a particularly attractive proposition. Lars Holmqvist, Head of the European Association of Automotive Suppliers expressed it thus: 'I am 99 percent certain it won't carry on as Saab ... Saab, from a technology point of view, is Opel. It's standard, run of the mill, very normal technology.'[64] This view was echoed by others, who drew a distinction between a possible acquisition of Saab by Mahindra and

Mahrindra and Tata's acquisition of Jaguar Land Rover (JLR) three years earlier. Dipesh Rathore, Managing Director of IHS Global Insight, a consultancy, commented: 'I look at Saab and there is hardly anything to acquire. Europe could be a springboard to the US but you don't get major volumes out of Saab. Saab isn't as strong as JLR.'[65] The last comment pinpointed an uncomfortable truth about Saab. Even without a damaged brand, Saab had never at any point in its life exceeded global sales of 135,000 units – and ironically enough its best year for sales ever was 2006, its final 'normal' year before the 2007–8 crisis. The brand's ability to support the combination of sales volumes and prices necessary for sustainable operation had always been its Achilles heel. With the brand weakened through protracted uncertainty and now bankruptcy, and restrictions on licensing from GM, what was there apart from some European assembly plant capacity in a relatively costly location?

Saab's bankruptcy administrators were graphically candid about the situation. On 21 January 2012, Hans Bergqvist, one of the administrators, said in his first public statement since the bankruptcy: 'Saab is a patient who has long bled to death and the brutal truth is that the patient is dead. But the patient has not stopped bleeding.'[66] The deadline for bids for Saab's remaining assets was 10 April 2012. Three bids were received, believed to be Mahindra and Mahindra, Youngman and a mystery consortium from China and Japan with interests in electric vehicles.[67] Youngman's bid was reported to be $470 million.

By May, information started to emerge about the electric vehicles consortium. The two main parties in the group were reported to be Sun Investment, a Japanese firm concerned with environmental projects, and National Modern Energy Holdings, a firm based in Hong Kong with energy interests. A company, National Electric Vehicle Sweden AB, or NEVS was been formed for the purpose of obtaining Saab's assets. Mattias Bergman, a spokesman for the group, who later became President of NEVS said: 'We have placed a bid, and we want to buy Saab and build cars.' We're interested in what Saab's brand stands for, the innovation and competence in the company, and the production facility that's world class.'[68] By mid June Youngman had made an improved bid (which was rejected by the receivers) and NEVS became Saab's new owner. The CEO was to be Kai Johan Jiang, founder and owner of National Modern Energy Holdings and also an economic advisor to the government of China's Shandong province. NEVS' objective was to use Saab as a platform to build a company producing electric cars. Speaking at a press conference in Trollhättan, Mattias Bergman, the President of NEVS laid out a plan for Saab to be a world-leading company for electric cars.

Karl-Erling Trogen (NEVS chairman and a former head of Volvo's truck division,) presented a similarly upbeat message: 'We will match Swedish automobile design and manufacturing experience with Japanese E.V. technology and a strong presence in China ... Electric vehicles powered by clean electricity are the future, and the electric car of the future will be produced in Trollhättan.'[69] CEO Jiang argued that China offered opportunities for Saab: 'Chinese customers demand a premium electric vehicle, which we will be able to offer by acquiring Saab.'[70] Speaking in 2013, Bergman summarized the assets that NEVS acquired. These included that rights to the Saab 9-3 (including GM's Epsilon 1 platform), the still incomplete Phoenix platform, a portfolio of trademarks and patents, the tooling, including supplier tooling, to make the 9-3; equipment and facilities to test new powertrains; and a substantial amount of land and buildings.[71]

The stated plan was to develop an electric vehicle based on the Saab 9-3, initially for sale in China, but with global sales as the ultimate target. However, NEVS was cagey about many details, such as which companies it would be working with (it just said it would be using 'Japanese technology'), the price it paid for Saab, and the investment it would be making in Trollhättan.

Although the NEVS plan eliminated the problem of head-to-head competition with other, much stronger car makers, analysts were sceptical. The Saab 9-3 had not been designed for electrical propulsion; Saab had no expertise with electric vehicles; sales of electric cars were tiny; and many technological obstacles to the widespread adoption of electric cars remained. The outspoken Lars Holmqvist, former CEO of CLEPA, the European Supplier Association, captured the suspicions of many observers:

> They [NEVS] need to get a decent partner because there is no chance, no chance whatsoever, these guys will be able to build an electric car. They have no idea how to build cars ... [Jiang] seems to me like he was out there to save the world and I am always sceptical about people [like] that in the automotive industry.[72]

Later in June came more bad news, which was that the right to use the Saab brand name and griffin logo had not been included in the sale. Saab Automobile's former parent company, Saab AB, retained the rights to the name and therefore could withhold approval for its use. Saab AB felt they had been adversely affected by Saab Automobile's bad publicity and bankruptcy and were concerned to ensure that when the Saab name was used it was associated with 'high competence'. The griffin logo is also used on Scania commercial vehicles, now majority owned by Volkswagen, who also vetoed its use by NEVS. Saab AB later granted NEVS an exclusive licence to use the Saab name on its vehicles, but use of the griffin logo remained off limits.

The sale to NEVS was confirmed in August 2012. There was little news for a number of months, and then in early 2013 reports of the company's plans started to emerge in the Chinese media. It was reported that the City Government of Qingdao, through its investment company, had taken a 22 per cent share in NEVS, allegedly for $310 million. The plan included a substantial production facility in Qingdao, with a production capacity of 400,000 vehicles a year to exploit rising demand for electric cars in China. This demand was predicated on the back of ambitious government targets for electric vehicles, claimed to be 500,000 on the road by 2015 and 5 million by 2020.[73]

However, the project still required government approval to produce cars and, despite ambitious targets, sales of electric vehicles in

China remained low (around 15,000 in 2012 according to some estimates) and key infrastructure undeveloped. All this, of course, was on top of the problem of the 9-3 being an old model that had not been designed to be an electric vehicle, and an almost total lack of development capability on the part of Saab or its new owners.

Meanwhile, back in Sweden, in May 2013 NEVS announced that it intended to restart production of the petrol- and diesel-engined Saab 9-3s at Trollhättan later that year. By August, the company was reporting that about 200 employees and 100 consultants were working at Trollhättan. In September a trial vehicle rolled off the line, and at the start of December production restarted, albeit at a very low volume of around 10 cars a week – a tiny number, bearing in mind that under normal conditions the plant had been producing 30–40 vehicles an hour. Cars were offered directly to Swedish customers via the company's website.

For the first few months of 2014, low-volume production continued, with the cars finding buyers amongst diehard Saab enthusiasts. But in May there was more trouble and production was halted because the company did not have the cash to pay its debts. NEVS claimed that the Qingdao Investment Company had not fulfilled its commitment to provide finance and that as a consequence they had run out of cash.[74]

In August an unpaid supplier submitted a bankruptcy petition against NEVS, who in turn applied for short-term protection from creditors whilst it sought alternative sources of funding. NEVS claimed to be in discussions with two unnamed global car makers about taking a stake in the company. The pattern of three years earlier seemed to be repeating itself. As 2014 drew to a close, the *Financial Times* reported that Mahindra and Mahindra were close to sealing a deal to buy remnants of the company. The reasoning behind this seemed to rest on brand. In 2013 Mahindra told the *Financial Times*: 'We need brands, because the one thing you cannot build, if you want to grow globally at least – something that can take a lifetime, and we are in a hurry – is brands'.[75] As this book goes to press in 2015, it was reported that Saab had emerged from bankruptcy protection, but there was no news of a deal with Mahindra and Mahindra, or indeed with any other buyer.

ANALYSIS: LESSONS FROM SAAB?

Having recounted the story of Saab, we will now turn to the lessons Saab holds for survival and resilience in the auto industry. We will use our concept of the survival envelope to understand the Saab case, specifically the four key components of operations and management, scale, market reach and stakeholders.

Market reach

As we described in previous chapters, there is considerable overcapacity in the automotive industry, in the order of 30 per cent globally. This situation has existed for many years, and means that even though global sales have risen as new markets have developed, there is fierce competition, particularly in segments where several producers compete head-on. Car manufacturers thus have to find positions in the market that are large enough not only to support their day-to-day operations, but also to generate the substantial financial resources needed to develop new vehicles that are competitive in their cost, quality and performance. As we have seen, the development cost of a new model, on a stand-alone platform is huge, typically in the order of $1–$6bn.

At first sight, Saab appeared to possess many of the attributes that many textbooks of strategy urge companies to pursue – a distinct brand identity and, for much of its life a loyal, committed customer base, so much so that Saab has featured in analyses of 'brand communities' – a phrase reserved for products and companies (such as Apple and Harley Davidson) whose customers show especially high levels of loyalty and engagement. Although some commentators have been quick to point the finger at brand mismanagement by GM to explain Saab's demise, claiming that loyal customers abandoned the brand, this explanation is not supported by the raw sales data.

Table 6.1 *Saab's average annual sales (in units) per decade, 1950–2008*

	Average number of units sold per annum
1950–1959	6,742
1960–1969	42,404
1970–1979	83,245
1980–1989	101,018
1990–1999	99,189
2000–2008	124,344

As Table 6.1 shows, the best period of Saab's history for sales came in the last few years of its life. Indeed, the best year in Saab's entire history was 2006, with sales of over 135,000 units globally. Sales did fall in 2007 and 2008, as they did for the industry as whole, and dropped catastrophically in 2009 – almost certainly because of fears over Saab's future once GM announced its intention to sell or close Saab early in 2009.

Thus, although there is scant evidence of a customer exodus from Saab, it is clear that whilst Saab was more or less treading water at between 100–135,000 units a year from the 1980s onwards its main competitors were expanding quite rapidly. Audi, for example, virtually doubled its annual sales volumes between the late 1990s and 2010, from around 600,000 units to over 1.1 million, but did so by an aggressive proliferation of models into segments in which Audi had not previously had a presence.

So, in market terms, what was Saab's problem? Saab had a clear niche position, which by definition means that it would always find it difficult to sell large volumes of vehicles. But herein lies a conundrum for any brand that emphasizes its difference from the mainstream as a major element of its brand values. Too different from the mainstream and there will be insufficient buyers; not different enough and there will be an insufficient price premium to compensate for the lower volumes. This in many ways appeared to be one of Saab's most fundamental problems. Strong competition in the luxury segment from players like Audi, BMW and Mercedes meant that Saab products could not command sufficiently high margins to enable it to be sustainable on its modest sales volumes (unlike Porsche, for example, which can). This put Saab at a continued disadvantage against its larger competitors who were able to offset their development costs across many more units and therefore put much more time, effort and resource into development, of course, resulting in even more refined, competitive vehicles. Saab was therefore caught in a very uncomfortable place, between the low-volume, high-margin producers further upmarket, the other premium producers who enjoyed much higher volumes, and the non-premium, high-volume producers whose prices were much lower but from whose products Saab was not sufficiently different.

This problem was further exacerbated by two more factors: Saab's narrow model range and its limited global reach. For most of its life Saab only offered one or two models, at a time when market segments proliferated considerably. In desperation to reach new segments Saab (or strictly speaking, its then-owner, GM) succumbed to re-badging models designed and produced by other manufacturers such as the Subaru Impreza and Chevrolet Trailblazer, which apart from minor cosmetic items were indistinguishable from the originals. These models accounted for very few sales in the last few years of Saab's life and probably did more harm than good by undermining the authenticity of the Saab brand and attracted derisory nicknames such as the 'Saaburu' and 'Trollblazer'. In this respect, those who accuse GM of brand mismanagement have a point. Saab simply did not have products in segments that were enjoying considerable growth from the 1990s onwards such as SUVs, MPVs and, more recently, crossover vehicles, and with a financially marginal operation was not generating the resources to develop these.

Furthermore, in Saab's case the problem of limited market reach in terms of segment coverage was exacerbated by its reliance on just three mature, national markets, with around 60 per cent of sales concentrated in the US, the UK and Sweden. The UK and US were particularly exposed to the 2007–8 global financial crisis, so Saab's dependency on these markets and its lack of presence in markets less affected by the crisis was a twofold problem.

Thus Saab violated two key conditions for the resilience of an auto company with respect to market reach. Saab's two-model line-up meant that Saab did not have a presence in growing segments (such as smaller premium cars and SUVs). Its sales footprint was concentrated into three, rather mature, markets in which there was limited growth potential, and in which they were up against very strong competitors. Saab's presence in developing markets, such as China, was virtually non-existent. These structural conditions, combined with other conditions such as uncertainty about the company's future, gave Saab some major market vulnerabilities that manifested themselves as a precipitous drop in sales in 2009.

Scale

As we have seen, economies of scale are enormously significant in the auto industry. There are substantial fixed costs in operating a car company, and these interact with other conditions, such as exposure to the economic cycle, and mean that financially marginal companies are very vulnerable during downturns because they lack a substantial financial buffer to ride out the storm. This is over and above the challenge that marginality poses for the funding of renewal activities, such as new model development. The automotive industry typically suffers earlier and deeper recessions than other sectors,[76] as customers can usually postpone the purchase of cars in the face of financial uncertainty. So it was with Saab who saw an 80 per cent drop in demand between 2008 and 2009, from which it never recovered.

As we argued in Chapter 4, the importance of scale is not necessarily a simple case of 'bigger is better'. With multiple market segments and territories, car companies also need to be capable of delivering products at very high levels of variety, which can of course impede economies of scale. As we saw in Chapter 2, one way of squaring this circle is to try to achieve maximum variety on the surface whilst minimizing the variety of platforms and components underneath so that the standardization and economies of scale still exist, but not in areas particularly apparent to the customer. Joint model development programmes between auto firms is another route to achieve economies of scale in development.

As we can see from Saab's history, the use of some of these strategies started quite early in the company's history. Back in 1967, the V4 four-stroke engine for the 95/96 models was sourced from Ford of Germany. The engines for the early 99s were purchased from Triumph in the UK. The 9000 was a joint platform development with Fiat and Lancia. These were all pragmatic, workable solutions to the challenges of vehicle development, but they were also early symptoms of a car company that was not generating the resources to completely fund its development activities on its own. Whilst some companies grow out of this dependency Saab never did.

From this perspective, Saab's incorporation into a larger car maker was a logical and perhaps inevitable step in order to achieve economies of scale and access to engineering and technological resources that could not be attained as an independent entity. As Figure 6.1 shows Saab's total annual sales never exceeded 140,000 units, and that even this was split across two models from the early 1970s onwards. Saab's total volume across both its models was only about equal to the average sales per single model for many other Western European producers.[77]

Faced with this situation, it is not clear that Saab had a great deal of room for manoeuvre. Saab never looked likely to achieve scale through organic growth (as, for example, BMW did) and without this the decision was really down to the choice of partner/s or owner. Saab was not alone in this – no other small to medium-sized European car maker has survived without seeking the protection and support of a larger automotive group. However the Saab story demonstrated some of the risks inherent in niche producers being taken under the wings of larger corporations.

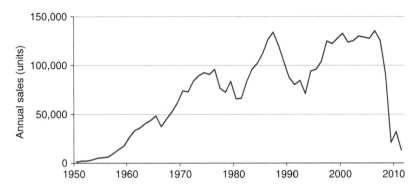

FIGURE 6.1 Saab's global sales, 1950–2011
Source: Annual reports

With respect to scale, Saab and GM were caught in a dilemma. On the one hand it was necessary for Saab to use GM technology and engineering resources in order to secure cost savings and achieve more frequent model renewals. On the other lay the need for Saab to stay sufficiently faithful to its own brand values and areas of distinctiveness to retain its position as a premium European brand. Between them, Saab and GM struggled to achieve this balance. From 1996 onwards, for 12 years in a row, Saab achieved annual sales in excess of 100,000 units. This was a record run for Saab (it had managed to exceed 100,000 units a year for only six years in a row in the 1980s) but it fell a long way short of GM's initial hopes of 250,000 units a year. Audi and BMW, in comparison, each exceeded 1,000,000 units per year during the same period.

To Saab purists, GM's use of mid-market platforms for Saab models undermined the Saab brand. The bind for GM, of course, was that as a high-volume producer of economy to mid-range cars GM simply did not possess platforms that were engineered with a premium European brand in mind – and indeed to have done so would likely have undermined its competitiveness in those high-volume markets. Thus GM's standard offerings sat uncomfortably with Saab's niche of quirky individualism, technological sophistication and premium positioning. Saab for its part resisted necessary attempts by GM to standardize and cut costs by sharing technology with its Opel and Vauxhall models. GM's late and ultimately ineffectual attempts to reach market niches that were new to Saab by rebadging GM and Subaru products for the US market clearly did not help either.

The Saab story, at least in part, can be seen as a failed attempt on the part of a niche producer and a global giant to satisfactorily resolve the underlying tension between the dual needs of distinctiveness in the market and economies of scale in design and production.

Operations and management system

Although the absence of scale and market reach is an important part of the story of Saab's failure, operational shortcomings seem much less significant. The 1980s Saab models were rather labour intensive to build, but during the 1990s GM succeeded in reducing the labour hours required to build a car by about half.

Throughout Saab's history, and certainly up to the GM years, the company's ability to design, build and produce competitive vehicles has not generally been questioned. Saab vehicles have generally received positive reports from motoring critics and have performed reasonably well in consumer tests, receiving particular acclaim for their combination of performance, safety and durability, particularly in the 1980s. The advent of GM-derived vehicles changed that somewhat, but primarily amongst motoring critics and testers. These of course are important opinion leaders, but as we have seen, Saab actually sold more vehicles per year under GM than at any other time in its history. Thus, as we saw in the previous section, the argument that brand mismanagement by GM drove loyal, devoted Saab customers away is not borne out by the sales data. Or if previously loyal Saab enthusiasts were driven away by GM's influence then they were replaced in even greater numbers by new customers.

Unlike Rover, where shortfalls could be seen in many areas of operational execution – from product development to manufacturing – Saab's failure does not appear to have been rooted in a dramatic lack of capability to design and build cars. Some readers might find this position uncomfortable, or even difficult to believe – surely if a company designs and makes good products, it will succeed?

The Saab story is interesting in terms of one of the basic arguments in this book – namely that operational and managerial capabilities alone do not necessarily provide a comprehensive explanation for success and failure. What would the advice to Saab's management have been? The orthodox answer would be to 'design and build better (or perhaps more mainstream) cars' but throughout its history the limited resources available to Saab made that problematic. The quirky distinctiveness that made Saabs so attractive to a fairly small subset of the global car-owning community perhaps inevitably made them less attractive to others. Unlike Volvo, that initially built a more broad-based following around safe, solid family cars and eventually diversified its range of models, Saab perhaps stayed with its two-model, large car line-up for too long and found itself in a position which was then very difficult to break out of. The Saab story is thus perhaps one of managerial omission – not so much being bad at what it did, but rather doing the wrong things. Or at least, continuing to do the same things as it had always done, as the world changed around it. Saab's competitors extended their model ranges, pushed into new global markets and market segments and grew their volumes in ways that Saab did not.

In our model of the 'survival envelope', the roots of the Saab failure lie not so much in the failure of operational subsystems as in the 'management system', particularly the processes of sensing how a complex environment is evolving and setting in train the processes to deal with this. Perhaps if Saab had been acquired by an auto firm with a set of platforms better suited to the European premium segment than GM's mid-market offerings, things could have been different – but the question of just how much volume Saab's brand could support would still have remained.

Stakeholders

Stakeholder support is important in that even organizations that are not especially strong operationally or commercially may be surprisingly resilient if they enjoy strong support from key stakeholders. Although Saab failed, which suggests a lack of stakeholder support, there is another perspective – that what is remarkable about Saab Automobile is not that it failed, but rather its resilience in terms of how long it took to fail.

We have seen that prior to General Motors taking full control, Saab Automobile was part of Saab AB, a technology conglomerate, which was in turn largely owned by Investor, an Investment Company established by the influential Wallenberg family in 1916. Although Investor had many interests, the history of Saab (the whole company, not just the car division) presents a picture of considerable continuity of direction and what would today be termed a 'stakeholder' orientation. As we described earlier in this chapter, illustrative of this is the position of Marcus Wallenberg (1899–1982), who dominated Investor from the 1960s and was still chairman of the company when he died in 1982. Significantly, Wallenberg was also a member of the Board of Saab from 1939, and chairman of Saab's Board from 1968 until 1980. Wallenberg's perspective is captured by the following observation: 'Marcus Wallenberg often remarked "let there be music" – meaning that all the many elements of a decision should form a harmonious whole, to the benefit of the nation, the Company and the individuals involved' (The Saab-Scania Story, 1987). Wallenberg's stubbornness and patience is credited with enabling Saab to weather a number of crises, in which short-term considerations (such as returns on investment) were apparently put aside in favour of the long-term goal of building up the technological expertise of the company. Partly to reduce its exposure to the Swedish industrial sector, partly in search of increased returns, from the late 1980s onwards Investor orientated more towards high-growth unlisted companies.[78] The divestment of Saab Cars, first by selling 50 per cent of the company to GM in 1989, and some years later the remaining stake, was part of a wider process that eventually saw Scania, the trucks division of the company, sold to Volkswagen. But arguably this development meant that Saab Automobile was more exposed and under more pressure to justify itself financially than had previously been the case.

Within a huge company such as GM, Saab people felt that getting resources, in particular for product development, was a major challenge. Jan-Åke Jonsson put it thus:

> Saab was a part of GM and what that means specifically is that whereas Saab was not integrated into GM everywhere in some of the major areas it definitely was. And I would say one of the key items that impacts any car company is product development, you know the whole engineering side was integrated fully into General Motors, which meant that GM had a, call it an annual budget for engineering and investments ... And being an integrated part of engineering that meant that we had to fight for our resources together with everybody else, and then it is important to remember that GM sold around five/six million cars per year and Saab had 100,000. So in other words we were a tiny little player that had to fight for our fair share if you wish ... And that was particularly sad for Saab because we paid but we didn't get anything. In other words with the 9-5 that was 12/13 years when it was replaced. In our type of industry it was a way too long lifecycle.

The significance of stakeholders is further demonstrated by Jonsson's comments about GM's bailout by the US Government in 2009. The politics of the bailout were such that the benefits to the US were demonstrable. Given that GM was also cancelling a number of its North American brands (such as Hummer and Saturn) one can see the political argument against retaining a marginal European brand. It is also worth remembering that such was the scale of the crisis that the disposal of Opel/ Vauxhall was under active consideration, so that Saab lost the support of its owner–stakeholder under these conditions is not surprising.

GM was replaced by an enthusiastic owner in the form of Spyker and Victor Muller, but this all too graphically illustrated that the willingness of stakeholders to offer support must be matched with a capacity to do so, so when Saab's sales failed to recover at the predicted rate, Spyker rapidly ran out of cash. As in the case of Rover, it was another stakeholder group – suppliers who had not been paid and who lost confidence that they ever would be – who finally called time on Saab Automobile.

As this book goes to press, the story of stakeholder support – and perhaps of hope triumphing over experience – continues with NEVS and prospects of new investors from Asia, where hopes of a future for Saab as a producer of electric vehicles persist, but with little sign of the resources necessary to make this a reality.

7 Near misses: Chrysler and Nissan

In Chapters 5 and 6 we examined the failures of Rover and Saab, the two most significant car companies to fail within the last decade or so. However, equally significant to any understanding of resilience in the auto industry are the cases of those companies that experienced crisis but managed to survive. Indeed, in more or less every decade since the Second World War there are examples of car companies that experienced a significant crisis and that managed to survive. In this chapter we examine two examples of 'near death' experiences, Japan's Nissan (in 1999) and Chrysler in the USA (in 1979 and again in 2009).

Many car firms that are currently regarded as strong, industry leading enterprises have – at least once in their lifetimes – come close to collapse. Crises are a perennial feature of the motor industry and have afflicted auto companies across all regions of the globe. Toyota, for example, nearly failed in 1950. In the early 1950s the young Toyota Motor Company faced a serious drop in demand as credit from the Reconstruction Finance Bank was restricted and a recession hit the Japanese market at the same time. Toyota vowed to honour its lifetime employment contracts, but in the end had to lay off 2,146 workers through voluntary redundancy. The crisis forced company founder Kiichiro Toyoda to resign as president, after issuing a profuse apology to its workforce, and led to the division of Toyota's manufacturing and sales arms into two companies, a division which remained until 1982. Toyota's President Akio Toyoda summed up the nature of the industry, stating that 'Toyota has been hit by a crisis about once every ten years.'[1] This picture replicates itself at most major car firms: VW, for example, one of the largest car makers in the world at the time of writing, experienced existential crises in 1973–4, 1982–3 and

1992–4, made a €1bn loss in the US market in 2004, and announced a $5bn cost reduction programme in 2014.

In this chapter we describe two companies that have faced crises that led them to near-bankruptcy, but which survived: Chrysler, which has experienced a number of crises, but which was bailed out by the US Government in 1979 and 2009; and Nissan, which came close to bankruptcy in 1999 and was saved by entering an alliance with France's Renault. We then briefly review several crises that have hit car companies around the world since 1945.

CHRYSLER: THE COMEBACK KID

In this section we provide an analysis of Chrysler, which along with GM, went into Chapter 11 bankruptcy protection in 2009. Chrysler was bailed out by the US Government, who insisted that Chrysler tie up with a foreign partner as a condition of the rescue. Chrysler is of particular interest to our analysis of crisis and resilience, because it is an example of a company that has faced repeated crises and yet, so far, has managed to survive. The ups and downs of Chrysler are of course closely linked to the cycles of the North American car market, on which Chrysler has always been particularly dependent, with around 80 per cent of its output sold in North America. The significance of this dependency will become evident as we tell Chrysler's story; as one might expect, Chrysler's crises have generally occurred during the periodic, severe downswings in the US auto market, which are vividly displayed in Figure 7.1. Chrysler's US sales volumes are shown in Figure 7.2.

Chrysler has been particularly vulnerable to oscillations in the US market because of three interrelated factors: its smaller size relative to Ford and GM; its dependence on the US market; and its concentration of models in segments in which demand is particularly vulnerable to recession and oil shocks, such as larger cars, light trucks and SUVs. When these factors are overlaid with periodic operational and managerial shortcomings, we can see why Chrysler faced crises. When Figures 7.1 and 7.2 are viewed together it becomes apparent

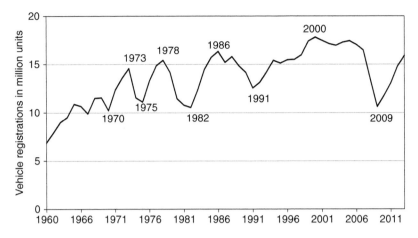

FIGURE 7.1 New vehicle registrations in the USA since 1960

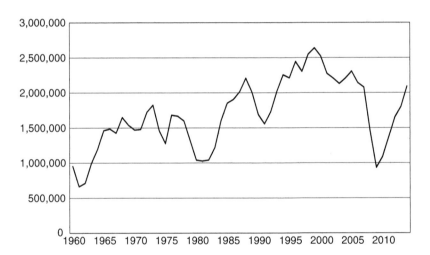

FIGURE 7.2 Chrysler's sales in the USA in units, 1960–2014
Source: Ward's Yearbooks, various years

that Chrysler has been hit harder by troughs than has the sector as a
whole, but has also rebounded more strongly during the peaks. For
example the trough-to-peak gain for the whole US market between
1991 and 2000 was +42%. For Chrysler, from 1991 to its slightly
earlier peak of 1999 the gain was +70%. On the way down, the whole
US market fell −40% between 2000 and 2009, but Chrysler's fall

was −65%. These are very substantial swings for any business to absorb, but are particularly challenging for a high fixed-cost operation like auto assembly. The figures explain Chrysler's reputation as a boom-and-bust company and also why it has attracted the nickname 'the comeback kid'.

From the perspective of resilience, as equally interesting as Chrysler's crises is its persistent ability to secure support at critical junctures, allowing it to live on despite its underlying weaknesses. These conditions place Chrysler in the interesting category of 'permanently failing' organizations, that is, those that repeatedly come close to collapse but never actually do so.

Over the years, there have been many accounts of events at Chrysler, as there have of the fortunes of GM and Ford and of the US auto industry as a whole. We analysed many of these in researching this book and those readers who wish to read more about the trials and tribulations of the US auto industry have a rich array of material to choose from, such as Yates (1983) Halberstam (1986) Ingrassia and White (1995) Vlasic (2011), Ingrassia (2011). There are also a few executive 'how-I-did-it' autobiographies of auto executives of which Iacocca's *Iacocca* (1986) is perhaps the best known. Many of these accounts are rich and colourful, often written by journalists rather than academics and benefit from extensive insider knowledge, obtained both on and off the record.

Many of these accounts follow the same basic narrative, which with minor variations typically goes something like: a once good company has slipped into decline because management took its eye off the ball with respect to products, processes or people (and often all three); better-managed competitors moved in and took market share, causing a crisis; a new CEO comes in and leads a transformation; the company's fortunes are restored. Apart from perhaps overstating the role of the heroic CEO, this narrative is quite persuasive when only a single crisis or episode is considered, but when several such episodes in the same company are examined sequentially, over a period of time, the hero-CEO narrative is less convincing. Typically, the turnarounds do not last and problems that were allegedly 'fixed' during one episode of reform mysteriously reappear by the next. Thus the cycle of fixing them (and writing books and articles about how it is done) begins all over again. In some cases the 'hero' of one period actually becomes the 'villain' of the next, as happened in the case of Lee Iacocca across successive accounts of the Chrysler story.

In terms of our model of resilience, the narrative of a transformative CEO typically focuses on what in Chapter 4 we described as the 'operations and management' element of competitiveness and resilience, ascribing improvements in performance to the CEO's ability to restore the company's operations to a competitive state from one that had become uncompetitive. The emphasis on management and operations down-plays (or even completely ignores) many of the other forces and factors that constrain performance such as settlements with stakeholders or market/product positions that cannot be quickly or easily changed. Whilst the quality of management clearly can and does impact on corporate performance, the size of the impact varies considerably according to the context within which the organization is embedded. For large, complex and highly embedded organizations such as car companies, it can be hard to untangle the impact of context and environment on performance from that of management action. One consequence of this is that CEOs who enjoy favourable environmental conditions are likely to be hailed as miracle-workers, whilst those who are unfortunate enough to be in post during a downswing are likely to carry the can for all that is wrong with the firm.

With this in mind, we will now present a short history of the US car company Chrysler, during which we shall further explore the question of management action vs context in understanding crisis and recovery.

Early period

The Chrysler Corporation was formed in 1925, some 15–20 years later than Ford or General Motors. At this time Chrysler absorbed the struggling Maxwell Motor Company, which had been established in

1904. As we described in Chapter 2, the US auto industry went through a period of rapid consolidation in its early years, with the number of auto manufacturers falling from 253 in 1908 to only 44 in 1929. Many of the auto firms that survived until 1929 disappeared altogether during the Great Depression of the 1930s.

Following GM (as described in Chapter 3), Chrysler segregated its offerings into different brands and levels as it evolved, with the Plymouth brand at the entry level, the DeSoto and Dodge brands in the mid-market (Chrysler acquired Dodge in 1928) and the Chrysler brand itself at the upper end. By the late 1930s, GM, Ford and Chrysler held over 80% of the US market between them, with GM in the clear lead with over 40% market share, followed by Chrysler and then Ford, who both held 20–25%. Chrysler held the number two position for market share until 1949, when it slipped into third place behind Ford. During the Second World War Chrysler's activities focused on the construction of military vehicles as part of the war effort, and the company branched into several other military-related areas such as radar and missiles, and in the late 1950s, boosters for spacecraft.

By the late 1950s and into the 1960s Chrysler's auto operations were under considerable pressure. The company had made significant losses in both 1958 and 1959 and its cars had developed a poor reputation for quality. By 1962 its share of the US market was down to 8.3 per cent. Moreover, unlike Ford and GM which had moved quickly into overseas markets and production between 1910 and 1930, Chrysler almost exclusively served the North American market. Correspondingly its production was also largely concentrated in North America, apart from some small local assembly operations in countries such as South Africa and Australia, where substantial tariffs on imported cars were in place. Chrysler's pattern of heavy reliance on the North American market largely persists today.

In 1961, Lynn Townsend, Chrysler's new and financially oriented CEO, embarked on a programme of internal reform and internationalization (Halberstam 1986). Internal reforms took the form of cuts, plant closures and the consolidation of divisions.

To try and restore customer confidence in the quality of Chrysler's vehicles Townsend insisted on a 5-year–50,000-mile warranty, although there was considerable anxiety within the firm about the cost of this. Townsend's efforts bore fruit and by 1968 Chrysler's domestic market share was up to over 18 per cent. However, Halberstam observes:

> On paper what [Townsend] was doing looked good; that was part of the problem. Subtly and inevitably, more energy went into what would look good on paper than what was good for the cars. He was preoccupied with what would drive the stock up; therefore so were all the men around him ... Chrysler gradually became caught in a vast and lethal self-deception
>
> (Halberstam 1986: 554).

The issue of managing appearances for the short term was epitomized by the 'sales bank', a euphemism for the vast stock of cars that had been built in the absence of orders from customers and dealers, in order to keep production numbers up and the manufacturing plants busy. Chrysler pressurized dealers to take cars that the dealers did not want and when this failed unsold cars were assigned to the Chrysler Financial Corporation to disguise the problem. By 1969 the sales bank contained over 400,000 unsold cars.

Under Townsend's influence and some 40 years behind Ford and GM, Chrysler began to move into Europe, whose auto market was at the time growing rapidly. Over a period of years, Chrysler took a controlling interest in France's Simca, 35 per cent of Spain's Barreiros and acquired the UK's Rootes Group. As an auto group Rootes was in many respects similar to BLMC/ Rover, as described in Chapter 5. The Rootes Group had been formed from a series of mergers and comprised a number of previously independent marques and faced the same challenges of integration.

These various acquisitions created Chrysler Europe – Chrysler's answer to the European subsidiaries of its rivals Ford and GM. Chrysler Europe initially comprised a multitude of brands – Simca, Barreiros,

Hillman, Humber, Sunbeam and Talbot, plus a couple of commercial vehicle brands. As was the case with BLMC at the time, Chrysler struggled to integrate and rationalize the portfolio of brands, models and operations that it had acquired, and like BLMC, lacked the resources to update its aging models. In private, Townsend described Chrysler's European acquisitions as 'dogs' but claimed he had little choice but to deal with them or risk being locked out of the international market (Halberstam 1986). Rather than making a positive contribution to Chrysler, its European arm was a net drain on its resources and finally collapsed in 1977. It was taken over by Peugeot-Citroën (PSA) in 1978, ending that particular foray of Chrysler into Europe.

Chrysler also created another international venture, in 1970, in the form of a tie-up with Japan's Mitsubishi Motors (MMC) which involved Chrysler taking a 15 per cent share in MMC. Throughout the 1970s, Chrysler imported Mitsubishi models and badged and sold these as their own, although as Mitsubishi began to sell more of its own models directly in the USA, the relationship with MMC came under increasing strain and was eventually wound down, although it was to re-emerge many years later.

The first bailout

In its home market of North America, Chrysler faced considerable pressure during the 1970s. Many of the incursions into the market by imports (principally by German and Japanese auto firms) during the 1960s and 1970s had come at the expense of Chrysler's share of the market. The sales bank of unsold cars had grown hugely, as had Chrysler's debt, which in 1970 hit $791 million, greater than that of GM, but GM was several times the size of Chrysler. Chrysler was particularly hard hit by the first oil crisis of 1974, and responded with layoffs and cutbacks in investment and in new product development. Townsend was pressured to resign, which he did, in 1975.[2]

In 1978 Lee Iacocca, formerly of Ford, became CEO of Chrysler, and reportedly was horrified by what he found, saying to a former colleague from Ford, who had joined Chrysler some months before,

'You son of a bitch, why didn't you tell me it was this bad?'[3] By 1979 Chrysler was in the grip of an acute financial crisis and was in danger of running out of working capital and defaulting on its credit agreements. In desperation, Chrysler sought $1.5 billion in US government aid to avert closure. Speaking at the Chrysler Loan Hearing in October 1979 Iacocca said:

> We [Chrysler] are the microcosm of all the things that are wrong ... we're just that big. Energy is impacting us, regulation is impacting us, runaway inflation on commodities are impacting us, imports are impacting us. We are a big city company with a lot of black employment, that's impacting us. I don't know where to turn. I ran it all out for this Committee. I've done the best I can, I'm committed to it, I'm going to turn it around, one way or another. I need your assistance now, and I need a vote of confidence. What else can I tell you?
>
> *(Chrysler Loan Hearing 18 October 1979)*[4]

Despite some opposition to the idea of a state rescue, Chrysler succeeded in securing loan guarantees to keep it afloat. But in order to do this various stakeholders had to make concessions. Labour agreed to changes that reduced wages costs by about $2 an hour; suppliers agreed to less favourable terms; and state and local governments agreed various concessions and support, including placing orders for military vehicles. Crucial to the rescue, especially in a strongly pro-market environment such as the USA, was Chrysler's ability to build a broad coalition of supporters. The fact that Chrysler still had a significant share of the domestic auto market and was a major employer was clearly important – indeed, at that time the Big Three collectively still held about 75 per cent of the US market and the Japanese automakers were not yet building cars in the USA. Iacocca claimed that half a million jobs and $10 billion in lost tax revenues and increased unemployment benefits were at stake were Chrysler to collapse. The fact that there was a Democrat president in the White House, elected in part on the blue-collar vote, was also significant.

The 1980s

The bailout prevented Chrysler's collapse and bought Chrysler's management some time to regroup. Chrysler's military division was sold to General Dynamics in 1982. A new line of fuel-efficient front-wheel drive cars, known as the K-cars was launched in 1981, which despite a slow start, went on to sell well. In 1983 Chrysler was able to pay off its loan from the US Government. In 1984 it launched its very successful Minivan (people carrier, in European terms), based on the K series platform, which also went on to sell very well. With the Minivan Chrysler essentially defined a new market segment, which it went on to dominate for many years.

As Figure 7.1 shows, the US vehicle market (including cars and light trucks) hit a trough of around 10 million units in 1982 in the wake of the second (1979) oil shock, but then grew rapidly for four consecutive years, peaking at over 16 million units in 1986. A rising tide lifts all boats and Chrysler benefited from this upswing, helped considerably by the right strategy in terms of product lineup in the form of the K cars and the Minivan, which were the right products for the prevailing conditions.

By the mid 1980s Chrysler was widely hailed as a great success story, which at one level of course it was, a case of recovery from extreme adversity. Importantly, from the point of view of the 'recovery' narrative, this was a time during which the Japanese automakers were advancing rapidly. Chrysler provided a story of fighting back, of the restoration of American prowess in the auto industry. Iacocca himself developed a very high public profile, appearing in person in Chrysler's TV commercials. He became one of the first global celebrity CEOs, publishing his autobiography (*Iacocca*) in 1984 and a follow up, *Talking Straight*, in 1988. He was renowned for his pro-American, anti-Japanese stance on many issues, a position that sat awkwardly with the fact that Chrysler's success partly relied on buying cars and components from Mitsubishi to be badged as Chrysler brands. During this period Chrysler extended its collaboration with Mitsubishi, forming 'Diamond-Star Motors' a joint venture company which built an assembly plant in the USA to produce both Chrysler and Mitsubishi models.

As Chrysler's financial health improved during the 1980s the company made a number of acquisitions. It acquired Gulfstream Aerospace, producers of corporate jets, in 1985 and Electrospace Systems, which produced communications equipment, in 1987. The declared intention of these acquisitions was to buffer Chrysler against the cyclicality of the automotive business.[5] Also in 1987 Chrysler acquired American Motors (AMC) for $1.5 billion, which became the Jeep-Eagle division of Chrysler. This brought the profitable Jeep brand into the Chrysler family, the Eagle brand being discontinued in 1998. The AMC acquisition also brought a potential early entry into the Chinese market though Beijing Jeep, AMC's joint venture in China, which had been initiated in 1979. This was one of the earliest forays into the Chinese auto market by a foreign automaker and perhaps was ahead of its time. By the mid 1990s Beijing Jeep accounted for around 10 per cent of the total Chinese market, but lack of investment and increasing liberalization of the market led to declining sales and in 2004 Beijing Jeep became Beijing Benz.

Chrysler acquired Lamborghini, the Italian maker of sports cars, in 1987 and also embarked on what turned out to be an expensive and ill-judged venture with Maserati. However, what Chrysler did *not* do was invest heavily in new models and technology at a time when its Japanese competitors were doing just that.[6]

The 1990s

The acquisitions of the late 1980s depleted Chrysler's working capital and as the US market on which Chrysler was so dependent turned down, as it did between 1986 and 1991 (see Figure 7.1), Chrysler's position quickly worsened with it. In late 1989 Chrysler announced that it would divest many of the companies that it had only recently acquired, beginning with Gulfstream and Electrospace. In a falling market, Chrysler once again faced financial difficulties, although not as acutely as in the late 1970s, and underwent a restructuring. Talks were held with Fiat of Italy about possible joint ventures, including the possibility of Fiat taking a stake in Chrysler, but ultimately these did not lead anywhere, although Chrysler agreed to distribute Alfa Romeos in the USA and did so from 1988 to 1995. Iaccoca also approached Ford to see if they would buy Chrysler, but Ford were not interested. The US car market reached the bottom of its cycle in 1991, with around 12.5 million units sold. Chrysler also hit the bottom in this year, selling only around 1.5 million units. In 1992, under pressure from the Board, Iaccoca, previously hailed as Chrysler's saviour, was forced into retirement. He was to reappear within three years as a party in an unsuccessful hostile takeover bid for Chrysler in 1995.

From 1991 through to 2000, the US market grew considerably, achieving an all-time high of 17.8 million units in 2000, an increase of 42 per cent from the trough of 1991. Chrysler's sales continued to be highly concentrated in the US market. Chrysler's product line-up of SUVs and pick-ups put the company in a good position to benefit from the booming demand for these products during the 1990s. Chrysler sales grew from the trough of 1991 to the peak in 1999 by a phenomenal +70 per cent. Also, although not large in volume terms, muscle cars like the Dodge Viper were good for the company's image amongst car enthusiasts, though not amongst environmentalists.

Back in the mid 1980s approximately two thirds of Chrysler's sales in the USA had been cars and one third 'trucks' (SUVS and pick-ups). By the mid 1990s this ratio was reversed (Ingrassia 2011). In a stroke of good fortune for Chrysler, Ford and GM, the Japanese auto producers initially failed to spot the rising demand for trucks and SUVs and as a consequence lost market share to their US competitors as the sales of these vehicles took off. Business books celebrating the turnaround and revival of the US auto industry began to appear, a marked contrast to the 1980s where a predominant theme amongst business commentators was how poorly the US auto producers performed relative to their Japanese counterparts.[7]

In the booming market of the 1990s Chrysler's profitability achieved record levels, independent surveys of quality showed considerable improvement in Chrysler's vehicles and Chrysler's product development processes, particularly its use of platform teams, attracted praise from industry analysts for the speed and efficiency with which they could bring new vehicles to market.[8] In 1997 *Forbes* magazine voted Chrysler 'Company of the Year', commenting:

> Think of them as buccaneers, fast, impudent, daring, flying the black flag, attacking and pillaging the big, slow Spanish galleons. That's Chrysler Corp., the Forbes Company of the Year ... we think the reality here is that Chrysler's good luck is being leveraged by a superb management team that has made smart, disciplined decisions.[9]

This was clearly a view shared at the time by Daimler in Germany which acquired Chrysler for $36 billion in 1998. Officially this was described at the time as a merger of equals, although the CEO of Daimler, Jürgen Schrempp, was later reported as saying that this was a ploy to make the deal acceptable to Chrysler. As we described in Chapter 2, the mood of the 1990s auto industry was very much that scale was critical to success and a spate of merger and acquisition activity was one consequence of this, manifested by the M&A activity of BMW and Rover, Nissan and Renault, GM and Fiat's alliance and the acquisition of premium brands such as Jaguar, Saab, Volvo and Land Rover by Ford and GM.

Merger with Daimler

Rather like BMW's acquisition of Rover, Daimler, by merging with Chrysler, added high-volume, mid-market products to its existing line up of premium products. The Daimler-Chrysler 1998 annual report described the new entity as: 'A new company with a proud combined heritage, with unparalleled products and brands, and with extraordinary opportunities that neither Daimler-Benz nor Chrysler alone could have dreamed of.'

The intention of the combined company was to achieve synergies across the board (valued at $1.4 billion for 1999), particularly in engineering and purchasing. The creation of a giant, truly global, car company was also clearly part of the agenda and in 2000 Daimler-Chrysler acquired a controlling interest in Mitsubishi Motors of Japan (a previous alliance partner of Chrysler) for US$ 1.9 billion, giving the company full operations in North America, Europe and Asia.

However, disappointment lay ahead. As has been documented in detail elsewhere[10] the hoped-for synergies failed to materialize. Reports of tensions and cross-cultural issues soon started to leak out of the merged firm. Daimler's uncompromising emphasis on technical excellence sat uncomfortably with the reality of Chrysler's mass market, build-to-a-price ethos. Like BMW and the acquisition of Rover, Daimler granted Chrysler considerable autonomy at the outset. However, as the peak of the US market passed, Daimler became increasingly concerned about Chrysler's dependency on trucks and SUVs and had increasing doubts about the strength of Chrysler's underlying capabilities. Far from achieving synergies, Chrysler's costs were actually rising, hitting earnings, which had a knock-on effect on Daimler-Chrysler's share price. In 2000, Chrysler lost $1.3 billion, at a time when the US auto market was at an all-time high (Figure 7.1). Bob Eaton, who had been Chrysler's CEO since 1992 took early retirement; his American successor lasted only a few months before he was dismissed and by the end of 2000 an executive from Daimler, Dieter Zetsche, became CEO of Chrysler. Zetsche began closing plants and cutting back production, further fuelling US–German tensions and leading some commentators to start referring to the company as 'Occupied Chrysler'.[11]

Chrysler enjoyed some product successes in the early 2000s (such as the PT Cruiser, launched in 2000 and the 300, launched in 2004) but by 2005 Chrysler was facing headwinds. Other companies now had products in the minivan market that Chrysler had previously dominated. Japanese producers were going after the SUV and trucks segments. Daimler executives were frustrated and concerned about Chrysler, not only for operational reasons, but also the high legacy health care and retirement costs that Chrysler, along with Ford and

GM, faced. By 2006 fuel prices were on the rise and Chrysler's continuing dependency on trucks and the US market began to assert itself. Chrysler lost $1.5 billion in the third quarter of 2006 and rumours that Daimler was seeking to sell Chrysler began to circulate.

Cerberus

These rumours were confirmed officially in early 2007. Initially, a number of potential purchasers were in play. One suitor, perhaps surprisingly given its own mounting difficulties, was GM who saw opportunities to add Chrysler's brands to its own collection whilst making big savings by eliminating duplicate functions. GM was prepared to offer Daimler 10 per cent of its shares in exchange for Chrysler, but a condition of GM's interest was that Chrysler agreed plant closures and changes to health care and pensions benefits with the UAW *before* any sale. Ingrassia describes the problem in a nutshell:[12] 'On the surface Chrysler was a powerful industrial machine that built and sold more than 2.6 million vehicles a year . . . but 90% of its sales were in the intensely competitive North American market.' Daimler was not prepared to let the UAW have a right of veto of the sale, so GM was out of the running. A new owner, given time, could revise the product portfolio and try and diversify into international markets, but the problem of long-term obligations for the health care of current employees and retirees was huge – and estimated at the time to be around $19 billion. Renault-Nissan and Hyundai also took a look at Chrysler, but neither proceeded.

In the end, the main parties interested in Chrysler were four private equity houses, of which two, Blackstone and Cerberus Capital Management, were the strongest contenders. Cerberus' view was that in early 2007 the auto industry was already at the bottom of the cycle, so that there was little downside to the deal. They believed that Daimler had mismanaged Chrysler by creating too much bureaucracy and by trying to force a higher volume of sales than the Chrysler brands and products could support. Over and above the business case for the acquisition, a certain degree of patriotism was evident in

Cerberus' position, with apparently genuine intentions of restoring an American icon by making Chrysler an American-owned company once more. In August 2007 Cerberus bought 80.1% of Chrysler for $7.4 billion (just 20% of what Daimler had paid nine years earlier). Daimler retained a 19.9% share and in addition contributed $650 million towards Chrysler's health care costs.[13]

Cerberus' ownership of Chrysler was to be short lived. Bob Nardelli, who had previously been CEO of Home Depot was brought in to lead Chrysler and to focus on taking out cost and restoring profitability. Slow-selling models were eliminated and there were further job losses. However, as the Chrysler–Cerberus deal was being finalized early signs of the impending financial crash were starting to show. The market for debt, Cerberus' main source of capital, had already started to dry up and a number of banks who were underwriting the debt ended up holding it themselves. This meant that Chrysler was lightly capitalized at the outset. There was therefore not much time available to execute a turnaround; already in a weak position, Chrysler was now extremely vulnerable to worsening market conditions.

Cerberus' plan had been to follow the standard private equity pattern of quick and vigorous change. However, they had embarked on this without apparently fully recognizing some of the difficulties and constraints that confronted them, leading to strained working relations within Chrysler. Chrysler's new product pipeline had been starved of investment whilst Daimler was searching for an exit, meaning that Chrysler desperately needed new models but had neither the time nor money to develop these itself. To address this, Chrysler sought a partner from whom it could buy and rebadge a small car (as it had done with Mitsubishi many years before), a move remarkably reminiscent of Rover's plight in the late 1970s.

Extensive discussions took place with Renault-Nissan, which demanded a 20 per cent stake in Chrysler in exchange for providing Chrysler with a model. This was a price Chrysler were not prepared to pay. Chrysler also had discussions with Fiat, with a view to Fiat providing a small car, and with GM, to whom they offered a full-blown merger. However, GM was in deep financial trouble of its own, and when news leaked out of the Chrysler–GM talks investors and analysts reacted negatively to the prospect of merger, effectively closing off that option. To make things even worse, Daimler began agitating to dispose of its remaining 19.9 per cent share in Chrysler. Cerberus, who thought that they had bought cheaply and near enough to the bottom of the cycle to weather any storm, were finding Chrysler such a burden that they were prepared to give the company away in order to be free of it.[14]

The second bailout: 2009

In September 2008 the global financial crisis began to really bite. Lehman Brothers went under, the US insurers American International Group (AIG) had to be bailed out by the US Government, as were the two major home loan companies Fannie Mae and Freddie Mac. In many countries across the world liquidity dried up. In the most exposed economies, banking systems were threatened with collapse. Outside of the financial sector, auto companies were particularly exposed to the crisis. Many auto purchases are made on credit, so sales plunged as credit tightened. Auto companies who operated their own finance and credit services (from which more money was often made than from the sale of the cars themselves) struggled to raise the capital they needed in order to advance loans to purchasers. And as share (stock) prices fell and consumer confidence collapsed, potential buyers deferred purchases – a toxic combination of conditions.

The 2008 financial crisis was unprecedented in its scale and reach, and profoundly affected many economies and industries. The extreme nature of the crisis and its impact on the auto industry shines a bright spotlight onto the auto industry dynamics and reveals much about the nature of resilience in the auto industry. The crisis represented a very deep 'trough' and therefore demonstrates, in exaggerated form, the issues that auto firms are likely to face at the bottom of any economic cycle. All auto firms suffered, including Toyota which made its first loss in 59 years.[15] However, the firms with the lowest cash reserves, mostly due to their inability to earn and retain sufficient resources during the good times, were the ones most exposed. It is at this point that the ability to call on stakeholder support is crucial – either from investors who provide additional equity or banks or other lenders who are willing and able to provide loans.

In late 2008 Chrysler and GM were both getting close to running out of cash to pay their bills. GM in particular claimed that their difficulties were due to circumstances beyond their control, but public confidence in the underlying ability of both companies to adequately manage themselves out of the crisis, even with financial support, had largely collapsed. On top of this, many financial institutions were themselves in trouble and not necessarily able to provide such support even if they had wanted to. Faced with this situation, the Big Three, led by GM, turned to the stakeholder of last resort – the US government.

In mid November 2008 the CEOs of GM, Ford and Chrysler, plus the head of the UAW went to Washington to argue their case for support under the Troubled Asset Relief Program (TARP) that had been set up by the US Government to support financial institutions in order to avoid a collapse of the financial system. Their first appearance, on 18 November, was before the Senate Committee on Banking, Housing and Urban Affairs. The hearing, in which the four were questioned by a mix of 21 Democrat and Republican senators, did not go well. The auto executives failed to convince the Committee that they had the situation under control, or even that they knew exactly how much state support would be needed to see them through the crisis.

A second hearing before the House Financial Services Committee held the next day was even worse. Overnight it had emerged that the three CEOs had each flown down from Detroit to Washington by private corporate jet. This received massive coverage in the media and the symbolism of private air travel sat very badly with requests for taxpayer support for the companies that the CEOs represented. Pro-market, anti-union Republicans considered government support for failing companies to be objectionable on principle. So was support for an industry whose troubles those on the right of the political spectrum saw as due to unsustainably favourable working conditions on the part of unionized labour. Democrats were concerned about levels of executive pay, particularly when plants were being closed and jobs cut – and of course the UAW was a major Democrat supporter. Environmentalists objected to Detroit's gas-guzzlers and long-term hostility and resistance to pro-environment policies. At this point, stakeholders who were supportive of the auto firms were noticeable primarily by their absence.

Ford, who had shown rather more foresight than GM or Chrysler, had raised money ahead of the crisis (partly by selling off its Aston-Martin, Jaguar and Land Rover subsidiaries, with Volvo to follow) and decided to go its own way without government support. It accepted a 'safety net' of government line of credit, but did not intend to use this unless it had to – and did not do so. Ford was subsequently to enjoy considerable public support for eschewing a bailout.

Congress was unable to reach agreement on the form and terms of a bailout so in December the outgoing President, George W. Bush, took executive action and announced $13.4 billion of government loans for GM and $4 billion for Chrysler. In a speech to the nation on 19 December Bush made it clear that:

> The terms of the loans will require auto companies to demonstrate how they would become viable. They must pay back all their loans to the government and show that their firms can earn a profit and achieve a positive net worth. This restructuring will require meaningful concessions from all involved in the auto industry – management, labor unions, creditors, bond holders, dealers, and suppliers. In particular, automakers must meet conditions that experts agree are necessary for long-term viability, including putting their retirement plans on a sustainable footing, persuading bond holders to convert their debt into capital that

companies need to address immediate financial shortfalls, and making their compensation competitive with foreign automakers who have major operations in the United States.

Chrysler and GM were given three months to come up with viable recovery plans. In January 2009 George Bush completed his term as President and Barak Obama succeeded him.

When the plans arrived, Chrysler was asking for an additional $5 billion in loans in addition to the $4 billion granted by Bush in December. The plan proposed that some older models be phased out, some assets sold and fixed costs reduced. However, it did not mention job cuts or plant closures. Future products were heavily dependent on an unspecified alliance with Fiat of Italy.

Obama had set up an automotive task force whose role was to evaluate the plans of GM and Chrysler and advise the President on the rescue. The task force did not deem Chrysler's plan to be viable.[16] On 30 March Obama announced that neither the GM nor Chrysler plans went far enough to justify further public investment, but he gave both companies more time to 'work with creditors, unions, and other stakeholders to fundamentally restructure in a way that would justify an investment of additional taxpayer dollars'. The conditions attached to Chrysler were tough. The task force concluded that Chrysler could only survive if it had an international partner – specifically, Fiat – and gave it 30 days to reach an agreement with Fiat. A successful agreement with Fiat, the President promised, could unlock up to a further $6 billion of government loans. Without this, there would be no support for Chrysler. Obama also sent a clear message that the Chapter 11 bankruptcy code could be used as a 'tool' to assist restructuring.

Thirty days later, on 30 April, Obama announced that Chrysler and Fiat would indeed be partners, and that Chrysler would enter Chapter 11 'to clear away its remaining obligations'. In a month of frantic negotiations Chrysler, Fiat and members of the Auto Task Force had, to use the language of our resilience model, managed to renegotiate Chrysler's 'settlements' with a whole range of stakeholders. With respect to *labour*, the bulk of health care liabilities were transferred to a VEBA (Voluntary Employee Beneficiary Association) with Chrysler donating 55 per cent of its (largely worthless) shares to this. Eight plants were to be closed, 10,000 further jobs cut and 800 dealerships axed.[17]

Financiers and previous owners also took a hit. Cerberus came away with nothing, having lost all its investment. The banks gave up about 70 per cent of the money they were owed by Chrysler; Daimler gave up its 19.9 per cent stake and made a further contribution to the VEBA. Fiat agreed to contribute technology in exchange for an initial 20 per cent stake. The Government of Canada, in which Chrysler has manufacturing facilities, also provided support.

President Obama described this surge of stakeholder support as follows:

> over the past month, seemingly insurmountable obstacles have been overcome, and Chrysler's most important stakeholders – from the United Auto Workers to Chrysler's largest lenders, from its former owners to its suppliers – have agreed to make major sacrifices ... Now, this partnership was only possible because of unprecedented sacrifices on the part of Chrysler's stakeholders, who are willing to give something up so that this company – and all of the men and women whose livelihoods depend on it –-might see a better day. Chrysler's management, and in particular, its CEO, Robert Nardelli, have played a positive and constructive role throughout this process. The United Auto Workers, who had already made painful concessions, agreed to further cuts in wages and benefits; cuts that will help Chrysler survive, making it possible for so many workers to keep their jobs and about 170,000 retirees and their families to keep their health care. Several major financial institutions, led by J.P. Morgan, agreed to reduce their debt to less than one-third of its face value to help free Chrysler from its crushing obligations. The German automaker, Daimler,

agreed to give up its stake in Chrysler and contribute to the company's pension plan, further easing Chrysler's financial burden. And countless Americans across our country will be making major sacrifices, as well, as a result of plans to consolidate dealers, brands, and product lines.

Whatever the politics behind this statement, the basic facts are clear – that as Chrysler hit bottom, some very deep, long-established stakeholder 'settlements' were fundamentally re-written. Chrysler had survived.

Commentary

The Chrysler story is a fascinating case of crisis and resilience, not least because the company has been in and out of crisis so often. Chrysler provides a powerful illustration of the various factors that can both support and undermine resilience.

In terms of Chrysler's operations and management, the picture is certainly not all bad – bear in mind that in 1997 Chrysler won the *Forbes* 'Company of the Year' award and was praised for 'a superb management team that has made smart, disciplined decisions'. Not all the company's products have been successful and product quality has, at times, certainly not been class-leading. But at times in its life Chrysler has been able to develop and produce models that have been innovative and market-leading in their own ways, and have sold well – the front wheel drive 'K' cars, the minivan and the Chrysler 300 for example. During some periods in its history Chrysler's business processes have been held up as a shining example – for example its product development processes in the 1990s. All of which suggests that, although they are not consistently class-leading, it is apparent that Chrysler's operational processes per se do not tell the whole story of why the company has repeatedly faced crises.

Market reach, however, has clearly been a long-term issue for Chrysler. Chrysler remained focused on the North American market and did not venture into what was for a while the major growth market in the world – Western Europe – until the 1960s. This was 40 years or more behind Ford and GM, by which time most of the companies available for acquisition were, in the words of Chrysler's then CEO, 'dogs'. Unsurprisingly, Chrysler's venture into Europe was unsuccessful, leading Chrysler to withdraw from Europe in the late 1970s after years of losses.

Chrysler had a relatively early relationship with a Japanese auto producer via its activities with Mitsubishi Motors, but there is little evidence that it was able to learn a great deal from Mitsubishi – an opportunity forgone. Its acquisition of AMC gave Chrysler a very early entry into China – perhaps too early, in that doing business in China was very much uncharted water in those days – but the opportunities offered by being an early mover in China appear to have been lost.

The net effect is that for most of its life Chrysler has been an auto company that predominantly produces and sells cars in North America. It has therefore been very exposed to the swings of the US auto market, which was the first car market in the world to reach full maturity and which since the 1960s has been characterized by considerable cyclicality, driven by the economic cycle. Although Ford and GM have also been exposed to this cyclicality, Chrysler has lacked the cushioning effect of Ford and GM's international markets and operations.

Along with Ford and GM, Chrysler has suffered as Japanese auto producers have taken a progressively larger share of the North American market. Areas in which Chrysler has had strength have tended to be in the larger segments (Minivans, pick-ups and SUVs) in which demand is perhaps even more vulnerable to the economic cycle than in other segments – the K car of the 1980s was really the main exception to this. Consequently, when the 2008 financial crisis hit, Chrysler was particularly poorly placed to weather it. As the smallest and weakest of the Big Three, Chrysler faces a greater challenge in resourcing the development of a full range of competitive vehicles compared to its larger competitors.

These factors together go some way towards explaining Chrysler's relatively precarious position, but how has Chrysler continued to survive not one, but two, near-death experiences? The answer to this seems to lie in stakeholder support. In both 1979 and 2009 there was a remarkable mobilization of stakeholder support, including from government. At first sight this seems rather paradoxical – as a fierce proponent of free market principles, the USA would be one of the last places one would expect to see a government bailout of a failed company. Bush's announcement of the first tranche of aid (19 December 2008) is revealing in this respect:

> On the one hand, government has the responsibility not to
> undermine the private enterprise system. On the other hand,
> government has a responsibility to safeguard the broader
> health and stability of our economy. Addressing the challenges
> in the auto industry requires us to balance these two
> responsibilities. If we were to allow the free market to take its
> course now, it would almost certainly lead to disorderly bankruptcy
> and liquidation for the automakers. Under ordinary economic
> circumstances, I would say this is the price that failed companies
> must pay. And I would not favor intervening to prevent the
> automakers from going out of business. But these are not ordinary
> circumstances.

Here the message is one of 'extraordinary circumstances demanding extraordinary measures', hence paving the way for invention, despite an ideological aversion to such action. Obama largely maintained this line, by making support contingent on a set of reforms so difficult and painful (the funding of employee and retiree health care, for example) that generations of executives and union leaders within the auto industry had shied away from them. In his speech of 30 April 2009 Obama invoked a sense of national interest and pride to legitimate the rescue of Chrysler:

> Now, these are challenging times for America's auto industry
> and for the American people. But I am confident that if we as a
> nation can act with the same sense of shared sacrifice and shared

purpose that's been shown by so many of Chrysler's stakeholders, if we can embrace the idea that we're all in it together – from the union hall to the boardroom to the halls of Congress – then we will succeed not only with Chrysler, we will not only see our American auto industry rise again, but we will rebuild our entire economy and make the 21st century another American Century. We have made great progress. We can make great American cars. Chrysler and GM are going to come back. And I am very confident that we're going to be able to make once again the U.S. auto industry the best auto industry in the world.

Of course, political rhetoric may be one thing and concrete action another, but a cross section of US stakeholders – labour, financiers and others – did indeed make sacrifices, albeit under intense pressure from the US Government, to enable Chrysler to survive. We argue that fundamentally it was this re-writing of stakeholder settlements that prevented Chrysler from going under in both 1979 and 2009.

NISSAN: THE POWER OF ALLIANCE

In 1999 Nissan faced bankruptcy. For the previous two decades Japanese superiority in manufacturing had been widely publicized, as we described in Chapter 2. Yet now the second largest Japanese car manufacturer was in financial difficulty and subject to a foreign takeover. Often, ailing Japanese companies had been rescued by their 'keiretsu' partners. With Nissan this was not the case, partly because the group of which it was a part, headed by the Fuji Bank, was itself in a weak position in the late 1990s. The takeover of Nissan by a foreign company came as a profound shock to the Japanese public.

Background to the crisis

The crisis at Nissan in 1999 had a long gestation period. After the Second World War many Japanese manufacturers benefited from funds that were available to support exports and national economic growth. Nissan, which through its wartime assistance to the military found itself close to the source of these funds, used them to build up substantial production capacity. The easy availability of these funds meant that profitability was not necessarily an overriding priority. When the Japanese bubble burst in 1990 and the Japanese auto market started to contract, Nissan was burdened with overcapacity and, crucially, a lack of experience in managing costs and financial performance under difficult conditions. Nissan lost global market share in almost every year during the 1990s, its production dropped, and in seven out of the eight years of the 1990s the company suffered serious financial losses. It was not that one single event triggered the crisis at Nissan; rather that the situation by the late 1990s was a culmination of a gradual erosion of competitiveness.

The alliance with Renault

The alliance between Nissan and Renault, signed on 27 March 1999, is the largest scale and most enduring example of a tie-up to date. As part of this alliance, Renault initially acquired 36.8 per cent of Nissan stock, which was increased to 44.4 per cent in 2001, when Nissan also acquired 15 per cent of Renault's stock. A principle at the outset was that the two brands should retain their individual identities and brand names, but share expertise and areas of strength in areas where it made sense to do so; for Renault these lay in design and management, for Nissan manufacturing and engineering.

There were five main causes for Nissan's distressed financial state, which were described in the 1999 Nissan Revival Plan (NRP). These were:

(1) a lack of a clear profit orientation
(2) an insufficient focus on customers and a misplaced preoccupation with chasing competitors
(3) lack of cross-functional, cross-border and intra-hierarchical lines in the company[18]
(4) lack of a sense of urgency, and
(5) absence of shared vision or common long-term plan.

The NRP proposed far-reaching restructuring measures designed to address these five problems. New product development was placed at the heart of Nissan's revival. A key objective was to release resources from non-strategic, non-core activities and re-invest these in Nissan's core business, while at the same time reducing Nissan's debt. The initial timeframe set for achieving these ambitious goals was three years.

A key phrase of the NRP was *reduction*. The plan was to reduce purchasing costs by 20%; product development lead times by 50%; the number of platforms in use by 50%; the number of manufacturing plants in Japan from seven to four; capacity by 30%, administration and sales costs by 20%; distribution subsidiaries by 20%; and total retail outlets by 10%. In addition, fixed overhead costs were reduced, global financial operations were centralized, 21,000 jobs cut world-wide, and land, securities, and non-core assets shed. In Japan itself, the most radical reform proposed by the NRP was the cutting of keiretsu ties with Nissan suppliers, an important part of the very fabric of buyer–supplier relations in much of the Japanese auto industry. Nissan planned to reduce the number of affiliated companies in which it held shares from 1,394 to only 4 – a clear dismantling of Nissan's keiretsu in pursuit of more competitive, cost-effective parts supply. In the terms of our model, this represented a breaking of existing stakeholder settlements, in this case settlements with suppliers.

Benefits of the alliance

The alliance provided Nissan with benefits at a number of levels. First and foremost, it provided new capital. Without this Nissan would have run out of cash completely, with catastrophic consequences. Operationally, the alliance offered the opportunity for the two companies to share platforms, reducing development and manufacturing costs and also to reap benefits from economies of scale in purchasing. Furthermore, the global market reach of the combined company was increased considerably – Renault's strengths in Europe and Latin America complemented Nissan's in Japan, the USA and China. The

Alliance had much better coverage of global markets, important both for scale and also as a hedge against economic peaks and troughs in particular regions and markets.

A further dimension to the alliance concerned the politics and process of change. Being strongly embedded in the keiretsu system with its associated obligations and relationships, Nissan executives inevitably found it difficult to reform these from within. The perception in Japan that it was easier for a foreigner, someone from outside the system, to execute the necessary reforms – to close plants, reduce capacity in Japan and shake up suppliers. Carlos Ghosn, Renault's CEO who was nicknamed 'le cost cutter', was able to do this.

From 1999 onwards Nissan engaged in vigorous cost cutting, closed three out of seven domestic manufacturing plants and sold off non-core assets. By 2001 Nissan had reinvigorated its financial situation and achieved the Revival Plan one year ahead of schedule. Also in 2001, the alliance established the Renault-Nissan Purchasing Organization (RNPO), a joint purchasing company tasked with driving and developing purchasing strategy for both companies, and Carlos Ghosn who up to then had been Nissan's COO was appointed President and Chief Executive Officer of Nissan, a position which, at the time of writing in 2015, he holds concurrently with that of CEO of Renault.

In 2002, Nissan acquired a 15 per cent equity stake in Renault and Renault increased its stake in Nissan to 43.4 per cent. Formed on 28 March 2002, Renault-Nissan BV[19] was set up, equally owned by Renault and Nissan, responsible for the strategic management of the Renault-Nissan Alliance (RNA). From its inception Renault-Nissan BV was tasked with managing two joint companies; the RNPO, mentioned above, and RNIS (Renault-Nissan Information Services) which was tasked with designing and operating the Alliance's information systems.

When the RNPO was initially set up, the costs of similar components sourced by both Renault and Nissan from the same sources were compared. The conclusion was that Nissan was paying up to

20 per cent more than Renault for equivalent parts. Although Japan's historically close ties between buyers and suppliers have generally been assumed to have a positive impact on performance, when one of our doctoral students, Merieke Stevens, interviewed CEO Carlos Ghosn in 2001 his evaluation of Nissan's keiretsu system was rather different to the conventional wisdom at the time. Ghosn commented: 'Nissan was abused by its suppliers by not delivering their best performance ... the obligation to buy from suppliers in which Nissan held shares confused supplier ties.'[20] The Nissan vice president for supply chain management held a similar position:

> There is no doubt that at the end of '99 the performance of Nissan suppliers was terrible. Certainly in terms of ... to what extent they shared the benefits with Nissan ... Nissan was getting a bad deal, either because the supplier was poor, or because the supplier was taking most of the benefit.[21]

Ghosn argued that 'cosiness' had led to complacency, and that a lack of monitoring of suppliers had resulted in a purchasing price disadvantage relative to Renault, a view echoed by the vice president for supply chain management:

> The pre-99 situation was unsustainable in its cosiness and its inefficiency because of a lack of tension ... It was far too comfortable ... there wasn't any tension to promote performance improvement ... In a situation where relationships will be too long term there are barriers to entry [for] some of the new suppliers or more agile suppliers ... Can you imagine in this situation of high trust the sourcing of components in low cost countries, or leading cost countries? It would not have happened ... because there is no drive, no impetus to change.[22]

In an attempt to reduce its costs, Nissan sold its shares in most of its keiretsu suppliers and requested that they reduce costs by 30 per cent over three years. (See Stevens (2010) for a detailed account how as part of these reforms Nissan overhauled the organization of its purchasing department.) The previous system whereby purchasers had been in charge of individual supplier firms disappeared and purchasing managers were put in charge of product groups and given clear individual performance indicators based on purchasing cost reductions. Previous personal ties between Nissan staff and suppliers were discouraged. In 2001 for example, all the traditional midyear gifts received by Nissan staff from suppliers were returned, with a note that these would not be accepted any more. None were sent the following year. The purchasing cost reduction target of 30 per cent announced in 1999 was in fact achieved in 2001.

In the case of BLMC/Rover in Chapter 5 we saw how the merged company struggled to rationalize and integrate its operations following the 1968 merger. In the RNA there is a dedicated team which focuses on 16 areas identified as priorities for cooperation. These include joint powertrains, common module technology and platforms, research and advanced engineering, manufacturing, purchasing, IT and marketing. RNA estimated the total synergies of the Alliance were £2.1bn in 2012 (£1.6bn of which was product related), and are expected to further increase over the coming years (estimated at £4bn in 2016).

Centres of excellence are based around the two companies' historic areas of expertise; Renault specializes in diesel engines and manual transmissions, while Nissan specializes in gasoline engines and automatic transmissions. Rachel Konrad, an RNA spokeswoman, stated their objective: 'We have an internal goal of 4 billion euros in synergies in 2016' (Bloomberg 2012). With respect to the integration of production, Table 7.1 shows the countries in which the Alliance has manufacturing operations, either in vehicle assembly or powertrain. Given that the two companies were both large and mature prior to establishing their alliance, the modest degree of overlap is quite remarkable.

In 2013, the Alliance had manufacturing operations in 29 countries. Renault had a presence in 16 of these, Nissan in 19, meaning that manufacturing is only duplicated in 6 countries, with the

Table 7.1 *Renault-Nissan production sites. Source: Renault-Nissan Alliance (2013)*

Country	Renault Group products	Nissan products	Vehicle assembly	Powertrain manufacture
Europe				
France	x		x	x
Portugal	x			x
Romania	x		x	x
Russia	x	x	x	
Slovenia	x		x	x
Spain	x	x	x	x
Turkey	x		x	x
United Kingdom		x	x	x
Americas				
Argentina	x		x	x
Brazil	x	x	x	x
Chile	x			x
Colombia	x		x	
Mexico		x	x	x
United States		x	x	x
Africa				
Egypt		x	x	
Kenya		x	x	
Morocco	x		x	
South Africa	x	x	x	x
Asia				
China		x	x	
India	x	x	x	x
Indonesia		x	x	
Iran	x		x	
Japan		x	x	x
Malaysia		x	x	x
Philippines		x	x	x
South Korea	x	x	x	x
Taiwan		x	x	x
Thailand		x	x	x
Vietnam		x	x	

associated benefits in terms of costs. In terms of their manufacturing footprint at least, Renault-Nissan appears to have found a balance of maximum reach from near-minimum resources.

The Alliance started making extensive use of platform sharing, the advantages of which were described Chapter 2. Launched in 2002, Nissan's small car, sold as the March in Japan and the Micra in Europe, was the first vehicle built on the common 'B' platform, and by the end of that year five different Alliance models were built on this platform. The expansion of B platform vehicles at Renault and Nissan was further driven in subsequent years by the use of common powertrain and electronics components. In 2012, no fewer than 37 models were built on the B platform. RNA-wide platform development and sharing has been further expanded since the inception of the B platform. For example the joint 'C' platform is the basis for the Renault Megane, Scenic and Fluence models, as well as the Nissan Qashqai and Rogue. For 2013, the alliance plans to build 26 models on this C platform. By the end of the decade, the vast majority of the Alliance's production volume will be based on only 4 platforms: the B platform and its successor the B2 platform, the C and its successor the CMF1 platform, and the D and V platforms, with each of these platforms carrying between 1–2 million units per annum.

Since 2009, RNA has been working on a new philosophy for common parts, named 'Common Module Family' or CMF. In this context, modules are a set of parts and derivatives that can be applied to different car models and powertrains, which require common mechanical and electronic architecture. The common module family technology is expected to cut engineering and process costs 30–40 percent and spending on parts 20–30 per cent by 2020 (*Automotive News*, 2013).

RNPO is the Alliance's largest common organization, and is responsible for the Alliance's purchasing strategy. It is tasked with negotiating prices with suppliers on behalf of both Renault and Nissan. RNPO has delivered significant financial benefit for the Alliance. Since 2009, RNPO has handled all of Renault and Nissan's purchasing, compared to just 30 per cent shared purchasing in 2001. RNA states: 'Our aim is to cut the number of our suppliers globally as we develop our product line at the international level' (*Automotive News*, 2013). Common module family technology is expected to reduce the expenditure on components between 20–30 per cent by 2020.

According to Renault-Nissan BV, further non-product synergies are achieved in the areas of logistics, customs and trade, and information systems infrastructure. In the area of logistics, a unified team is tasked with commonizing packing, shipping and other logistical functions achieving €220 million in synergies in 2011. A dedicated customs and trade team has reduced customs duties and administrative costs that each company incurred separately, and the estimated synergies amount to approximately €50 million. Renault and Nissan also share common information systems infrastructure, data centres and licences.

In terms of financial outcome, the Alliance has stabilized both firms' performance, as Figure 7. 3 shows. While the global financial crisis did leave a considerable mark, as it did for virtually all car firms, overall financial performance since 2000 has returned to levels comparable to the industry average.

Commentary

The Nissan case is revealing, in terms of both precursors to crisis and to recovery from it. Operationally, Nissan performed reasonably well on measures of manufacturing efficiency and product quality in the decades leading up to the crisis, although it lagged Toyota, the class leader, and motoring aficionados regarded many of its products as rather dull, albeit worthy and reliable. Consistent with our arguments in Chapter 4, Nissan does not appear to represent a case in which a fundamental inability to design and build cars to competitive standards was responsible for the company's near-failure.

Rather, Nissan is an example of a company in which constraints on change and adaptation led it to slide slowly, almost imperceptibly towards a financial crisis, aggravated in the 1990s by the stagnation of

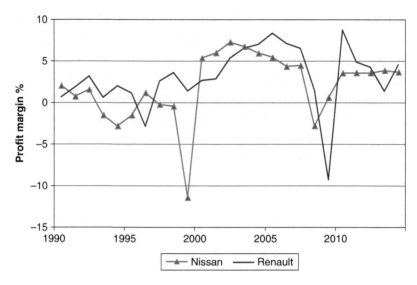

FIGURE 7.3 Profit margins at Renault and Nissan since 1990
Source: Annual reports

the Japanese economy. In this respect, the very strength of certain stakeholder relations – particularly with suppliers, and to some extent labour – may have discouraged earlier adjustments, and therefore meant that adjustment, when it came, had to be all the more brutal. It was easier for an outsider, in the form of Ghosn, to break existing stakeholder settlements (for example with suppliers, by bringing to an end Nissan's close, cooperative relations with its suppliers, and with labour in the form of job cuts and plant closures in Japan) than it was for those who were part of the system to do so – an observation which commentators have also made about labour relations and the GM and Chrysler rescues. The breaking of these settlements, particularly with suppliers, released resources that eased Nissan's financial position, albeit at the expense of the suppliers, and permitted investment in future models.

Also significant have been economies of scale, achieved through joint activity between the two companies – via platform sharing, joint purchasing and other activities. In market terms, Renault's market strength in Europe complements Nissan's in Asia and North and

South America. However, aside from Nissan's Infiniti luxury brand and Renault's low-cost Dacia brand, both Renault and Nissan operate in intensely competitive mid-market segments where margins can be lean.

Finally, one of the most remarkable features of the Alliance, which is in its 16th year as we go to press, is how successful and enduring it has been – an unusual achievement in an industry that is littered with failed merges and alliances. Our interpretation of this is that the Renault-Nissan Alliance has rather delicately managed to navigate its way through many of the obstacles that often trip up mergers, acquisitions and alliances between automakers. It has kept the two brands separate (perhaps helped by limited regional overlap of markets at the outset) which has meant otherwise painful and political rationalization and integration has been avoided. It has managed to realize economies of scale in some areas (such as purchasing and platform-sharing) allowing scale economies comparable to those of the largest car companies in the world. This has been facilitated by the fact that the respective powertrain architectures are very similar, and by the fact that the brand positioning of the two companies is not so different so as to make such sharing problematic (as was the case with BMW and Rover, or Daimler and Chrysler, for example). In doing so, Renault-Nissan appears to have found an effective approach to resolving the economies of scale vs market reach dilemma.

OVERVIEW OF CRISES

Chrysler and Nissan are just two examples of major crises that have occurred in the global automotive industry since 1945. To conclude this chapter, we review a cross section of major crises experienced by car firms around the world in the post-war period (see Table 7.2). The table is not exhaustive, but is rather intended to illustrate actual and near-bankruptcies, that is, events sufficiently serious to threaten the continued existence of an auto company. We have used 'chronic shortage of cash' as our ultimate indicator of crisis – the point at which a company has used all its capital and is at, or close to, the

Table 7.2 *Examples of crises and bankruptcies in the global car industry since 1945*

Year	Firm	Reasons for the bankruptcy or near-bankruptcy
1949–50	Toyota	Reduced credit and recession lead to drastic reduction in demand. Toyota is forced into using redundancies to downsize. Manufacturing and Sales companies are split, and remain so until 1982. Toyota returned to profitability as the Japanese market picked up again, and did not post an operating loss again until 2009.
1958–59	BMW	In 1958 BMW's losses meant that it only narrowly avoided a takeover by Daimler-Benz. Capital for new products was provided by Herbert Quandt. The new 1600, 1800, 2000 series BMW models launched in 1961, and became a commercial success.
1975	BLMC	The failing national car champion was nationalized after a series of loss-making years. Cash injection for 'product-led recovery'.
1979–80	Chrysler	In 1979, Chrysler ran out of cash and was forced to turn to the US Government for support. A $3.6 billion aid package was provided. The funds supported the development of the K-car.
1992	Volkswagen	Following Carl Hahn's expansion strategy in the late 1980s, the recession of 1990 left VW 'two weeks away from bankruptcy'. New CEO, reduction in headcount, cuts in prices to suppliers, consolidation of product development, cost reduction.
1997	Kia	In 1997, Kia was pushed into bankruptcy protection due to its large debt. It faced production overcapacity and the Asian financial crisis provided a trigger. Hyundai's acquisition of Kia Motors in 1998 marked the beginning of the company's turnaround. A wide-ranging

Table 7.2 (*cont.*)

Year	Firm	Reasons for the bankruptcy or near-bankruptcy
		restructuring programme led to the closure or sale of under-performing affiliates.
1999	Nissan	Nissan made losses every year from 1993, apart from 1997. With poor sales in key markets, Nissan's corporate debt spiralled and by 1999 Nissan was struggling to raise more capital. Merger discussions took place with Ford and DaimlerChrysler, until Nissan entered an alliance with Renault in 1999.
2001–04	Fiat	Fiat was loss-making from 2001 to 2004, losing €4.8bn pre-tax in 2002 alone. It recapitalized in 2003, and in 2005 GM paid US$2bn to exit from a planned merger between the two firms.
2005	MG Rover	MG Rover ran out of cash as sales declined and no partner could be found. The firm was liquidated and the remaining assets auctioned off to Nanjing Automotive.
2008–10	GM	The global financial crisis of 2007–8 causes sales of autos to fall dramatically, particularly in the US market. GM loses US$30.9bn in 2008, and turns to the US Government for aid. It seeks Chapter 11 bankruptcy protection by June 2009. The US Government provides US$51bn in funds, which GM repays by April 2010.
2008–11	Chrysler	Chrysler, then owned by Cerberus, a private equity house, runs out of cash and turns to the US Government for aid. It enters Chapter 11 in April 2009, and receives a total US$12.5bn in government funds, conditional on a partnership with Fiat.
2009–11	Saab	As part of its global restructuring under Chapter 11, GM sells Saab to Dutch sports car maker Spyker. Spyker fails to restore sales and runs out of cash. No new investor can be found and Saab declares bankruptcy in 2011.

Table 7.2 (cont.)

Year	Firm	Reasons for the bankruptcy or near-bankruptcy
2014	Peugeot-Citroën	Following losses during 2008–9, PSA briefly returns to profit but loses €5bn in 2012, and €2.3bn in 2013. The French Government initially provides a €3bn bridging loan, and in 2014 agrees to a take a part-stake (14%) in PSA. PSA's Chinese JV partner Dongfeng takes the same share in the firm (14%).

limit of its ability to raise more. It is at this point in time that the stricken firm starts consuming its assets to sustain its operations (e.g. by selling off parts of the firm), something which clearly is not sustainable. There are of course other events that may be labelled crises, such as major financial losses in a particular period, large-scale recalls, safety or quality issues, industrial action, but these do not necessarily pose an immediate threat to the continued survival of the firm.

Our purpose in exploring this broader range of crises is to gauge the extent to which our four cases of failure and survival – Rover, Saab, Chrysler and Nissan – exhibit patterns that are found more widely across the auto industry.

A number of points emerge from Table 7.2. The first point concerns the sheer range of car companies that appear in the table. These include car makers who had reasonable, and sometimes very good, products at the time they experienced the crisis. This lends support to one of our main arguments, namely that neither the experience of crisis, nor the ability to survive it, map cleanly onto the fundamental ability of auto companies to design, make and sell cars competitively. There are clearly other factors in the mix, some of which may link back to decisions made – or avoided – many years previously, some of which may be due to the nature of the auto industry itself, such as its persistent overcapacity which erodes profitability, and the vulnerability of car sales to economic cycles.

While the reasons for entering a crisis are common – generally an economic recession in key markets – there are several exit routes from the crisis periods that we can observe. First and foremost, and virtually inevitable in any case, is internal reform. A stricken firm generally suffers from cash-burn, and thus needs to reduce its cost base. VW, Toyota and Fiat[23] are good examples of how this has been achieved. Recovery in these cases is generally a combination of the economy recovering, reduced cost, and new models coming online. Second is the route through merger, whereby the stricken firm joins forces with, or is taken over by, a competitor. Nissan, Kia, Chrysler (in 2009) and PSA are examples of this route. Renault-Nissan and Kia are two examples where mergers have presented a viable route; however, as we will discuss in the next chapter, while mergers provide access to capital and expertise, they only appear to offer a lasting solution under certain, rather unusual, conditions. Third is the route of seeking stakeholder, typically, state support, as in the case of Rover (1975), Chrysler (1979 and 2009), GM (2009) and PSA (2014). The state can be a guarantor for survival, however it is also bound by changes in government (as happened in the case of the Thatcher government, where privatization became a mantra) and regulation (e.g. through EU competition laws). Finally, there is the possibility of liquidation, as in the case of Rover and Saab, discussed in the previous chapters.

In our 13 examples of crises, we observe 11 successful recoveries. In only two cases – Toyota and VW – was survival effected by internal reform, and even then in both cases there was a change of CEO. Thus, the evidence strongly suggests the need for external resources – which may be capital, know-how, or simply a fresh perspective – for the recovery of a stricken company. Four crises were resolved through some form of merger, acquisition or alliance and five by state support. PSA, and Chrysler's 2009 rescue, each involved a combination of both these, with a tie up with Fiat in Chrysler's case and with Dongfeng in the case of PSA. If BMW and Fiat are also classified as companies that received external support, then 9 of the 11 crises were resolved with external assistance – an overwhelming majority. This assistance can come from difference sources (the French Government and a Chinese automaker in the case of PSA, or close shareholders as in the case of BMW), and be given for very different reasons (preserving jobs in France or acquiring an option on a European auto brand). From the point of view of a stricken company, the key issue is the ability to secure such assistance. It is instructive to note that the final months of Rover and Saab were dominated by desperate, and ultimately fruitless, searches for a partner. Our two major cases of survival, Nissan and Chrysler, both survived because they were able to find such a partner.

Having examined two failures and two 'near misses' in detail we shall now draw the threads together and consider the implications of our findings for the future shape of the auto industry.

8 The future shape of the industry

In this chapter we revisit our key findings and lay out the implications of these for understanding crisis, resilience and survival in the auto industry. We shall first look at what our cases show about how auto firms get into crisis, and then how they get out of a crisis – or fail to do so. We then present a 'resilience index' that – by drawing on information from a variety of publicly available sources – quantifies the likely resilience and the strategic vulnerabilities of the world's major car companies. We then look at the implications of a major disruption in the industry – such as a significant shift towards alternative powertrains – for the resilience of existing auto companies.

WHY DO AUTO FIRMS GET INTO CRISIS?

Our argument thus far has been that many analyses of the auto industry, implicitly or explicitly, assume that resilience, failure and survival can be explained by the capability of car companies to design, make and sell cars to competitive standards. This view is persuasive and is based on a Darwinian notion of survival-of-the-fittest. We accept that such capabilities are significant, but of themselves they only go so far in explaining the current shape of the auto industry, and are limited in their ability to predict the future shape of the industry. To provide a more comprehensive picture, we must invoke a number of additional factors (explained in full in Chapter 4) if we are to understand the survival prospects of an auto firm.

The first is the industry characteristic of *overcapacity*. The economic, social and symbolic importance of car manufacturing means that there are strong incentives to establish car manufacturing operations and even stronger obstacles to closing them, over and above the market forces of supply and demand. Thus nations whose

259

markets are large enough may use market access as a bargaining counter in order to pressure global car makers to manufacture locally and to force technology transfer with nascent local firms, as China has been doing since the mid 1980s. On the other hand, try as they might, not all governments can overcome global economic conditions and 'force' the development of a local car industry. In 2014, Toyota's announcement that it was to join Ford and GM and end car making in Australia marked the end of over 60 years of car making in the country – but without tariff barriers and other incentives, it is questionable whether Australia would ever have had a car industry of the scale that it once was, for as long as it did.[1]

The effect of these forces, coupled in some cases with the agendas of the owners of car companies (some of whom may have objectives other than short- to medium-term return on investment), has been to create and sustain long-term overcapacity in the industry. Even in emerging markets that are growing quickly there is a tendency for global car makers to pile in rapidly, leading to over-supply if an economy temporarily falters.

This overcapacity interacts with two further characteristics of the auto industry, namely its high fixed costs and the susceptibility of demand for cars to rise and fall with the economic cycle. This puts automakers in a difficult position. First, persistent overcapacity erodes margins because globally there are too many car makers, with too much capacity, chasing too few customers – even accounting for the fact that global demand has grown enormously and more or less continuously since 1945 (see Figure 2.1) with average annual growth in production of 2.5 per cent since 1960. Thus, the margins of most car companies are not particularly high. Second, the susceptibility of auto demand to the economic cycle means that car makers experience significant peaks and troughs in sales – coupled with modest margins, losses during downturns in demand are almost inevitable. A loss in a downturn is not necessarily a problem as long as sufficient money is earned during the good times to provide cover during the bad, but if not, periodic cash crises can ensue. A company such as Chrysler represents an extreme example of this problem, and in Chrysler's case largely explains the company's characteristic boom-and-bust cycle.

However, although overcapacity and cyclicality explain the vulnerability of car companies at the bottom of the economic cycle, they are not the whole story. Some car companies experience financial crises more often, and more profoundly, than others. Why is this? At least two other factors come into play, which are captured by the concept of *market reach*. The auto market is huge and global – 68 million passenger cars and 22 million commercial vehicles in 2014. But these aggregate figures hide a plethora of different vehicle segments, as well as a multitude of national and regional markets. Competition is more intense in some segments than others, and therefore margins are lower. Some segments may boom whilst others stagnate or decline. The same goes for national economies – in 2009 demand for vehicles (cars and light trucks) in the USA fell to around 10 million units, which represented a huge drop compared to its peak of around 17 million units in 2006 – but whilst this was happening, growth in the Chinese market roared ahead.

What this means is that the sales footprint of car companies has a profound effect on their profitability and on the overall volatility of demand that they face. Companies whose products occupy segments where there are few credible competitors (for example the German premium brands such as BMW, Mercedes and Audi) or have a strong presence in markets where demand is buoyant (e.g. VW and GM in China) are all likely to enjoy better margins than those which do not. In the case of volatility of demand, companies whose sales are concentrated in particular countries, regions or segments will enjoy the effects of local booms but suffer the consequences of busts much more profoundly than those which have a more dispersed sales footprint. Again, Chrysler is a case in point. It has always been very dependent on the North American market, with around 80 per cent of its sales there. The North American auto market is profoundly cyclical (Figure 7.1) and Chrysler's rising and falling sales obviously reflect this. But Chrysler's products are also concentrated in the larger sedan, light truck and

SUV segments, which although enjoying higher margins in the good times tend to suffer dramatic declines in demand in the bad times. Saab was very dependent on two fairly large, semi-premium models, with sales concentrated in just three markets – Sweden, the UK and the USA, all of which suffered badly during the financial crisis. Saab's new owner in 2010 was a small, lightly capitalized entrepreneurial firm so it is not surprising that the money ran out before market demand recovered – especially as Saab was financially marginal, at best, even during less troubled times.

Combined with long-term overcapacity, market reach goes some way to explaining why some auto firms are resilient and others susceptible to crisis and why this vulnerability may, at a particular point in time, be only loosely connected to a company's ability to design and build cars. It could of course be argued that being in a poor position with respect to market reach is not a failure of operations but a failure of strategy, through poor decisions about product portfolios and target markets. This is a persuasive argument, which highlights other critical features of the auto industry, namely *lag* and *path dependency*, that is, how decisions made in the past have a constraining effect in the future. Entering a new auto market is a significant undertaking, involving understanding and conforming to local tastes and regulatory conditions, establishing distribution, service and parts networks and building product and brand awareness. There may be windows of opportunity as auto markets develop which mean that it is easier to develop a presence in a market at certain times, after which gaining a foothold is much harder. This was clearly the case with BLMC/Rover, and the UK car industry as a whole, which for too long focused on soft, empire markets for exports to the neglect of the rapidly growing continental European market – a position aggravated by the UK's exclusion from the European Common Market in the 1960s. As markets liberalized in the 1960s and 1970s BLMC (Rover) found its preferential access to the empire markets disappearing, just as the increasingly capable Japanese auto companies began to push overseas. Continental European competitors had recovered from the war and were much stronger, and were experienced in producing appropriate vehicles for the continental European market. At the same time BLMC started to feel the full brunt of foreign competition in its home market. In BLMC's case there were also genuine deficiencies in their ability to design and produce cars competitively, exacerbated by post-merger integration and labour relations issues, but even without these, market circumstances were already very difficult for the company. Such situations are rarely the result of a single executive error, however much hero-manager books might like to portray them as such; rather they are the consequence of many decisions (or non-decisions), made over a long period. But once established, the pattern exerts profound constraints on executive action.

Scale, or lack of scale, also has a significant impact on resilience. The auto industry requires a large investment in facilities, manufacturing equipment (such as robots) and tooling for steel body parts – all of which are large fixed costs that have to be spread across as many units produced as possible. The low overall profitability of the industry means that minimum economies of scale are high. When demand drops on the downward slope of the economic cycle, firms often struggle to generate enough volumes to recover their fixed or sunk costs. Being able to command higher volumes thus represents a major competitive advantage in this industry, which in turn presents a formidable barrier to entry.

Some readers might think we are painting a rather hopeless picture, in which management teams are trapped by the past, while facing pressures for volume and scale. However, the stories of Ford, GM, Toyota and VW in Chapter 3 show that individual companies can succeed by configuring their operations in ways that are appropriate for the time. Toyota, by being able execute its operations efficiently, was able to grow from making less than 10,000 vehicles per year in the 1950s, to being the world's largest auto producer at 10,000,000 units 60 years later. As we described in Chapter 3, different management paradigms have produced considerable competitive advantage for the firms that pioneered them, and subsequently, have changed established practices in the entire industry. But management teams clearly do not enjoy a blank slate – managing an auto company is perhaps akin to navigating a very complicated obstacle course.

HOW DO AUTO FIRMS SURVIVE CRISIS?

Structural features of the auto industry – specifically, high fixed costs, persistent overcapacity and cyclicality – mean that auto companies are periodically prone to crisis. The impact of this can be softened or exaggerated by an auto company's market reach, which can act as a hedge against economic peaks and troughs in particular markets or segments, and can boost margins, if auto companies are able to find markets and segments where fewer competitors are fighting for the same customers. However, crises can neither be easily avoided, nor escaped from, once they strike.

Given this, the interesting question is not so much 'Why do auto firms experience crisis?' as 'In the light of auto industry conditions, why don't more auto companies fail?' In this section we will consider three main responses of firms to crisis – radical self-help, in which a firm recognizes the crisis that it faces and takes the steps to get itself out of trouble; M&A, in which the firm merges with or is acquired by another auto firm; and rescue by supportive stakeholders. Rescues generally involve a combination of all three of the above actions, to varying degrees.

Radical surgery

As we saw in Chapter 7, of the cross section of firms in Table 7.1 which have experienced crises, relatively few were able to escape from crisis purely on the basis of their own efforts. This is not surprising – given that our definition of crisis is 'an imminent shortfall in cash with no immediate prospect of further support', it stands to reason that a firm in crisis will have exhausted most of the possibilities that it is aware of and has the capacity to enact. However, examples can be found. In 2008–9 in the face of the collapsing US auto market, Ford's situation was not radically different to that of Chrysler and GM, both of whom had to be bailed out by the US Government. Yet Ford took a different route. By 2006, the existing CEO, William Clay 'Bill' Ford Jr, recognized that he could not fix the problems facing the company and sought a replacement for himself –which he found in Alan Mulally, from Boeing. Bill Ford stayed on in the company as Executive Chairman and the Ford family, who controlled the company through their 40 per cent voting rights, were prepared to 'bet the company' on a strategy that enabled it to ride through the crisis without Government support – essentially by taking on a very large amount of debt using all of the firm's assets as collateral before the capital markets froze up and by selling its European brands – Aston Martin, Jaguar, Land Rover and Volvo. The company also eliminated its Mercury brand and focused its resources on its core 'Blue Oval' brand.[2] However, turnarounds such as this are rather unusual, and in Ford's case were taken on the cusp of a crisis, rather than once the crisis was in full swing. But the basic principles illustrated by the Ford self-help approach carry more general lessons about injections of resources to buy time and to support corrective actions. In Ford's case the resources funded a vigorous programme of new model development for a greatly reduced portfolio of brands and divisions. In terms of our model of resilience, the interesting long-term question for Ford is whether this rationalization has reduced its market reach to an extent that makes it hard to achieve the volume of sales across segments and regions necessary for long-term stability and resilience.

Ford's recovery case is also interesting in that it also illustrates a number of processes that we see in other firms that are under stress. During the late 1970s and throughout the 1980s, Rover sold off many operations and assets in order to try to get down to a manageable, sustainable core. This certainly simplified the management task of running the company, and helped generate resources. But by definition, the parts of a business that are sold are the ones for which buyers can be found, which are likely to be the more attractive propositions. Therefore there is a risk that what remains are the weaker parts of the business. In the case of Rover, when BMW decided to withdraw, the profitable Land Rover was sold to Ford and BMW itself retained the new Mini. What was left were the volume cars – the aging 25/45 series; the newer, but rather slow-selling 75, all competing in very crowded segments of the market in which there were strong competitors. There was also no product development capability left to speak of, even if there had been funding to develop new models (which there wasn't). Perhaps what is most surprising is that Rover survived for five years after BMW pulled out, despite these conditions. We speculate that this pattern of 'slow break up' is a defining characteristic of failing auto firms, and a warning sign of eventual collapse.

Fiat is another case of how radical surgery – in the form of asset sales, balance sheet restructuring slimming down the business to focus on the core operation, and stabilizing revenues – has led to an internal resolution of its crisis. In 2004 it had €10bn of debt, lots of peripheral activities and falling market share and volumes. Its CEO Sergio Marchionne sold some non-core assets (such as component plants and Fiat Avio), rebuilt the balance sheet (€4bn debt to equity swap with some banks) and reorganized Fiat's product plan to stabilize market share. Fiat returned to breakeven in its European operations, although many analysts questioned its long-term ability to generate sufficient capital to fund its product development needs in the long term. Fiat's subsequent union with Chrysler, and overtures to GM in 2015, indicate its long-term vulnerability.

Merger and acquisition

A second route out of crisis is merger and acquisition, in which stronger firms either take over smaller or weaker ones, or two or more firms with relative weaknesses in particular areas combine with a view to filling the 'gaps'. GM's development via acquisition in the early twentieth century is an example of the first approach, the Renault-Nissan Alliance an example of the latter. In terms of resilience, mergers can work by:

(a) improving operations and management, by a more capable firm transferring its skills to a less capable one;

(b) increasing scale, either through increasing absolute volumes or through platform and component sharing;

(c) increasing market reach, by either adding market segments or territories that one or other of the parties was unable to penetrate with their own resources.

Mergers and acquisitions can fail to meet their objectives due to implementation difficulties in any of these areas. What is interesting in terms of resilience in the auto industry is how hard it is to execute auto mergers effectively. As Carlos Ghosn the joint Renault and Nissan CEO declared, 'It is not validated by any example in the car industry that this [a merger] works. Not one example. And saying something different is just rubbish.'[3]

Saab and Rover show that it can be difficult to integrate different companies' business strategies and modi operandi without the partners losing their corporate identity. A merger may offer shelter to a weak company. But it can also reduce a previously autonomous firm to a division within a large company where it becomes interchangeable with other parts in a production network. Saab shows the danger of brand dilution, loss of unique identity and consequent decline, aggravated by use of its brand on other GM models.[4] The auto mergers that have worked best possessed *complementarities* in multiple dimensions. Take the coupling of Renault and Nissan, for example, illustrated by Table 8.1. In 1999, Nissan was almost bankrupt, while Renault was a mid-size manufacturer with some innovative products but only a limited geographical reach (largely focused on Europe, including Eastern Europe and Russia, and South America). One firm was strong where the other was weak, and vice versa, and that as a result, the fit between them was relatively clean.

One could not say the same for the failed alliance between GM and Fiat, which ended by GM paying Fiat for the privilege of *not* buying Fiat's remaining shares, or the DaimlerChrysler merger, which

Table 8.1 *Areas of complementarity in the Renault-Nissan Alliance*

	Renault	Nissan
Core capabilities	Design	Manufacturing
Strong market presence	Western Europe Eastern Europe Latin America	Japan North America Australasia China
Low or no market presence	USA Asia (all markets)	Latin America Eastern Europe
Product line-up and architecture	Front-wheel drive Low degree of platform sharing Strong presence in commercial vehicle market No trucks or 4×4	Generally front-wheel drive Low degree of platform sharing Several SUVs and light truck models Limited presence in commercial vehicle market
Brands	Renault (volume) Dacia (entrance-level)	Nissan (volume) Infiniti (luxury)

destroyed no less than €40bn of Daimler's stock market value.[5] Daimler and Chrysler employed very different product architectures (front-wheel drive at Chrysler and rear-wheel drive at Mercedes, which meant that only a single vehicle was ever shared between the two firms: the 'Crossfire', a rebadged Mercedes SLK). The two firms also had radically different brand identities and market positioning, so that even joint purchasing was problematic.

In the case of BMW-Rover the acquisition looked sensible on paper. Rover's 'British' flavour promised to complement the BMW range, and enhanced BMW's portfolio by adding Land Rover and Mini. Meanwhile, Rover should have benefited from BMW's skills and discipline in engineering, as well as from its deep pockets. But it was not to be. Rover's losses dragged the overall group down. The lesson for BMW from its unfortunate episode with Rover was that the skills involved in designing and making premium brand cars are quite different to those required to successfully acquire and integrate other auto firms. Clearly, a powerful, large and cash-rich partner is not of itself a sufficient condition for survival.

Critical to the success of an alliance or merger between two car companies is the scope for synergy by pooling resources, sharing knowledge and economies of scale. In the absence of these, long-term success is unlikely and eventually the stronger partner will discard the loss-making subsidiary. This happened with GM and Saab, BMW and Rover, and Daimler and Chrysler. A key element in successful automotive mergers is 'complementarity', that is, where both firms gain something from the partnership. This can come in many forms: access to technology, access to capital for investment, lower cost by sharing platforms and components, but also non-production synergies, such as access to new markets.

Although difficult, this is not impossible. The Volkswagen Group has acquired other auto firms and integrated these whilst maintaining separate, distinctive brands. Within the Group there is extensive sharing of platforms, powertrains and parts across brands in the Group (Audi, Seat, Skoda and VW) whilst allowing each brand an identity appropriate to its particular market. This creates economies of scale and means that lower-volume models can be offered at a profit, thereby maximizing market reach without major cost penalties.

Fiat-Chrysler revisited
Viewed through the lens of the survival envelope, the merger of Fiat and Chrysler partially addressed the limitations of scale and market reach that each company faced whilst independent. At the time of writing, the combined output of the merged entity is in excess of 4 million units. This is less than half that of global leaders such as VW and Toyota, but enough to place FCA 8th in the world by volume. It also means that FCA has reasonably strong positions in the USA and Europe, and via Fiat's operations in Brazil, in Latin America.

However, margins in Brazil are set to fall as other car makers move in and FCA does not have a strong presence in China. The advantages of market reach for FCA appear largely to lie in the form of a hedge against downturns in the European or US markets. This has been demonstrated by the post financial crash recovery in the US market which has meant that the Chrysler side of the operation has been able to make money again and has therefore supported the still-weak European operation. But this does not alter the fundamental economics – the hedge may improve resilience in the short term, but Fiat and Chrysler are both in relatively weak positions across the whole economic cycle. So when one is supporting the other through a downturn, this will be draining resource away from the temporarily stronger side of the operation – resource that could be used for new model development, or the entry to new markets, or any of a number of things that could build strength in the long term. Both of these firms have struggled to fund renewal in the past and this does not bode well for the future. FCA may have built some resistance to short-term perturbations by pooling risk across its US and European operations, but possibly at the price of longer-term development. Our resilience model suggests that FCA is more a case of arrested decline than a fundamental turnaround of fortunes.

The advantages of the merger operationally are also unclear. Chrysler and Fiat engineer their vehicles for very different markets and segments, and apart from some transfer of know-how with respect to smaller, more economical powertrains from Fiat to Chrysler, it is not clear how the merger will result in either reduced costs through economies of scale, or higher prices through enhanced capability. Early re-badging of Fiat products as Chryslers was symptomatic of an absence of room for real manoeuvre, as were some wildly optimistic J-curve sales forecasts for sales of Alfa Romeo and Jeep made in 2014.[6]

Rescue by supportive stakeholders

Our detailed cases show that the auto industry is embedded in a complex net of stakeholders: workers, unions, customers, shareholders and capital markets, and of course, various national and regional governments. These stakeholders all bring their own motives and priorities to the table, over and above the profitable manufacture and sale of motor vehicles – favourable employment terms, a good return on investment, economic development, and so on. These motives can support the core activity of designing and making cars, but also be a distraction.

One of the most common 'alternative agendas' of car making concerns employment. Car plants are large employers, so national and regional governments encourage the establishment of car plants and may give financial and other support to secure continued employment. Recent examples include the rescue of GM and Chrysler under the TARP programme in the USA, and the French government's stake in PSA in 2014.

Rover illustrates this clearly. Under successive Labour governments, there was a real reluctance to embrace labour reforms and downsizing. While this support was instrumental in keeping Rover alive, it also slowed reforms and restructuring that might have made the company more competitive. Under the Thatcher (Conservative) government during the 1980s, the focus shifted to privatization (albeit overlaid with a reluctance to sell national icons to foreigners), and Rover represented a very public example of this policy. Margaret Thatcher's comment on the sale of Rover to British Aerospace in 1988 ('Best of all, it is British') illustrates the degree to which non-commercial considerations shaped strategic and commercial decisions.

WARNING SIGNS OF CRISIS

There are a number of tell-tale signs of underlying weakness that indicate that a firm may be approaching a crisis. One such sign is the 'permanently optimistic forecast'. The reasons for this are typically as follows. First, the firm is under-performing and the constraints within which it is embedded mean that little can be done to provide immediate alleviation of this. Second, management therefore feels the need to promise something to secure continued stakeholder support. Third, because the firm faces constraints, the most plausible story is often one of 'change-just-around-the-corner' – often in terms of big increases in sales. Examples of such forecasts abound. Three recent examples include:

(a) Carlos Ghosn's initial promise of the sale of 1.51m electric vehicles by 2016. By 2013 Ghosn admitted that Renault-Nissan was 'four to five years behind' on this plan. Between 2010 and 2013 Renault and Nissan had sold a combined 120,000 electric cars, the majority of which were one model, the Nissan LEAF.
(b) VW's sales target of selling 800,000 units pa in the US market by 2018. In 2014 it sold less than half that, while sales have declined continuously since 2012.
(c) Sergio Marchionne's prediction that Alfa Romeo will reach 400,000 units annual sales by 2014, a five-fold increase on existing sales at the time, and thus contribute a major component of the volume growth necessary for Fiat-Chrysler's recovery. Equally implausible growth was forecast for the Jeep brand.

Organizations in distress thus tend to produce very favourable predictions, whose purpose is to promise better times in the future – the 'permanently optimistic' forecast. Within stricken organizations, forecasts (like restructuring plans) are often used to convey a positive message about the future and mask the difficulties of the present. Throughout Rover's history, there were recurrent forecasts of sales-based recoveries to come which never arrived. Lord Stokes, speaking on the future of British Leyland at the launch of the Allegro in 1973, said: 'This is the beginning of a very exciting era for British Leyland, and I think our designers, engineers and production men are going to provide you with a British motor industry of which you will be very proud ...' Less than two years later, the company had collapsed and had to be taken into public ownership.

Another Rover executive put it thus:

When I came here in 1974 we had to put a corporate plan together. And everybody did J-curve planning – the past had gone down but

the future was going to get better, and the business previously
had had 50% market share ... People just wanted you to drive plans
that looked better. So people produced plans – which no-one
believed – but that just got you off the hook, **so there was that
characteristic in the business, which was a complete ability to deny
history and assume that although the past was bad, the future
would be better.** (Our emphasis.)

Another Rover executive captured the sense of denial, in which anything
other than an optimistic forecast led to a highly unpalatable conclusion:

when you're trying to justify programmes, or a business in a general
sense, there are some things that, if you believe the downside
forecast, you'd say, 'Well, we're not in business'. You psych yourself
into the position where you say, 'Give us the forecast that will keep
us in business and we'll do everything to achieve the forecast' ...
We used to get into life crises because the pessimistic view wasn't
enough to sustain anything, so you do what you do.

Figure 8.1 illustrates an overly optimistic forecast, also known as a
'J-curve'. Note that the essence of a J-curve narrative is that the

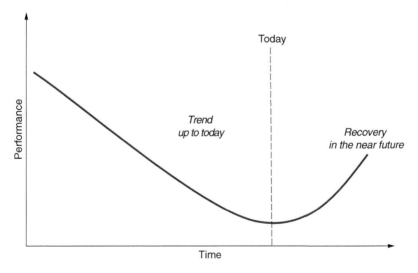

FIGURE 8.1 The 'J-curve' phenomenon

current downward trend is about to end and that things will start improving – soon, but not immediately. This pattern is typical of situations when high expectations, or simply a vital need for continued support, meet a set of difficult-to-surmount constraints. It is no surprise, then, that permanently optimistic forecasts are such a feature of the auto industry.

However compelling this graphic may look, if neither the strategy nor the constraints change, neither will the long-term picture. J-curves are one of the most compelling signs that a firm may be entering crisis – because they demonstrate the need to create a narrative that depicts a brighter future, diverting attention from the constraints of the present.

IMPLICATIONS FOR THE FUTURE SHAPE OF THE AUTO INDUSTRY

Thus far we have concentrated on identifying the factors associated with entry into crisis and recovery from it. A legitimate criticism of what we have covered so far is that it has been conducted with the benefit of hindsight. A particular cue that all is not well is just one piece of information amongst many at the time, weighed up and acted on, or disregarded, according to the best understanding of the decision-makers at the time. As we saw in the case of Rover, decision-makers may be overloaded by so many demands that information is not given the attention that it requires – especially if the message it contains is unwelcome. When looking back after the event we have the knowledge of what happened next – a benefit which decision-makers do not have at the time.

In this section, we use our model of resilience to consider the likely shape of the auto industry in the future. In doing this we seek to address the question: which auto firms are likely to be most resilient to crises, and thus most likely to survive?

We have constructed a 'resilience index', and applied this to 14 leading auto firms (Table 8.2). The auto companies that do not appear in the table do not do so because it was not possible to obtain data for them on one or more of the resilience measures – this typically applies to companies that are part of larger industrial groups and whose results are not reported separately. This includes, for example, Mazda, Mitsubishi, Volvo and Jaguar Land Rover. Where a single company has multiple brands (such as VW and GM) data for the whole group are used. The index draws on publicly available data to generate proxy measures for the four main components of our model of resilience – operations, scale, market reach and stakeholder support. We start with a health warning – we have tried to capture some quite complex, subtle processes using publicly available data. We have had to skate over some significant areas because suitable proxy data are not available. In others, the data that are available need to be interpreted carefully and overly mechanical 'readouts' avoided.

In terms of *operational capability*, we use two measures, revenue per employee and the ranking for the JD Powers quality survey. The revenue per employee measure provides an approximation for productivity, with the caveat that it is influenced by vertical integration, which it not easy to correct for. Thus, for example, an auto firm that engages in only vehicle assembly and buys in everything else will need fewer employees than one which performs many more operations in-house. The assembly-only firm therefore will look better on the measure of revenue per head than the one that is highly vertically integrated. In the past, there were significant differences in vertical integration between auto companies and between car-producing regions; however, during the 1990s greater outsourcing became the norm (partly due to US giants GM and Ford spinning off their in-house divisions), so this should be less of an issue now than it once was. The measure of quality picks up the incidence of defects as identified by the customer and is therefore sensitive to care, thoroughness and accuracy in processes of design and manufacture. We have not included any measure of the efficacy of the *management system* (the corporate processes of control, coordination and so on) on the grounds we could not identify a sufficiently robust measure for which data are readily available.

We measure *scale* in two ways – by total vehicle production, in units, and by the average production volume by per platform. The rationale for using the platform measure lies in Chapters 2 and 4 – that a fundamental challenge for auto firms is to simultaneously maximize variety (and hence market reach) and economies of scale (thereby minimizing costs). Well-executed platform strategies (shown by high production volumes per platform) provide a more subtle indication of economies of scale than total simple volume of units produced.

Market reach is gauged in two ways. The first is the Herfindahl–Hirschman index, which measures the distribution of sales across national markets. Simply put, a company whose sales are dispersed relatively evenly across many countries, thereby reducing its reliance on the health of any single economy, will score relatively well on this index. This measure is significant because of the problem of economic cycles for the auto industry – those companies whose bets are spread most widely across multiple countries are less likely to be vulnerable to troughs. One word of warning about this measure – we have used dispersion of sales across *countries*, rather than entire regions. On this measure a company like Renault, whose sales are spread across many countries in a region such as Europe, scores very well – despite the fact that it has no presence in the USA or Japan, other than through its partner Nissan. Where countries in a region move through the economic cycle in unison (as happened in Europe following the global financial crisis) the hedging effect of dispersion is clearly eroded.

The second measure of market reach is percentage of sales that are in the five markets that have shown the fastest growth in the period 2008–2013 – China, Brazil, India and Thailand. We have also, with some reservations, included the USA as this market has shown rapid growth since 2008. However, the US growth represents an upswing after a deep trough in a mature market, rather than the long-term growth and development of a new market. A strong presence in growth markets is important in the context of overcapacity – auto firms that are early movers into emerging markets face many challenges, but also may enjoy the benefits of reduced competition – at least for a while.

We have not included any measures of market segment coverage (e.g. small cars, SUVs, premium models, etc.) in our measure of market reach. Although it is very desirable to do so, it is difficult to do so in a simple, clear way given the huge number of combinations of segments and markets.

Although all three measures of operations, scale and reach have their challenges, *stakeholder support* is the most difficult to gauge in a clear, simple and transparent way, for a number of reasons. Companies have multiple stakeholders – labour, suppliers, customers, financiers – any or all of whom can provide support at times of need. Assessing the likelihood that these stakeholders will actually provide help when the chips are down is problematic – in 2008–9 Chrysler and GM went through many nail-biting months as their bailouts were discussed, debated and negotiated by their stakeholders, and the final outcome was by no means clear or assured at the outset. As we have observed, stakeholder support, particularly in a crisis, often involves the breaking and re-negotiation of existing settlements with stakeholders. There is therefore often a highly political element to the process – outcomes evolve from a myriad of interactions and interpretations amongst the actors concerned and are therefore difficult to predict in advance with any great confidence. Again, the 2009 rescue of Chrysler is instructive in this respect. On paper, Chrysler was a company that had persistent weakness, was located in a strongly free-market political and economic environment, had been bailed out before and was seen by some powerful players to embody much of what was wrong with the USA. Logically, Chrysler should *not* have been bailed out. But it was, conditional on a deal with Fiat, under the banner of saving an American icon and American jobs. In this case, patriotism trumped free market ideology – just.

Faced with these issues, we have opted for two financially orientated proxies for likely stakeholder support – credit rating (derived from Moody's credit ratings) and closely held shares as a percentage of total shares. We use credit rating as an indicator of capital market confidence in the ability of a company to meet its obligations to its financiers. Our logic is that such confidence will be a factor in determining whether support is offered, although this measure does not of course pick up perhaps the most important stakeholder support of all, that is, support that is provided in spite of poor short- to medium-term prospects according to normal financial criteria. 'Closely held shares' typically refers to (voting) shares that are held by shareholders who are close to the company and which are not traded publicly, as common shares are. Examples of closely held shares include cross-holdings of shares by companies in the same keiretsu group in Japan; or family-held shares with special voting rights (as in the case of the Ford family, who hold 40 per cent of the voting rights in Ford, or the 62 per cent voting rights held by the Quandt family in BMW). We use closely held shares as a proxy for a long-term commitment to the firm, likely to be manifested as a propensity to provide support in the face of financial and other adversity. In the case of Honda and Toyota, on paper their shareholdings appear quite dispersed but closer inspection reveals that many of the shares are held by 'friendly' bodies who have either business relationships with them or who see themselves as very long term investors.

For each measure we have converted the raw scores into z-scores, which express each company's position in terms of the distance above or below the mean score of all companies on that measure, and then combined all four measures, giving equal weight to each, to provide a simple 'league table' of resilience and vulnerability.

To be clear, we argue that a company's position in the table is an estimation, based on the proxy measures of our model of resilience, of (a) the probability that the company is likely to find itself seriously challenged in the medium to long term and (b) its propensity to survive a crisis should one hit. In essence, Table 8.2 provides a summary of a company's profile in terms of its operational performance, scale, market reach and stakeholder support.

No company tops the table on every single measure, indicating how difficult it is to have strengths in every single area. This of itself shows why companies who may not be particularly strong operationally show remarkable resilience – the effects of scale (being big) and market reach (being in the right places at the right time) can have a considerable compensating effect.

The 'star performers' of the table are Hyundai, Toyota, Honda, GM Ford and BMW, all of whose resilience quotients are, cumulatively, more than one standard deviation above the average. Those in the lower zone of the table (on average more than one standard deviation below) are Fiat-Chrysler, Daimler, Renault and PSA. While one could devote an entire book to each of the car firms' respective positioning in the index and the underlying reasons for this position (and arguably many books have attempted to do so), it is instructive to point to the core reasons for some of the firms' respective positions.

At the top of the league table is Hyundai Motors. Modelled after Toyota, stringent in its organization and near-militaristic in its operational execution Hyundai has strong operational capability. It has hired key talent from VW for its product design, and in many ways represents a powerful hybrid between Toyota and VW. Its most recent growth occurred during recent years of austerity following the 2008 global financial crisis, with small economical cars and long warranties, and some commentators see Hyundai's rise as a consequence of the austerity of the post-financial crisis recovery years.

The next places in the table are taken by Toyota and Honda, testimony to the fact that excellence in operational execution still matters, and provides a competitive advantage. Toyota's foothold in the hybrid market means that it is well equipped to defend its leading position and Japan provides a large local market for low-emission vehicles (as we noted previously, 30 per cent of sales of new cars in Japan are hybrids).

GM and Ford are in 4th and 5th place, respectively. Structural reforms to fix legacy health care costs have now taken place, and their respective scale and global market reach (especially GM's) should provide resilience. It is conceivable that both firms may slowly slip down the global league table of global production, and in GM's case fall further behind VW and Toyota. GM's ability to seek and

Table 8.2 Index of the likely resilience of selected major car manufacturers

Company[1]	Total revenue per employee in '000 US$.[2]	JD Powers quality ranking for best-selling sedan vehicle, 2014 model year.[3]	combined z-score	Total vehicle production in 2013.[4]	Average production volume per platform in 2013.[5]	combined z-score	Dispersion of sales across markets.[6]	Percentage of sales in top five global growth markets in 2013.[7]	combined z-score	Moody's credit rating, per firm, 2013.[8]	Closely held shares as percentage of total equity.[9]	combined z-score	Resilience Index
Hyundai Motor Group[10]	730.52	4.22	1.54	7,233,080	637,671	1.62	8.42	0.53	0.40	65	26	-0.04	3.52
Toyota Motor Company	630.45	4.00	0.95	10,324,995	316,255	1.03	6.07	0.44	-0.46	85	55	1.08	2.60
Honda Motor	518.90	3.33	-0.10	4,298,390	402,479	0.38	5.99	0.65	0.10	80	48	0.81	1.19
General Motors Company	721.89	3.11	0.45	9,628,912	370,616	1.10	7.04	0.72	0.56	50	0	-0.95	1.17
Ford Motor Company	770.47	3.22	0.74	6,077,126	191,830	-0.04	7.85	0.63	0.53	55	40	-0.12	1.11
BMW AG	746.94	3.00	0.44	2,006,366	238,394	-0.52	9.70	0.37	0.30	75	62	0.88	1.11
Volkswagen AG	381.08	3.00	-0.94	9,379,229	346,583	0.98	6.60	0.49	-0.18	70	71	0.88	0.74
Nissan Motor Company	610.56	2.89	-0.18	4,950,924	208,635	-0.16	7.34	0.54	0.13	70	0	-0.32	-0.52
Tata Automotive	627.95	3.56	0.52	1,062,654	57,987	-1.26	5.12	0.75	0.12	45	60	-0.10	-0.72
Zhejiang Geely Holding Group[11]	610.42	3.33	0.24	969,896	118,870	-1.08	2.88	0.66	-0.69	45	100	0.57	-0.94
Fiat-Chrysler Automotive	447.28	3.00	-0.69	4,681,704	177,439	-0.31	5.95	0.62	-0.01	35	31	-0.91	-1.91

Daimler AG	501.30	2.89	−0.59	1,781,507	85,376	−1.06	8.55	0.34	−0.10	70	0	−0.32	−2.06
Renault SA	379.21	3.00	−0.94	2,704,675	256,391	−0.35	10.33	0.13	−0.19	50	15[12]	−0.69	−2.18
PSA Peugeot Citroën[13]	492.87	2.00	−1.46	2,833,781	253,392	−0.34	7.78	0.25	−0.52	40	28	−0.79	−3.11
Mean	583.56	3.18		4,852,374	261,566		7.12	0.51		60	38	
Standard deviation	132.57	0.53		3,239,465	149,780		1.92	0.18		16	30	

Notes:

[1] Suzuki, Mazda and Mitsubishi are omitted from this table as their credit ratings have been withdrawn or are not available. SAIC, Dongfeng, FAW and Changan are included in the figures for their respective joint-venture partners.

[2] Converted from annual reports into USD. 2014 data. Source: S&P Global IQ.

[3] Source: JD Powers, 2015. Figures for Renault and PSA are taken from the 2013 IQS survey in the UK.

[4] Source: OICA 2014.

[5] Source: IHS Global Insight.

[6] Using an inverted Herfindahl-Hirschmann index of a firm's share across markets, 2013 data. Source: World Motor Vehicle Data 2014.

[7] Source: World Motor Vehicle Data 2014. Growth markets are defined as those with largest absolute increases in vehicle sales, 2008-2013. These markets are China, USA, Brazil, India and Thailand.

[8] Converted to % with AAA as 100% and C as 0%. Source: Moody's 2014.

[9] Estimates where no data has been published. Sources: various. Close shareholding is % of equity held by 'friends' or affiliates (e.g. families with special voting rights, companies with a relationship, or national and/or regional governments).

[10] Workforce figure combines Hyundai Motors and Kia Motors. Source: Annual reports, 2014.

[11] Workforce figure combines Geely Automotive and Volvo Cars Corporation. Source: Annual reports, 2014.

[12] Renault owns 43% of Nissan. Although the companies are very interdependent we have not counted these as 'closely held shares'.

[13] Workforce figure for automobile division only. Source: Annual report, 2014.

colonize markets has been a key strength that compensates for GM's operational mediocrity, something that has been criticized by analysts for the best part of three decades. Ford on the other hand is very competent operationally and as such is likely to hold its position in the USA and Europe. However, its 'back-to-basics' strategy may limit its market reach and is unlikely to develop Ford's penetration of emerging markets at the same rate as that of its competitors.

BMW appears as the strongest European manufacturer, which in itself is not a surprise given its strength of brand and strong skills in design and execution of premium products. These limit direct competition and therefore protect BMW's margins. The greater surprise is that it comes in ahead of VW which is five times its size. VW is capable of executing brands very well, and uses platform-sharing to its advantage. It also shares a very strong position in China with GM. But VW has a weak position in the USA, and its financial performance is not as stellar as the company's rhetoric would suggest: high costs in execution due to internal complexity are an issue, as seen by the €5bn cost reduction programme announced in 2014. Product proliferation in pursuit of market reach, it seems, may have exceeded the optimal economic trade-off for VW.

Daimler's relatively lowly position in the table is surprising. Daimler is challenged on several fronts – having low productivity (the company announced a major cost cutting programme in 2014, seeking to cut €3.5bn per annum by 2020[7]), mediocre quality as rated by customers, moderate scale, and sales quite concentrated in a few regions (USA and Europe). The strength of Daimler's brand – a measure of the support of customers as a stakeholder group – offsets many of these drawbacks. Should Daimler enter a crisis, however, our index suggests that it is not as well placed as other firms to weather the storm.

Renault and Nissan still report their accounts separately, and hence feature individually in our index. Nissan is the stronger of the two on the index, but if treated as one, they would still remain in Nissan's place in the rankings, with the combined enterprise performing at the industry average. Renault on its own appears vulnerable. Renault-Nissan made a large bet on electric vehicles, but missed the grand sales projections for EVs that it announced. If the electric vehicle bet does not pay off, the learning may largely benefit the rest of the auto industry, while Renault-Nissan bears the cost.

Jaguar Land Rover, owned by Tata Motors, has seen a very strong growth in a favourable global market, selling around 425,000 units in 2013 (348,000 Land Rovers, 77,000 Jaguars). It recently opened its first own engine plant, and has embarked on an ambitious new platform programme that will see its product portfolio increase considerably into SUV, cross-over vehicles and 'D-segment' (BMW 3-series/Audi A4) vehicles. However, Jaguar Land Rover's sales should be seen against those of BMW which produced over 400,000 X1s, X3s and X5s in 2013, from a standing start in the 4×4 market in 1999. BMW's total output was 1.6 million in 2013, four times that of Jaguar Land Rover. There are no obvious operations synergies between Jaguar Land Rover and its parent Tata, and Land Rover's current success probably owes more to Ford's period of ownership (2000–2008) than to Tata's. A key question is whether Jaguar Land Rover will be able to deliver the revenue, engineering capability and brand strength to sustain itself without occasional, and substantial, cash injections from its parent. Tata Motors combines an extremely heterogeneous set of automotive operations, which does induce a certain degree of uncertainty into Tata's position in the index.

Volvo, now owned by China's Geely, is in a difficult place: its brand is not-quite-premium and its markets are historically focused in the USA and Europe (and moreover, amongst particular groups of consumers in each). Volvo's sober, understated brand values do not sit very comfortably with large sections of the Chinese market where most of the hopes for volume growth lie. The question is how long it will take for this to become apparent, and how Geely will deal with it if and when it does. Volvo is still small, so suffers from lack of scale economies, but growth and internationalization will help. Volvo has also started sharing parts with Geely, via purchasing in China, and claims a 30 per cent reduction in the cost of parts.

The final places in the index are taken by Fiat-Chrysler and PSA, reflecting the strategic issues facing both firms. Chrysler remains weak outside the USA and with Fiat does not offer obvious synergies, despite the rhetoric to the contrary. Chrysler must be at risk in the next US downturn, and Fiat is unlikely to have the resources to support it (unless Fiat's position in Europe and its other markets improves to an implausibly significant degree). Chrysler is also unlikely to command much US government support. Jeep will live on in some form, possibly under the wing of another company (as Land Rover has), but Chrysler's volume cars business must be at risk in the medium to long term. One likely trajectory for Chrysler is the path Rover followed, with the volume cars dying out and other firms taking on the stronger brands (Land Rover and Mini in Rover's case, Jeep in Chrysler's). Fiat, on the other hand, is not strong in markets outside of Southern Europe and a few emerging economies. The operational synergies with Chrysler are questionable and there has already been some cross-badging of existing Chrysler vehicles that suggests a degree of desperation. Fiat enjoys strong support in Italy, but the Italian state faces severe economic and political difficulties, so Fiat's home market is unlikely to be an engine for growth.

PSA is dependent on the middle-to-lower end of the mature European market where it is head-to-head with some strong players. PSA has no presence in the USA, and is not particularly strong in emerging markets, having had a troubled early start in China. Strong labour unions in France make reform difficult. The interventionist French state may continue to provide a safety net in terms of stakeholder support – but at the price of limiting the firm's strategic options, for example by insisting that production stays in France.

The resilience index presented in this chapter has applied and quantified our conceptual model presented in Chapter 4. The purpose of the index is to identify the firms that are most – and least – able to withstand adverse conditions in the future. As our examples of Rover and Saab have shown, car companies do not die suddenly, but tend to enter a spiralling decline that sees their assets erode as successive crises eat away at their substance. Some of the firms in the lower part of the resilience league table may have already entered this protracted cycle of decline.

WILL ELECTRIFICATION RADICALLY DISRUPT THE AUTO INDUSTRY?

The automotive industry appears to be on the verge of a technological shift: the traditional internal combustion engine (ICE) burning petrol or diesel fuel faces increasing challenges due to environmental and energy security concerns. The ICE has served the world very well by providing cheap, safe and reliable propulsion and will continue to do so for some time to come. It will also remain the dominant powertrain for long-haul freight transportation, and off-highway applications (such as construction), where high energy density is paramount. In the case of personal mobility, the industry seems to be approaching a point of inflection with electric, or electrified propulsion technology to be more precise, now entering the mass-market vehicles. The electrification of the powertrains expressed in mild hybrids, plug-in hybrids and range-extended electric vehicles is still in the intermediate stage. It is not yet clear what design of powertrain will fully displace the ICE altogether. The current contenders are electric vehicles charged on the grid, and fuel cell vehicles using hydrogen as fuel. Other technologies may still enter this race.

Electric cars do not yet achieve acceptable standards in terms of range, performance and cost. The early signs are of very poor residual values for electric vehicles, due to fears about the cost of replacing batteries indicating that the motoring public is not yet ready to embrace them. However, if and when this point comes, the map of the auto industry will be re-written. Most change will occur in the supply base in areas such as battery technology, fuel systems and powertrain as well as in the servicing and support infrastructure. For car companies, making the switch from vehicles propelled by internal combustion engines to electric ones will be a significant change effort, and this may shuffle the pecking order of the industry. The major players should all be able to access the appropriate technology – many are already in alliances in order to do so – and so the technology of itself is unlikely to be a critical success factor. However, some auto firms will be better and faster at mastering the new skills involved in the design, production and support of electric vehicles and hence gain advantage over those that are less proficient. Smaller, weaker players may struggle with the scale of the task and the associated switching costs and disappear, probably becoming sub-brands under the wing of larger firms. Until public confidence in issues such as range and battery recharging infrastructure is established, there is likely to be a transition period during which hybrid, dual-fuel vehicles will proliferate. Some companies such as Toyota already have a head start in this space.

Unlike industries like mobile telephony, where a firm such as Apple can enter from a related sector and can capture a large market share within a single product generation, moves towards electrification in the auto industry are likely to play out differently. The 'embeddedness' of the sector means that incumbents in the auto industry are in the best position to assimilate and exploit new technology. Thus it is unlikely that the advent of new powertrain technology will see significant new entrants who disrupt the industry – in the same way as Apple disrupted the personal electronics sector. This is in particular the case for firms whose main markets have strict regulatory regimes, such as Japan and Europe. In Japan, by 2014, 30 per cent of passenger cars (excluding kei-class cars) were using hybrid powertrains, which amounts to 1.5 million units per annum alone. Being able to command such volumes due to government-induced adoption represents a huge advantage to Toyota, Nissan and Honda. Equally, we see European producers in a strong position due to the continued emphasis on emissions reduction, achieved through downsizing and light hybrid technology (kinetic recovery systems, small batteries that power auxiliary electric motors that can propel the car during urban cycles, and aid petrol or diesel engines during acceleration).

The greatest challenge for electric vehicles remains the source and storage of energy. In the future, an entirely new storage technology such as redox flow batteries (which, technically, are more fuel-cell than battery) might displace both electric battery and fuel cell vehicles, to become the new dominant powertrain design. Current battery technology, although improving, performs poorly in terms of energy density and recharging times, thus reducing the utility of the vehicle outside of short-range urban duties. Just as electric vehicles lost out at the start of the twentieth century, their weaknesses are again hampering their adoption. The technologies most likely to be the next dominant sources of energy provision and propulsion are a new generation of batteries (such as metal–air batteries), redox flow cells (that use two rechargeable liquids to generate a current), or hydrogen fuel cells. The storage of hydrogen remains the largest obstacle to its adoption, but a step change in liquid organic hydrogen carrier (LOHC), which would allow hydrogen to be stored within a compound, just like petrol, could shift the balance in its favour.

Profits from today's cars, powered by internal combustion engines, effectively have to pay for the R&D of their replacements. Faced with uncertainty over which technology will become the new dominant design, auto manufacturers are hedging their bets. Most are experimenting with electric vehicles and/or fuel cells, but in terms of mainstream production the hybrid represents an obvious interim stage that is likely to dominate the next decade, and quite possibly until the mid twenty-first century.

A further sea-change stems from increased connectivity of the vehicle to the rest of the world (such as GPS, 3G/4G, the internet and other data services). The latter will enable autonomous vehicles to gradually become feasible, and stable enough to be granted regulatory approval. Here, early experiments by Apple with its 'iCar' concept and Google's self-driving car are instructive. As BMW's board member Peter Schwarzenbauer succinctly put it, arguing that the auto industry was now more exciting than at any time in the past 30 years:

Two worlds are colliding here. Our world, focused on hardware and our experience in making complex products, and the world of information technology which is intruding more and more into our life. The winners will be those companies that understand how to build intelligent hardware ... We need to get away from the idea that it will be either us or them ... We cannot offer clients the perfect experience without help from one of these technology companies.

Thus there are several conceivable directions for the automotive industry. The ability to integrate traditional ICE and alternative powertrain technologies effectively will be significant at least in the medium term. So far, most alternative powertrain vehicles are produced in separate facilities, on bespoke platforms. Hybrids are mostly electrified versions of existing ICE vehicles, to which the new powertrain architecture has been added.

Whilst this model prevails, we can expect considerable continuity – and the same applies to the incorporation of other technologies, such as information and autonomous vehicle technologies. What is clear is that two key aspects will drive the change of powertrain technology in the auto industry: the oil price, and the regulators' ability to push forward regulatory change when faced with strong car industry lobbies. For the purpose of this book the most significant point is that a large-scale shift in the dominant technology may lead to some reshuffling amongst the car firms, and will create winners and losers. As we said earlier, the automotive industry is hard to disrupt, so incumbents are in a strong position to reap the benefits of this shift by assimilating and exploiting new technologies; however it is also clear that being able to efficiently produce a large variety of ICE-powered vehicles is unlikely to deliver a sustainable competitive position in the long term. Incumbent car firms have accumulated an enormous knowledge and asset base geared at providing ICE-powered cars, so a shift away from the ICE will directly threaten those firms unable to generate sufficient profits to pay for this transition. The weaker firms are likely to be hit by yet another wave, this time of technological change, which will eat away at their coastlines.

FINAL THOUGHTS

Being able to design, produce and sell products is a fundamental capability for any successful company, so it is not surprising that many previous analyses of the auto industry have focused on operational execution, especially productivity and quality, as explanations of success. However, this perspective does not explain why mediocre performers survive, apparently against all odds, and why very strong performers do not achieve global domination. Operational performance is important, but our research shows that operational performance is only *one* of the factors that matter. Predictions that only six OEM groups will be left by the end of the twentieth century proved to be incorrect. As of 2015, there are 36 vehicle manufacturers in the world, and 13 auto firms each produce more than 1 million passenger cars annually.

In the 120 or so years since its establishment, the car industry has proved remarkably resilient to disruption. Unlike many industries, the auto industry still comprises a range of firms that have their origins in the early days of the industry. Apart from Hyundai, which was founded in 1967, virtually all top-10 car firms date back to the first decades of the twentieth century. Few industries show such longevity in their line-up of firms. The reasons for this stability lie partly in the steadily growing demand for the car – a product that in its essential elements has not radically changed over the past century: a steel body to house around four passengers, set on four wheels, powered by an internal combustion engine. Demand for the type of personal mobility supplied by the automobile is likely to continue to rise for a number of decades, as more countries industrialize and develop. There will be local variations in patterns of demand, and some segments of the population may increasingly turn their backs on vehicle ownership (in heavily urbanized environments, for example), but for small groups, such as friends and families, it is difficult to envisage an alternative to the automobile that is better suited to carrying 2–7 people pretty much anywhere, anytime, at relatively low cost. The same argument applies to light commercial vehicles, which form the bedrock of much economic activity.

Cars are a prime example of a technology that is heavily *embedded* in most economies and societies. This means that change is likely to be slow and incremental because cars touch and enable many aspects of people's lives, all of which must absorb and adjust to any change. Independently of economic considerations, cars also serve as important 'identity items' – not just to drivers, but also to those that own the firms that make them, and to governments and communities who host car making. Cars are large, visible and relatively expensive items, and represent status as well as mobility. This function is unlikely to change. This means that – irrespective of pressing environmental and energy concerns – the car industry as we know it, with most of its incumbent firms, is likely to be around for some time to come.

Appendix

In this appendix we show selected operational and financial data for the main case firms discussed in Chapters 5–7

ROVER

		1968	1969	1970	1971	1972	1973	1974	1975
Company		BLMC	BLMC	BLMC	BLMC	BLMC	BLMC	BLMC	BLMC
Production	Car production in '000s	1,050.0	1,083.0	788.7	868.7	916.2	875.8	738.5	605.1
Workforce	in '000s	188.3	196.4	199.5	193.7	190.8	204.2	207.8	191.5
Financials	Turnover in million GBP	973.6	970.0	1,021.0	N/A	1,281.0	1,564.0	1,595.0	1,868.0
	Profit/Loss in million GBP	37.9	40.4	3.9	32.4	31.9	51.3	2.3	−76.1
	Profit after tax in million GBP	20.3	20.8	2.3	N/A	21.1	27.9	−6.7	−63.2

		1987	1988	1989	1990	1991	1992	1993	1994
Company		Rover	Rover	Rover	Rover	Rover	Rover	Rover	Rover
Production	Car production in '000s	471.5	474.7	466.6	417.4	360.0	339.1	356.3	369.6
Workforce	in '000s	N/A	N/A	N/A	41.9	N/A	N/A	N/A	34.2
Financials	Turnover in million GBP	3,096.0	N/A	N/A	N/A	N/A	N/A	N/A	4,477.7
	Profit/Loss in million GBP	N/A	N/A	N/A	N/A	N/A	N/A	N/A	279.0
	Profit after tax in million GBP	−21.6	N/A	N/A	N/A	N/A	N/A	N/A	N/A

Notes: BLMC refers to British Leyland Motor Corporation (later just 'BL'), AR to Austin
Source of data: Annual reports, Companies House, Ward's World Motor Vehicle Data, various

1976	1977	1978	1979	1980	1981	1982	1983	1984	1985	1986
BLMC	BLMC	BLMC	BLMC	BLMC	AR	AR	AR	AR	AR	Rover
687.9	651.0	611.6	503.8	395.8	413.4	405.1	473.3	383.3	465.1	404.5
183.0	195.0	192.0	177.0	157.0	126.0	108.0	103.0	96.0	78.0	N/A
2,892.0	2,602.0	3,073.0	2,990.0	2,877.0	2,869.0	3,072.0	3,421.0	3,402.0	3,415.0	3,412.0
70.5	3.1	15.3	−112.2	−387.5	−332.9	−222.7	67.1	−73.3	−110.3	N/A
47.0	−5.0	−11.0	−119.0	−391.0	−339.0	−230.0	−74.0	−73.3	−125.6	−455.6

1995	1996	1997	1998	1999	2000	2001	2002	2003	2004	2005
Rover	Rover	Rover	Rover	Rover	PVH	PVH	PVH	PVH	PVH	PVH
350.4	345.5	364.4	303.8	227.7	174.9	163.1	142.9	136.1	107.6	29.1
37.3	39.3	38.8	38.7	31.4	14.4	5.0	5.1	4.6	N/A	N/A
5,331.9	6,251.8	6,324.1	5,482.1	4,801.2	2,310.5	1,320.7	1,493.3	1,307.1	N/A	N/A
−50.5	−100.3	18.6	−570.5	−2,138.6	542.7	−227.3	−69.8	−92.6	N/A	N/A
N/A	N/A	N/A	N/A	N/A	N/A	N/A	N/A	N/A	N/A	N/A

Rover, PVH to Phoenix Venture Holdings (MG Rover).
years; Williams et al. (1994).

SAAB

		2000	2001	2002	2003	2004
Production	Total units produced	132,803	123,755	125,045	130,034	128,826
Workforce		8,722	7,619	7,444	6,226	5,580
Financials	Revenue (MSEK)	23,660	23,830	23,547	23,613	22,669
	Inventory on hand (MSEK)	1,319	1,205	1,235	1,091	899
	After tax profit (MSEK)	−341	12	−4,368	−4,767	−3,503
	After tax profit margin (%)	−1.44	0.05	−18.55	−20.19	−15.45

Source of data: Annual reports. Ward's World Motor Vehicle Data, various years.

CHRYSLER

Note: due to Chrysler's frequent changes in ownership since 1998, and the resulting changes in the way its results are reported, it is virtually impossible to assemble a meaningful longitudinal view of Chrysler's operational and financial performance. Chrysler became a private firm in 2007, after being divested by Daimler. Since 2009 it reports its results as part of Fiat-Chrysler-Automotive.

Chrylser LLC and DaimlerChrysler		1991	1992	1993	1994
Production	Global production in million units				
Workforce	Global headcount in thousands				
Financials	Revenue (million)	$28,162	$35,501	$43,600	$52,235
	EBIT (million USD)	$854	$902	$4,677	$6,767
	Operating profit (million)				

FCA US LLC		2003	2004	2005	2006
Production	Global production in million units	2.55	2.65	2.76	2.55
Workforce	Global headcount in thousands	93.1	84.4	83.1	80.7
Financials	Revenue (million USD euro)	€ 136,437	€ 142,059	€ 149,776	€ 151,589
	EBIT (million USD)				
	Operating profit (million)	−€ 506	€ 1,427	€ 1,534	−€ 1,118

Source of data: Chrysler annual reports 1991–1997, DaimlerChrysler annual reports

2005	2006	2007	2008	2009	2010	2011	2012
127,593	135,365	125,397	90,281	20,791	32,048	12,871	0
5,137	4,689	4,338	4,129	3,241	3,833	N/A	N/A
21,082	24,208	21,722	15,641	6,080	819	N/A	N/A
1,203	1,286	1,360	2,322	1,434	N/A	N/A	N/A
−4,120	−3,185	−2,122	−4,444	3,929	−218	N/A	N/A
−19.54	−13.16	−9.77	−28.41	64.62	−26.62	N/A	N/A

1995	1996	1997	1998	1999	2000	2001	2002
2.62	2.76	2.90	2.98	3.18	2.96	2.68	2.75
112.5	114.2	112.3	126.8	129.4	121.0	104.0	95.8
$53,195	$61,397	$61,147	bankruptcy	€148,243	€160,278	€150,422	€147,408
$4,444	$7,099	$5,563					
			€4,212	€5,051	€501	−€5,281	€609

2007	2008	2009	2010	2011	2012	2013	2014
2.58							
N/A							
N/A	$48477	$30,360	$41,946	$54,981	$65,784	$72,144	$83,057
	−$3,588	−$5,765	$763	$2,134	$2,855	$3,208	$2,851
N/A							

1998–2006, FCA US LLC for 2009–2014, S&P Capital IQ, Belzowski (2009:220).

NISSAN

		1980	1981	1982	1983
Production	Global production (million units)				
	Domestic production (million units)	1.74	1.94	1.86	1.82
Financials	Total sales (million USD)	14.66	16.61	15.67	17.15
	After tax profit (million USD)	1.19	0.95	1.11	0.99
	Operating margin (%)	8.1	5.7	7.11	5.76

		1993	1994	1995	1996
Production	Global production (million units)	3.12	3.05	2.68	2.73
	Domestic production (million units)	1.75	1.52	1.34	1.51
Financials	Total sales (million USD)	55.70	56.76	62.08	55.54
	After tax profit (million USD)	−0.06	−1.41	−1.12	0.38
	Operating margin (%)	−0.12	−2.48	−1.81	0.68

Source of data: Annual reports, Ward's Motor Vehicle Data, various years.

1984	1985	1986	1987	1988	1989	1990	1991	1992
		2.71	2.69	2.78	2.83	3.15	3.20	3.17
1.86	1.85	1.86	1.77	1.80	1.73	1.97	2.02	1.95
18.14	19.40	27.51	29.56	33.09	34.84	39.00	44.18	50.54
0.65	1.08	0.52	−0.11	0.34	1.35	2.62	0.94	1.16
3.6	5.58	1.9	−0.38	1.04	3.87	6.71	2.12	2.29

1997	1998	1999	2000	2001	2002	2003	2004	2005
2.74	2.75	2.47	2.40	2.48	2.43	2.59	2.88	3.29
1.41	1.51	1.35	1.21	1.14	1.09	1.19	1.24	1.20
55.10	50.16	57.84	55.49	48.51	46.48	57.84	71.31	79.99
1.63	0.64	0.96	0.77	2.31	3.67	6.24	7.92	8.03
2.95	1.28	1.67	1.38	4.77	7.89	10.8	11.1	10.04

Notes

CHAPTER I WHY A BOOK ON CORPORATE RESILIENCE?

1 Foster and Kaplan 2011

2 We study the global automotive industry as it has been the nexus of many innovations over the past century. It has transformed the way we live and work, and it is a global industry that virtually everyone on the planet is touched by. In this book we have attempted to cover the evolution of this industry over the course of more than a century. The industry produces more than 80 million units every year, and features a complex network of manufacturers and suppliers that feed the global market for its products. It turns over US$3bn every year, and by our estimates, directly employs 5 million workers in vehicle assembly alone, plus a multiple of that in the component supply chain, retailing and other services. Trying to reduce such a complex industry to a few select data points is very challenging, yet we felt it was necessary to underpin our qualitative insights from the many interviews we have conducted over the past decade with empirical data-points on operational, financial and customer-facing data.The main challenges we faced in this venture are listed below. They are not meant to serve as an apology for data inadequacy and potential error, but rather we ask the reader to consider our data in relation to these challenges. We are aware that data across sources shows inconsistencies, for the reasons outlined above. As a matter of principle, we have presented the unchanged source data, where possible, so as to provide consistency within individual figures.

   a. Firm ownership: It is not always clear who the 'car manufacturer' actually is. The many mergers and acquisitions, stakes, and joint ventures require considerable subjective judgement as to when a firm is 'controlled', and thus part of, another. Renault for example holds 44 per cent of Nissan, and while both firms report separately, they operate closely together. VW on the other hand holds 19.9 per cent of Suzuki, and it is not clear what influence or synergy applies here. Worse still, the largest car manufacturers in China, FAW, SAIC, Dongfeng and Changan, all operate mostly as joint-venture partners for foreign firms, in particular VW, GM, Ford and PSA. First Auto Works, for example, leads the market with cars produced in their joint ventures with VW and GM. Dongfeng (Second Auto Works) collaborates with PSA and Nissan. Should their output be attributed to either foreign or local partner, or both? We have opted for the first option, as these firms largely provide the design and branding of the vehicles. But other approaches are equally valid.

b. Product classification. A major problem is the lack of a coherent product classification. It is not clear what a passenger car is, vis-à-vis a light commercial vehicle, light truck or even a kei-car. These classifications are often made for taxation purposes and bear little resemblance to the utility, and utilization, of the product. A particular problem here is the US market, where best-selling SUVs are sold as 'light trucks', and classified separately, even though these vehicles are virtually all used as passenger cars. We will use 'passenger cars' (comprising vehicles predominantly used by individuals for personal transport) and 'commercial vehicles' (comprising light commercial vehicles, trucks and buses) as main categories. It should be noted however that these classifications are subject to interpretations. Thus, the volume of passenger car production for the USA will seem low, as many vehicles used as passenger cars are classified as light trucks. Furthermore, often subjective judgement is needed when distinguishing a new model from a facelift, or simply a superficial vehicle 'refreshment'. The problem of commonality and carry-over of component applies also to the distinction of platforms. What is a unique platform? No clear guidelines are available.

c. Firm heterogeneity. While all the firms we cover in this book are car manufacturers, there is a considerable degree of heterogeneity across these. Some have large financing arms, others do not. Some have large commercial vehicle operations, others do not,. And of course, firms operate in different segments of the car industry: volumes tend to be much lower in the premium segments, while margins are respectively higher, changing the minimum viable scale needed to survive. Most large car firms offer products across all vehicle segments, but there are extreme cases like Tata, which has both a low-entrant automotive operation, as well as a high-end luxury arm (JLR). Thus, although technically all firms are part of the same market, their morphology differs considerably.

d. Sales and registrations. Sales figures are prone to errors to a surprising degree. The reasons are that a manufacturer may account for a 'sale' when a finished vehicle passes into the ownership of the National Sales Company (NSC), which is a legal entity that is different from the factory, while both of course belong to the vehicle manufacturing firm. The vehicle can then be 'sold' to a dealer, and eventually is 'sold' again, when a customer buys it. Only at this point (with the exception of pre-registrations), is the vehicle registered. This process can take several months, hence a vehicle is quite likely to be produced in the preceding year to that in which it enters service. Hence one can find surprising differences between 'sales' and 'registration' figures, which are also often corrected retrospectively.

e. Reporting regimes and currency fluctuations. As is the case for any research that seeks to compare the performance of global firms, the problem of difference in financial reporting, the financial year and, of course, the effect of currency fluctuations causes some unavoidable distortions.

f. Shifts in geographic regions and free trade zones: Observing the automotive industry over the course of more than a century also requires the consideration of major political developments: the establishment of the European common market, and currency, free trade agreements like Mercosur, NAFTA, and soon possibly TTIP, and of course the break-up of the Eastern bloc, all have induced major shifts in production and demand footprints.

3 Peters and Waterman 1982

4 Womack et al. 1990

5 Collins and Porras 1994

6 Collins 2001

7 Examples in this genre include Williams et al. 1994 and Froud et al. 2006 and the GERPISA network. See http://gerpisa.org/en for GERPISA's website. For a recent GERPISA book see for example Freyssenet 2009.

8 Freeman 1984

9 Reason 1997

10 Oliver et al. 2008

11 Estimates vary, but consistently state a global overcapacity of 25 per cent or more. Actual capacity utilization is hard to calculate, as line speed adjustments and shift patterns distort the actual figures. For more detail see for example Mohr et al. 2013 or OECD 2013.

CHAPTER 2 THE EVOLUTION OF A GLOBAL INDUSTRY

1 More precisely, we calculated the combined production of passenger cars and commercial vehicles, from 1900–2014 to be 2,893,301,978 units.
2 Holweg et al. 2009a
3 See Hounshell 1984, Maxcy and Silberston 1959 and Rhys 1972 for detailed reviews of the evolution of the automotive industry.
4 Halbertstam 1986
5 *Automotive News* 1996 '100 Events that shaped the industry', Detroit.
6 BBC TV 1989 'Nippon'.
7 Froud et al. 2002
8 www.europolitics.info/eu-japan-eu-raises-japanese-car-import-quotas-to-meet-new-demand-artr160788-44.html, retrieved April 2015.
9 Holweg, M. 2007
10 Pascale and Athos 1981, Schonberger 1982 and 1986, Monden 1998
11 Womack et al. 1990. For a history of IMVP also see Holweg 2007.
12 This drew heavily on the work of Clark and Fujimoto, who published their own book on the topic in 1991.
13 Clark and Fujimoto 1991
14 Oliver et al. 1994
15 Jerry Flint (27 July 2004). 'Ford's Premier Automotive Goof'. Backseat Driver. Forbes.
16 Vlasic and Stertz 2000
17 Williams et al. 1992, Williams 1994.
18 *Automotive News* 2012, 'Top 100 Global Suppliers'.
19 Cusumano and Nobeoka 1998
20 Lutz 2011
21 Data on product development cost is highly sensitive. We estimate that the price tag to develop a new vehicle starts around $1 billion. According to John Wolkonowicz, Senior Auto Analyst for North America at IHS Global, 'It can be as much as $6 billion if it's an all-new car on all-new platform with an all-new engine and an all-new transmission and nothing carrying over from the old model' (www.autoblog.com/2010/07/27/

why-does-it-cost-so-much-for-automakers-to-develop-new-models/, retrieved April 2015). We would argue that this represents the upper limit of the range.

22 Holweg et al. 2009b

23 Martin Winterkorn's speech at the Annual Media Conference and Investor Conference on 12 March 2015. www.volkswagenag.com/content/vwcorp/ info_center/en/talks_and_presentations/2015/03/Part1.bin.html/ binarystorageitem/file2/1+Rede+Winterkorn+englisch+inkl+Verbrauch. pdf, retrieved March 2015

24 Source: International Council on Cleaner Transportation, icct.org. Data sources for the chart: US: Baseline performance: US EPA, Light-duty automotive technology, carbon dioxide emissions, and fuel economy trends: 1975 through 2013. Table 9.1, page 110. Online available at www. epa.gov/fueleconomy/fetrends/1975-2012/420r13001.pdf EU: Baseline performance: European Commission Car CO_2 Monitoring data (2009): http://eur-lex.europa.eu/LexUriServ/LexUriServ.do?uri=CELEX: 52010DC0655:EN:HTML Japan: Baseline performance: JAMA 2010, The Motor Industry of Japan: www.jama-english.jp/publications/MVS2010.pdf; MLIT, www.mlit.go.jp/common/000990330.pdf China: Baseline performance: China Automotive Research and Technology Center though internal communication and ICCT internal 2010 database for Chinese light-duty vehicles

25 Medawar 2011

CHAPTER 3 COMPETING IN A GLOBAL INDUSTRY

1 The motor industry has made a dramatic transition over the last century. From small workshops that had crafted customized vehicles for the affluent few, to Ford's mass-produced Model T that made motoring available to the large public, and to the Toyota Production System that proved to the world that high productivity and high quality can be achieved at the same time. Many researchers have studied these transitions in the motor industry, trying to understand how these changes could happen in such a short time. Historians such as David Hounshell, Allan Nevins and Lawrence White for example debate the drivers and enablers of the change from the craft production of the late nineteenth century, which was prevalent at the time (Nevins 1954; Nevins and Hill 1957; White 1971; Hounshell 1984), and Womack et al. and Takahiro

Fujimoto give a detailed account of the lean production paradigm as a contrast to the mass production approach (Womack et al. 1990; Fujimoto, 1999).

2 Ford and Crowther 1922
3 Hounshell 1984
4 Personal conversation with Robert Hall in 2004.
5 White 1971; Rhys 1972
6 Drucker 1946
7 Hounshell 1984
8 Sloan 1963: 69
9 Quote by Taichi Ohno, the father of the Toyota Production System
10 Ohno 1988: 79
11 Cusumano 1985
12 Ohno 1988
13 Quoted in Cusumano 1985
14 Ohno 1988: 75
15 Shingo 1988
16 Fujimoto 1999: 50
17 Oliver et al. 2007
18 Reuters News

CHAPTER 4 CONCEPTS: STAKEHOLDERS, OPERATIONS
AND CONTEXT

1 Pfeffer and Salancik 1978
2 Granovetter 1985
3 Freeman 1984; Freeman, Rusconi et al. 2012
4 Freeman, Harrison et al. 2010: 26
5 A turning point for Detroit: If GM's deal with the UAW is ratified, the Big Three could have a future after all, *The Economist* 27 September 2007
6 Womack et al. 1990: 9 and 256
7 Womack et al. 1990
8 Williams et al. 1994: 323
9 PriceWaterhouseCoopers 2013
10 Oliver et al. 2007
11 Clark and Fujimoto 1991
12 Cusumano and Nobeoka 1998
13 Walker and Guest 1952; Beynon 1975; Hamper 2008

14 Womack et al. 1990

15 Schmenner and Swink 1998

16 Holweg and Pil 2004

17 Womack et al. 1990

18 Womack et al. 1990

19 Williams et al. 1992

20 Williams 1994

21 Oliver et al. 1996; Holweg and Pil 2004

22 Williams et al. 1989; Delbridge and Oliver 1991

23 Cuckow and Oliver 2011

24 Lamming 1993

25 Holweg and Pil 2004

26 Beer 1972, 1984, 1994

27 Porter 1996

28 Galbraith 1974

29 Ashby 1956

30 Liu and Dicken 2006

31 Froud et al. 2002

32 MacDuffie and Fujimoto 2010

33 Liu and Dicken 2006

34 Olcott and Oliver 2014

35 Nishiguchi and Beaudet 1998

36 Freeman et al. 2004

37 Farjoun and Starbuck 2007

38 Farjoun and Starbuck 2007: 542

CHAPTER 5 ROVER: INSIDE A FAILING CAR COMPANY

1 A very good website on the history of the company can be found at www. aronline.co.uk/.

2 Brady and Lorenz 2001

3 Brady and Lorenz 2001

4 BBC News, http://news.bbc.co.uk/1/hi/business/5186314.stm

5 BBC News, http://news.bbc.co.uk/1/hi/business/6497959.stm

6 Owen 1999

7 Edwardes 1983

8 *The Guardian*, www.theguardian.com/news/2003/nov/22/ guardianobituaries.highereducation

9 Reason 1997
10 Ashby 1956; Beer 1984
11 Beer 1994

CHAPTER 6 THE FAILURE OF SAAB AUTOMOBILE

1 Saab-Scania 1987
2 Saab-Scania 1987
3 Chatterton 1980
4 Audi has used the slogan ever since 1971.
5 Bayley 1986
6 Fisher 1985
7 Data from www.saab.com
8 Source: www.saab.com
9 Strach and Everett 2006
10 Strach and Everett 2006
11 *Ward's Auto*, http://wardsauto.com/flashback/wardsauto-flashback-december-2014
12 Source: www.saab.com
13 Source: www.saab.com
14 *Which?* (1998)
15 Stach and Everett 2006
16 Strach and Everett 2006
17 *The Economist*, 29 January 2009
18 *The Economist*, 18 June 2009
19 Strach and Everett 2006
20 Ingrassia 2011: 175
21 *Just Auto*, 18 February 2011
22 *Just Auto*, 19 February 2009
23 *Just Auto*, 23 February 2009
24 *Just Auto*, 19 February 2011
25 *Just Auto*, 19 May 2011
26 *Just Auto*, 17 March 2010
27 *Just Auto*, 17 March 2010
28 *Just Auto*, 12 January 2010
29 *Just Auto*, 27 Jan 2010
30 *Just Auto*, 2 Feb 2010

31   Source: www.detectivemarketing.com/victor-muller-saabs-will-be-saabs-again/
32   Strach and Everett 2006
33   *Just Auto*, 2 February 2010
34   *Just Auto*, 17 March 2011
35   *Just Auto*, 3 March 2010
36   *Just Auto*, 27 May 2011
37   *Just Auto*, 24 June 2010
38   *The Independent*, 13 June 2011
39   *Car Magazine*, 3 June 2010
40   *The Guardian*, 13 November 2010
41   *Just Auto*, 4 August 2010
42   *Just Auto*, 12 August 2010
43   *Just Auto*, 29 October 2010
44   *Just Auto*, 29 September 2010
45   *Just Auto*, 29 October 2011
46   *Just Auto*, 6 January 2011
47   *Just Auto*, 12 January 2011
48   *Just Auto*, 1 March 2011
49   His contract specified that he could retire at 60 on full benefits, which came into effect the day he resigned, so to many commentators his resignation was not necessarily a sign of his disagreement with Victor Muller. However, in June 2011 the two union representatives also resigned, sparking renewed rumours about dissent in Saab's board.
50   *Just Auto*, 30 March 2011
51   *Just Auto*, 1 April 2011
52   *Just Auto*, 28 April 2011
53   *Just Auto*, 18 April 2011
54   *Just Auto*, 13 May 2011
55   BBC News, www.bbc.co.uk/news/uk-england-hampshire-15887821
56   *Just Auto*, 7 September 2011. See also the court application for 'Ansökan om företagsrekonstruktion' of 7 September 2011, which includes balance statements for Saab Automobile AB, and its subsidiaries.
57   www.saabsunited.com/2011/09/ttela-se-transcription-of-the-press-conference.html
58   'Exklusiv intervju: Muller tror inte på kineserna', *Teknikens Värld*, 30 November 2011

59 www.reuters.com/article/2011/12/06/gm-saab-idUSN1E7B50LC20111206, 6 December 6 2011.

60 Statement by James Cain, GM spokesman

61 'Saab-Lofalk is ready to give up on the reconstruction', *Dagens Industri*, 6 December 2011

62 Victor Muller quoted on TTELA online, 9 December 2011

63 *Chicago Tribune*, www.chicagotribune.com/classified/automotive/sns-rt-us-sweden-saabtre80511d-20120106,0,6571809.story)

64 *Chicago Tribune*, www.chicagotribune.com/classified/automotive/sns-rt-us-sweden-saabtre80511d-20120106,0,6571809.story)

65 *Financial Times*, http://blogs.ft.com/beyond-brics/2012/01/09/a-sahib-for-saab/#ixzz1j2SCAodm

66 www.thelocal.se/38644/20120122/

67 Justauto.com, http://www.just-auto.com/news/three-saab-bids-in-but-staff-still-owed-money_id122151.aspx

68 *Automotive News*, www.autonews.com/article/20120525/COPY01/305259865#ixzz1w6uObclO

69 *New York Times*, www.nytimes.com/2012/06/14/business/global/buyer-is-found-for-saab-automobile.html?_r=

70 http://evworld.com/news.cfm?newsid=28148

71 https://www.youtube.com/watch?v=52pBROVa5EY

72 http://uk.autoblog.com/2012/06/20/saab-rescue-swedes-don-t-believe-it/

73 *China Daily*, www.chinadaily.com.cn/cndy/2013-01/14/content_16110849.htm

74 Reuters, www.reuters.com/article/2014/05/20/saab-nevs-idUSL6N0O649M20140520

75 *Financial Times*, www.ft.com/cms/s/0/b3add3fc-8067-11e4-9907-00144feabdc0.html?siteedition=uk#axzz3MWGkqLzt

76 Holweg et al. 2009a

77 Pil and Holweg 2004

78 Investor AB, www.investorab.com/about-investor/investor's-history/

CHAPTER 7 NEAR MISSES: CHRYSLER AND NISSAN

1 25 June 2009. www.toyota-global.com/company/toyota_traditions/company/dec2009_feb2010.html http://www.toyota-global.com/company/toyota_traditions/company/dec2009_feb2010.html

2 Halberstam 1986

3 Halberstam 1986: 561

4 https://www.youtube.com/watch?v=ZMMlG0TaKHg

5 *New York Times*, www.nytimes.com/1987/06/20/business/company-news-chrysler-sets-deal-for-electrospace.html

6 Ingrassia and White 1995

7 Ingrassia and White 1995

8 Cusumano and Nobeoka 1998

9 Forbes, www.forbes.com/forbes/1997/0113/5901082a.html

10 Ingrassa 2011; Vlasic 2011

11 Ingrassia 2011

12 Ingrassia 2011: 198

13 Vlasic 2011

14 Vlasic 2011

15 Ingrassia 2011

16 Vlasic 2011

17 Vlasic 2011

18 While at the Nissan Headquarters there may have been a lack of cross-functional and cross-sectional interaction, at Nissan's technical centres this was not the case. Fujimoto for example argues that at Nissan's product development centre in Atsugi cross-sectional and cross-functional teams existed long before the NRP (Fujimoto 2004: 31, 32).

19 BV (Besloten vennootschap) is a closed limited liability company under Dutch law.

20 Stevens 2010

21 Stevens 2010

22 Stevens 2010

23 In 2005 Fiat extracted $2 billion from GM to terminate a 'put' option and hence also benefited from an external injection.

CHAPTER 8 THE FUTURE SHAPE OF THE INDUSTRY

1 This phenomenon is commonly referred to as the 'Dutch disease', whereby the local currency of countries that are exporting large quantities of raw materials appreciates, and thus renders manufacturing exports uncompetitive internationally.

2 Hoffman 2012

3 Reuters 2011

4 For example, the Saab 9-2-X and the 9-7-X products, which are rebadged Subaru and Chevrolet products, respectively.

5 *Manager Magazin* (in German), www.manager-magazin.de/magazin/artikel/a-473215.html, and http://www.manager-magazin.de/unternehmen/missmanagement/a-482843.html, and Der Spiegel, http://www.stern.de/wirtschaft/news/daimler-chrysler-supermanns-harte-landung-520139.html

6 Most prominent of these J-curves forecasts was Marchionne's forecast of Alfa Romeo selling 400,000 units globally in 2014. Actual sales in 2014 were 65,000 units, and the target deadline was moved to 2018. See also: www.ft.com/cms/s/0/d7d12858-9ba9-11e4-b6cc-00144feabdc0.html

7 http://deutsche-wirtschafts-nachrichten.de/2014/07/17/daimler-chef-zetsche-baut-spar-programm-aus/

Bibliography

Abernathy, W. and Clark, K. (1983) *The Competitive Status of the US Auto Industry. A Study of the Influences of Technology in Determining International
Industrial Competitive Advantage.* National Academies Press.

Allen, G. C. (1970) *British Industries and Their Organization.* Longmans.

Ashby, W. R. (1956) *An Introduction to Cybernetics.* Chapman & Hall.

Batchelor, J. (2001) Employment Security in the Aftermath of the Break-up of the
Rover Group, Warwick Business School Working Paper Series, No. 342.

Bayley, S. (1986) Marketing Vorsprung durch Technik. In S. Bayley, *Sex, Drink and
Fast Cars: The Creation and Consumption of Images,* pp. 87–112. Pantheon

Beer, S. (1972) *The Brain of the Firm – The Managerial Cybernetics of Organization.* John Wiley & Sons.

Beer, S. (1979) *The Heart of the Enterprise.* John Wiley & Sons.

Beer, S. (1984) The viable system model: Its provenance, development, methodology and pathology. *The Journal of the Operational Research Society* 35 (1):
7–25.

Beer, S. (1994) *The Heart of Enterprise.* John Wiley & Sons.

Belzowski, B. (2009) Can Chrysler survive its reinvention? In M. Freyssenet (ed.)
The Second Automobile Revolution. Palgrave.

Beynon, H. (1975) *Working for Ford.* EP Publishing.

Brady, C. and Lorenz, A. (2001) *End of the Road: BMW and Rover: A Brand Too Far.*
Financial Times Prentice Hall.

Carver, M., Seale, N. and Youngson, A. (2015) *British Leyland Motor Corporation
1968–2005: The Story from Inside.* The History Press.

Central Policy Review Staff, 1975. *The Future of the British Car Industry.* HSMO.

Chatterton, M. (1980) *Saab: The Innovator.* David and Charles.

Church, R. (1994) *The Rise and Decline of the British Motor Industry.* Cambridge
University Press.

Clark, K. and Fujimoto, T. (1991) *Product Development Performance: Strategy,
Organisation and Management in the World Auto Industry.* Harvard Business
School Press.

Collins, J. C. (2001) *Good to Great: Why Some Companies Make the Leap – and
Others Don't.* Random House.

Collins, J. C. and Porras, J. I. (1994) *Built to Last: Successful Habits of Visionary Companies.* Random House.

Crafts, N. F., Woodward, N. W. and Duckham, B. F. (1991) *The British Economy since 1945.* Clarendon Press.

Cuckow, N. and Oliver, N. (2011) Changing Patterns of Leanness: Stock Turns in the Japanese and Western Auto Industries 1975–2008 (with N. Cuckow). 18th EurOMA Conference, Cambridge UK, 3–6 July 2011.

Cusumano, M. A. (1985) *The Japanese Automobile Manufacturing Industry: Technology and Management at Nissan and Toyota.* Harvard University Press.

Cusumano, M. A. and Nobeoka, T. (1998) *Thinking Beyond Lean.* Simon Schuster.

Cusumano, M. A. and Takeishi, A. (1991) Supplier relations and management: A survey of Japanese, Japanese-transplant, and US auto plants. *Strategic Management Journal* 12 (8): 563–588.

Delbridge, R. and Oliver, N. (1991) Narrowing the gap? *International Journal of Production Research* 29 (10): 2083.

Delbridge, R. and Oliver, N. (1991) Just-in-time or just the same? Developments in the auto industry: The retailers' views. *International Journal of Retailing and Distribution Management* 19 (2): 20–26.

DETR (1998) *Efficient JIT Supply Chain Management: Nissan Motor Manufacturing (UK) Ltd, Good Practice Case Study 374.* Department of the Environment, Transport and the Regions.

Drucker, P. (1946) *Concept of the Corporation.* Transaction Publishers.

Dunnett, P. (1980) *The Decline of the British Motor Industry: The Effects of Government Policy, 1945–1979.* Croom Helm.

Edwardes, M. (1983) *Back from the Brink: An Apocalyptic Experience.* Collins.

Farjoun, M. and Starbuck, W. H. (2007) Organizing at and beyond the limits. *Organization Studies (01708406)* 28 (4): 541–566.

Fisher, A. B. (1985) Courting the well-heeled car shopper. *Fortune Magazine,* 5 August.

Ford, H. and Crowther, S. (1922) *My Life and Work: In collaboration with Samuel Crowther.* Cornstalk Publishing Company.

Foster, R. and Kaplan, S. (2011) *Creative Destruction: Why Companies That Are Built to Last Underperform the Market – And How to Successfully Transform Them.* Crown Business.

Freeman, R. E. (1984) *Strategic Management: A Stakeholder Approach.* Pitman.

Freeman, R. E., Harrison, J. S. et al. (2010). *Stakeholder Theory: The State of the Art.* Cambridge University Press.

Freeman, R. E., Rusconi, G. et al. (2012) Stakeholder theory(ies): Ethical ideas and managerial action. *Journal of Business Ethics* 109 (1): 1–2.

Freeman, S. F., Hirschhorn, L. et al. (2004) The power of moral purpose: Sandler O'Neill & Partners in the aftermath of September 11th, 2001. *Organization Development Journal* 22 (4): 69–81.

Freyssenet, M. (ed.) (2009) *The Second Automobile Revolution. Trajectories of the World Carmakers in the 21st Century*. Palgrave MacMillan.

Froud, J., Haslam, C. et al. (2002) Cars after financialisation: A case study in financial under-performance, constraints and consequences. *Competition & Change* 6 (1): 13.

Froud, J., Johal, S., Leaver, A. and Williams, K. (2006) *Financialization and Strategy: Narrative and Numbers*. Routledge.

Fujimoto, T. (1999) *The Evolution of a Manufacturing System at Toyota*. Oxford University Press.

Fujimoto, T. (2004) *Nihon no Monotukuri Tetsugaku (Japan's Manufacturing Philosophy)*. Nikkei Press.

Galbraith, J. R. (1974) Organizational design: An information processing view. *Interfaces* 4 (3): 28–36.

Granovetter, M. (1985) Economic action and social structure: The problem of embeddedness. *American Journal of Sociology* 91 (3): 481–510.

Greener, T. (2006) *Concentration of Resource and Effect (CORE) in BL Cars 1979–1981: Did It Ensure Survival?* University of Brighton Business School, Occasional/Working Paper Series, No. 6, April 2006.

Halberstam, D. (1986) *The Reckoning*. Open Road Media.

Hamper, B. (2008) *Rivethead: Tales from the Assembly Line*. Hachette Digital, Inc.

Heller, D. A. (2003) An inquiry into the role of interfirm relationships in recent organizational change initiatives in Japanese automobile firms. *Shinshu University Economic Review* 49: 45–88.

Heller, D. A, Mercer, G. and Fujimoto, T. (2006) The long term value of M&A activity that enhances learning organizations. *International Journal of Automotive Technology and Management* 6 (2): 157–176.

Hines, P. (1998) Benchmarking Toyota's supply chain: Japan vs UK. *Long Range Planning* 31 (6): 911–918.

Hoffman, B. G. (2012) *American Icon: Alan Mulally and the Fight to Save Ford Motor Company*. Three Rivers Press.

Holweg, M. (2007) The genealogy of lean production. *Journal of Operations Management* 25 (2): 420–437.

Holweg, M. and Pil, F. K. (2004) *The Second Century: Reconnecting Customer and Value Chain through Build-to-Order*. The MIT Press.

Holweg, M., Davies, P. and Podpolny, D. (2009a) *The Competitive Status of the UK Automotive Industry*. PICSIE Books.

Holweg, M., Luo, J. and Oliver, N. (2009b) The past, present and future of China's automotive industry: a value chain perspective. *International Journal of Technological Learning, Innovation and Development* 2 (1): 76–118.

Hounshell, D. A. (1984) *From the American System to Mass Production, 1800–1932: The Development of Manufacturing Technology in the United States*. Johns Hopkins University Press.

House of Commons Expenditure Committee (1975) *The Motor Vehicle Industry: 14th Report to the Expenditure Committee*, August 6th 1975. HMSO.

Iacocca, L. (1988) *Lee Iacocca's Talking Straight*. Bantam.

Iacocca, L. and Novak, W. (1986) *Iacocca: An Autobiography*. Bantam.

Ingrassia, P. (2011) *Crash Course: The American Automobile Industry's Road to Bankruptcy and Bailout – and Beyond*. Random House Trade Paperbacks.

Ingrassia, P. and White, J. B. (1995) *Comeback: The Fall & Rise of the American Automobile Industry*. Simon and Schuster.

Johnson, C. (1998) [1982] *MITI and the Japanese Miracle: The Growth of Industrial Policy, 1925–1975*. Stanford University Press.

Jones, D. T. and Prais, S. J. (1978) Plant size and productivity in the motor industry: some international comparisons. *Oxford Bulletin of Economics and Statistics* 40 (2), May.

Lamming, R. (1993) *Beyond Partnership: Strategies for Innovation and Lean Supply*. Prentice Hall.

Lewchuck, W. A. (1984) The role of British government in the spread of scientific management and Fordism in the interwar years. *Journal of Economic History* 44: 355–361.

Lewchuck, W. A. (1985) The return to capital in the British motor vehicle industry. *Business History* 27.

Lewchuck, W. A. (1986) The motor vehicle industry. In B. Elbaum and W. Lazonick (eds.), *The Decline of the British Economy*. Clarendon Press.

Lewchuck, W. A. (1987) *American Technology and the British Motor Vehicle Industry*. Cambridge University Press.

Lincoln, J. R. and Gerlach, M. L. (2004) *Japan's Network Economy: Structure, Persistence, and Change*. Cambridge University Press.

Liu, W. and Dicken, P. (2006) Transnational corporations and obligated embeddedness: foreign direct investment in China's automobile industry. *Environment and Planning A* 38 (7): 1229.

Lutz, B. (2011) *Car guys vs. Bean Counters: The Battle for the Soul of American Business*. Penguin.

MacDuffie, J. P. (1995) Human resource bundles and manufacturing performance: Organizational logic and flexible production systems in the world auto industry. *Industrial & Labor Relations Review* 48 (2): 197–221.

MacDuffie, J. P. (1997) The road to 'root cause': Shop-floor problem-solving at three auto assembly plants. *Management Science* 43 (4): 479–502.

MacDuffie, J. P. and Fujimoto, T. (2010) Why dinosaurs will keep ruling the auto industry. *Harvard Business Review* 88 (6): 23–25.

MacDuffie, J. P. and Helper, S. (1997) Creating lean suppliers: Diffusing lean production through the supply chain. *California Management Review* 39 (4): 118–151.

Maxcy, G. and Silberston, A. (1959) *The Motor Industry*. George Allen & Unwin.

Maynard, Micheline (2003) *The End of Detroit: How the Big Three Lost Their Grip on the American Car Market*. Currency/Doubleday.

Medawar, D. (2011) How Low is 'Low Carbon'? Reassessing Low Emission Vehicles. MPhil Dissertation, University of Cambridge.

Mohr, D., Müller, N. and Krieg, A. (2013) *The Road to 2020 and Beyond. What's Driving the Global Automotive Industry?* McKinsey & Company.

Monden, Y. (1998) *Toyota Production System: An Integrated Approach to Just-in-Time*. Engineering & Management Press.

Muellbauer, J. (1986) The assessment: Productivity and competitiveness in British manufacturing. *Oxford Review of Economic Policy* 2 (3).

Mueller, F. (1993) The role of know-how in corporate rejuvenation: The case of Rover. *Business Strategy Review* 4 (3): 15–24.

Nevins, A. (1954) *Ford: The Times, the Man, the Company*. Charles Scribner.

Nevins, A. and Hill, F. E. (1957) *Ford: Expansion and Challenge 1915–1933*. Charles Scribner.

Nevins, A. and Hill, F. E. (1963) *Ford: Decline and Rebirth 1933–1962*. Charles Scribner.

Nieuwenhuis, P. and Wells, P. (2007) The all-steel body as a cornerstone to the foundations of the mass production car industry. *Industrial and Corporate Change* 16 (2): 183–212.

Nishiguchi, T. (1989) Is JIT really JIT? Paper presented to the IMVP International Policy Forum, Pierre Marques, Acapulco, 7–10 May.

Nishiguchi, T. (1994) *Strategic Industrial Sourcing: The Japanese Advantage*. Oxford University Press.

Nishiguchi, T. and Beaudet, A. (1998) The Toyota group and the Aisin fire. *Sloan Management Review* 40 (1): 49–59.

OECD (2013) Medium-Run Capacity Adjustment in the Automobile Industry. OECD Economics Department Policy Notes, No. 21. November 2013.

Ohno, T. (1988) *Toyota Production System: Beyond Large-scale Production*. Productivity Press.

Olcott, G. and Oliver, N. (2014) Social capital, sensemaking, and recovery. *California Management Review* 56 (2): 5–22.

Oliver, N. and Delbridge, R. (1991) Beyond customer satisfaction: the changing face of car retailing. *International Journal of Retailing and Distribution Management* 19 (3): 29–39.

Oliver, N., Delbridge, R. et al. (1996) Lean production practices: International comparisons in the auto components industry. *British Journal of Management* 7 (1).

Oliver, N., Schab, L. et al. (2007) Lean principles and premium brands: conflict or complement? *International Journal of Production Research* 45 (16): 3723–3739.

Oliver, N., Holweg, M. and Carver, M. (2008) A systems perspective on the death of a car company. *International Journal of Operations & Production Management* 28 (6): 562–583.

Oliver, N., Jones, D. T., Lowe, J., Roberts, P. and Thayer, B. (1994) *Worldwide Manufacturing Competitiveness Study: The Second Lean Enterprise Report*. Andersen Consulting.

Owen, G. (1999) *From Empire to Europe: The Decline and Revival of British Industry since the Second World War*. HarperCollins.

Pascale, R. T. and Athos, A. G. (1981) The art of Japanese management. *Business Horizons* 24 (6): 83–85.

Peters, T. J. and Waterman, R. H. (1982) *In Search of Excellence*. Harper & Row.

Pettigrew, A. and Whipp, R. 1991. *Managing Change for Competitive Success*. Basil Blackwell.

Pfeffer, J. and Salancik, G. R. (1978) *The External Control of Organizations: A Resource Dependence Perspective*. Harper & Row.

Pil, F. K. and Holweg, M. (2004) Linking product variety to order-fulfillment strategies. *Interfaces* 34 (5): 394–403.

Pilkington, A. (1996) *Transforming Rover: Renewal Against the Odds 1981–1994*. Bristol Academic Press.

Porter, M. E. (1996) What is strategy? *Harvard Business Review*, November.

PWC (2013) The Global Innovation 1000: Top 20 R&D Spenders 2005–2013. From www.strategyand.pwc.com/global/home/what-we-think/global-innovation-1000/top-20-rd-spenders-2013.

Rattner, S. (2010) *Overhaul: An Insider's Account of the Obama Administration's Emergency Rescue of the Auto Industry*. Houghton Mifflin Harcourt.

Reason, J. (1990) The contribution of latent human failures to the breakdown of complex systems. *Philosophical Transactions of the Royal Society of London. Series B, Biological Sciences* 327 (1241): 475–484.

Reason, J. (1997). *Managing the Risks of Organizational Accidents.* Ashgate.

Reichhart, A. and Holweg, M. (2007) Lean distribution: concepts, challenges, conflicts. *International Journal of Production Research* 45 (16): 3699–3722.

Rhys, D. G. (1972) *The Motor Industry: An Economic Survey.* Butterworth.

Rover Task Force (2000) Interim Report to the Secretary of State for Trade and Industry, April.

Ryder, D. (1975) *British Leyland: The Next Decade.* Central Policy Review Staff, HMSO.

Saab-Scania (1987) *The Saab-Scania Story.* Streiffert & Co.

Sako, M. (1992) *Prices, Quality and Trust.* Cambridge University Press.

Saul, S. B. (1962) The motor industry in Britain to 1914. *Business History* 5 (1): 22–44.

Schmenner, R. W. and Swink, M. L. (1998) On theory in operations management. *Journal of Operations Management* 17 (1): 97–113.

Schonberger, R. (1982) *Japanese Manufacturing Techniques.* The Free Press.

Schonberger, R. (1986) *World Class Manufacturing.* The Free Press.

Segrestin, B. (2005) Partnering to explore: The Renault-Nissan Alliance as a forerunner of new cooperative patterns. *Research Policy* 34: 657–672.

Shingo, S. (1988) *Non-Stock Production: The Shingo System of Continuous Improvement.* Productivity Press.

Sloan, A. P. (1963) *My Years with General Motors.* Doubleday.

SMMT (1996) *The Motor Industry of Britain Centenary Book: 1896 – 1996,* edited by Sonia Seymour-Williams.

Stevens, M. (2010) Buyer–Supplier Relationship Management – Towards a Multi-Dimensional and Dynamic Approach. Ph.D. Dissertation, University of Cambridge.

Stevens, M., Holweg, M. and Pil, F. K. (2012) *Modulating between Relational and Contractual Approaches to Buyer Supplier Relations: A Case Study of Nissan.* Cambridge Judge Business School Working Paper Series.

Štrach, P. and Everett, A. M. (2006) Brand corrosion: mass-marketing's threat to luxury automobile brands after merger and acquisition. *Journal of Product & Brand Management* 15 (2): 106–120.

Sugimori, Y., Kusunoki, K. K. et al. (1977) Toyota production system and Kanban system; materialization of just-in-time and respect-for-human system. *International Journal of Production Research* 15 (6): 553–564.

Tillemann, L. (2015). *The Great Race: The Global Quest for the Car of the Future.* Simon & Schuster.

Tiratsoo, N. (1995) Standard Motors 1945–55 and the post-war malaise of British management. In J. Cassis, F. Crouzet and T. Gourvish (eds), *Management in the Age of Corporate Economy: Britain and France 1850–1990*. Oxford University Press.

Tolliday, S. (1988) Competition and workplace in the British automobile industry, 1945–1988. *Business and Economic History* 17: 63–77.

Utterback, J. (1994) *Mastering the Dynamics of Innovation*. Harvard University Press.

Vlasic, B. (2011) *Once Upon a Car: The Fall and Resurrection of America's Big Three Auto Makers – GM, Ford, and Chrysler*. William Morrow.

Vlasic, Bill and Stertz, Bradley A. (2000) *Taken for a Ride: How Daimler-Benz Drove Off with Chrysler*. Wiley.

Volpato, G. (1983) *L'industria automobilistica mondiale*. Padova, CEDAM.

Walker, C. R. and Guest, R. H. (1952) *The Man on the Assembly Line*. Harvard University Press.

Whipp, R. and Clark, P. (1986) *Innovation and the Auto Industry*. Pinter.

Whisler, T. R. (1999) *The British Motor Industry, 1945–94: A Case Study in Industrial Decline*. Oxford University Press.

White, L. J. (1971) *The Automobile Industry since 1971*. Harvard University Press.

Williams, K. (1994) *Cars: Analysis, History, Cases*. Berghahn.

Williams, K., Haslam, C. et al. (1992) Against lean production. *Economy and Society* 21 (3): 321–354.

Williams, K., Williams, J. and Haslam, C. (1987) *The Breakdown of Austin Rover: A Case-study in the Failure of Business Strategy and Industrial Policy*. Berg.

Williams, K., Williams, J. and Haslam, C. (1989) Why take the stocks out? Britain vs Japan. *International Journal of Operations & Production Management* 9 (8): 91–105.

Wilson, H. (1974) *The Labour Government, 1964–1970: A Personal Record*. Penguin.

Wolferen, K. G. van (1989) *The Enigma of Japanese Power*. Alfred A. Knopf.

Womack, J. P., Jones, D. T. and Roos, D. (1990) *The Machine that Changed the World: The Triumph of Lean Production*. Rawson Macmillan.

Wood, J. (1988) *Wheels of Misfortune: The Rise and Fall of the British Motor Industry*. Sidgwick & Jackson.

Yan, Y. P. (2008) Fostering a Chinese National Auto Champion – The Role of MG Rover, by Yuepeng. MPhil Dissertation, Judge Business School, University of Cambridge

Yates, B. W. (1983) *The Decline and Fall of the American Automobile Industry*. Empire Books: Distributed by Harper & Row.

Secondary data sources

Automotive News, Data Center. www.autonews.com/section/
datacenter11

Bernstein Research, various analyst reports. www.bernsteinresearch.
com

Companies House. https://www.gov.uk/government/organisations/
companies-house

IHS Insight, Global Production Database. www.ihs.com/industry/
automotive.html

JD Powers, IQS Quality survey data. autos.jdpower.com/ratings/
quality.html

Mergent Online, annual reports. www.mergentonline.com

Moody's. Credit ratings. www.moodys.com

NHTSA. www.nhtsa.gov

OICA, The International Organization of Motor Vehicle
Manufacturers, www.oica.net

Standard & Poor. Capital IQ. www.capitaliq.com

Standard & Poor. Credit ratings. www.standardandpoors.com

Thomson One. www.thomsonone.com

VOSA. www.gov.uk/government/organisations/vehicle-and-operator-
services-agency

Wards Automotive Yearbooks, 1950–2015. Penton Media, www.
wardsauto.com

World Motor Vehicle Data, 1970–2015. Penton Media, www.
wardsauto.com

Index